M000314144

The Performance of Projects and Project Management

In the increasing number of heavily projectized organizations, sustainable, commercial performance depends on their ability to measure and develop the performance of project management.

This involves developing new skills and capabilities, such as a learning approach across projects. It also involves transforming established approaches such as corporate governance to match the new project-oriented context and, finally, it involves learning to use projects to enable key organizational objectives, such as sustainability, as well as the project-specific outcomes.

The Performance of Projects and Project Management offers perspectives on all of these fundamental aspects of project performance. As such, it is an important book for those concerned with project strategy, project delivery and business sustainability.

Professor Laurence Lecoeuvre was formerly an International Director within the industrial sector and car industry (1984–2001). She joined SKEMA in 2001. After a few years as Business Programs Director, she is today Director of Project Management Department and Director of the PhD in Programme and Project Management. Laurence is mainly teaching project management fundamentals and research methodology. Her PhD focused on the links between project marketing and project management; she continues to develop her research on this topic but also on governance.

'This book captures a series of insights and perspectives of particular interest to project management academics and practitioners. It draws upon over a decade of valuable teaching and research by SKEMA's faculty. Its content is relevant, current and provides a sophisticated reference point for all readers. It will inform many "pracademics" for a long time. I thoroughly recommend it!'

Derek Walker, RMIT University, Australia

'There is increasing recognition of the interdependencies operating in project execution—cross-functional working, spanning organizational boundaries and engagement with wider organizational networks in successful project management. This book makes a significant contribution to understanding these interdependencies and how they are manifest in important topics of project management such as risk and governance.'

Hedley Smyth, The Bartlett School of Construction and Project Management, UCL, UK

The Performance of Projects and Project Management

Sustainable Delivery in Project Intensive Companies

Edited by Laurence Lecoeuvre

Routledge
Taylor & Francis Group

LONDON AND NEW YORK

First published 2017
by Routledge
2 Park Square, Milton Park, Abingdon, Oxon OX14 4RN

and by Routledge
711 Third Avenue, New York, NY 10017

Routledge is an imprint of the Taylor & Francis Group, an informa business

© 2017 selection and editorial matter, Laurence Lecoeuvre; individual chapters, the contributors

The right of Laurence Lecoeuvre to be identified as the author of the editorial material, and of the authors for their individual chapters, has been asserted in accordance with sections 77 and 78 of the Copyright, Designs and Patents Act 1988.

All rights reserved. No part of this book may be reprinted or reproduced or utilised in any form or by any electronic, mechanical, or other means, now known or hereafter invented, including photocopying and recording, or in any information storage or retrieval system, without permission in writing from the publishers.

Trademark notice: Product or corporate names may be trademarks or registered trademarks, and are used only for identification and explanation without intent to infringe.

British Library Cataloguing in Publication Data
A catalogue record for this book is available from the British Library

Library of Congress Cataloging in Publication Data
Lecoeuvre, Laurence.
The performance of projects and project management : sustainable delivery in project intensive companies / by Laurence Lecoeuvre.
pages cm
Includes bibliographical references and index.
1. Project management. 2. Industrial management—Environmental aspects. 3. Sustainable development. I. Title.
HD69.P75L4355 2015
658.4′04—dc23
2015025554

ISBN: 9781472421890 (hbk)
ISBN: 9781315554785 (ebk)

Typeset in Baskerville
by Swales & Willis Ltd, Exeter, Devon, UK

Printed in the United Kingdom
by Henry Ling Limited

... the idea grows, I developed it and all becomes increasingly clear, and the opera is really almost finished in my head, even if it is long, so that I can then, at a glance, see it in mind as a beautiful painting or a beautiful sculpture; I mean that in imagination, I don't hear parts one after the other in the order in which they will have to follow, I hear them all together at once ...

... l'idée grandit, je la développe, tout devient de plus en plus clair, et le morceau est vraiment presque achevé dans ma tête, même s'il est long, de sorte que je peux ensuite, d'un seul regard, le voir en esprit comme un beau tableau ou une belle sculpture; je veux dire qu'en imagination je n'entends nullement les parties les unes après les autres dans l'ordre où elles devront se suivre, je les entends toutes ensembles à la fois ...

Mozart, Wolfgang Amadeus (1756–1791)
(Extract of letter of W.A. Mozart to his father
in Mystérieux Mozart, *P. Sollers, Editions Plon, 2001)*

Contents

Figures

Tables

Contributors

Stefano Borzillo is Professor of Strategy and Knowledge Management at SKEMA Business School (Paris campus). His main research fields are communities of practice, knowledge creation and transfer in organizations. He obtained his PhD in Organizational Behavior from the University of Geneva (Switzerland) and was a Visiting Research Fellow at the Stern School of Business (New York University). Organizations where he conducted research on communities of practice include Siemens, Daimler, Oracle, IBM, PriceWaterhouse Coopers, Bearing Point, Swiss Re, Holcim, the World Bank, CERN (European Organization for Nuclear Research), the United Nations, the World Health Organization, the International Labor Office, Pictet Bank and the Lombard Odier Darier Hentsch Bank. He has also published in peer-reviewed journals such as *European Management Journal, Journal of Business Strategy, Management Learning, Knowledge Management Research & Practice,* and *Journal of Knowledge Management.*

Danièle Chauvel joined SKEMA as a Research Professor of Knowledge Management in 2010. Her professional background includes experience in academic research, managerial responsibilities in pedagogical engineering, senior executive education in an international environment and consulting practice in innovation and change management. She is an expert for EC (IST) and several think tanks, and her research is dedicated to the evolution of management principles, focusing on the role of knowledge management and its main trends and current development. She is the author of around 50 articles, chapters, grants or proceedings, and two books – *Knowledge Horizons: The Present and the Future of KM* (with C. Despres, Butterworth Heineman, 2000) and *Leading Issues in Innovation Research* (API, 2011).

Carole Daniel is an Associate Professor of Project Management at SKEMA. She holds a Master's in Management and a PhD in Management Science from Lille University. She is a certified consultant for MBTI® and Belbin®. She obtained an Evaluation Systems Diploma from ILI-Georgetown University, Washington, DC. After five years of professional experience in marketing and project management, she joined SKEMA to teach project management and team leadership. She has been a consultant for 13 years for international companies in the public and the private sectors. She is the Head of International Accreditations and the Executive MBA Program Director.

Pierre Daniel is the Deputy Director of ITEEM Engineering Master's degree in Technology, Management and Entrepreneurship, in partnership with Ecole Centrale de Lille. He is a trainer and consultant in the domain of complex programme management and strategic project management for international companies. He created the DevelopementModeling© methodology for analyzing, evaluating and managing complex projects and programmes. His research is dedicated to complex projects and programmes as dynamic systems and the entrepreneurial theory of control. He teaches Strategic Project Management in the MSc in Programme, Project Management and Business Development at SKEMA Business School. He regularly lectures in the MSc in Project Management at HEC Genève in Switzerland.

Régis Delafenestre is MS Supply Chain Management and Purchasing Scientific Director at SKEMA Business School for Lille and Casablanca. Régis teaches mainly basic principles of supply chain and operations and purchasing. He holds a Master's degree in Production and Operations Management and a PhD in Management, with a major in Supply Chain and Operations. His PhD concentrated on the supply chain tactical planning process with information and communication technologies. He continues to develop his research on this subject. He worked at Kohler Company for ten years as Supply Chain Manager and for ten years at Framatome Connectors International as Production Manager. He joined SKEMA in 2011.

Lorenz Gareis is Senior Consultant and authorized representative of RGC. His field of competency covers project and programme management, process management, change management and business analysis. He has profound experience as a consultant, trainer and project manager in various industries at a national and international level. He lectures in Project Management at the University of Applied Sciences, Vienna and the University of Applied Sciences Burgenland.

Roland Gareis graduated from the University of Economics and Business Administration in Vienna and gained his habilitation from the Department of Construction Industry at the University of Technology in Vienna. From 1979–1981 he was Professor of Construction Management at the Georgia Institute of Technology in Atlanta, then was Visiting Professor at ETH Eidgenössische Technische Hochschule, Zurich (1982), at the Georgia State University, Atlanta (1987) and at the University of Quebec, Montreal (1991). From 1986–2003 he was President of Projekt Management Austria, the Austrian Project Management Association and from 1998–2003 he was Director of Research of the International Project Management Association (IPMA). Since 1983 he has been Director of the postgraduate programme in International Project Management at WU Vienna and owner of Roland Gareis Consulting, Vienna. Since 2006 he has been the owner of Roland Gareis Consulting, Bucharest and from 2007 he has been Academic Director of the Professional MBA programme Project and Process Management at WU Vienna.

Jean-Charles Hainglaise has been working as a Project Manager and Consultant on industrial and international cooperation projects for 15 years. He also teaches project management in various environments and cultures. In 2005 he left the THALES group to create 'P Plus C', a company specializing in project management (consultancy and training). Since 2007 he has also been Associate Director of Global Consulting Group. He also volunteers on non-governmental organization projects in ecology. He graduated from the French School of Management of Lille (his master's specialized in Project Management).

Otto Husby is currently Project Director at Metier and is responsible for R&D and global business development. He has over 20 years of practical project management experience; working with offshore field development projects, IT projects, telecom projects, industrial projects and change projects. He has lectured in project management and participated in R&D project management programmes throughout his working career. He has also been responsible for Metier Academy's unique portfolio of project management learning products and blended learning approach, which is currently applied by many global project-oriented companies. He is currently working mainly with project governance and implementing 'best practice' project management in project-oriented organizations.

Waffa Karkukly is the owner and Managing Director of Global PMO Solutions, Inc. During her career she has been involved in leading strategic change programmes, quality and delivery improvement for projects, programmes and portfolios and every aspect of project management office (PMO) design, implementation and ongoing development for Fortune 100 and startups. She has a PhD in Strategic Program and Project Management and a Master's Degree in Information Technology. She is a regular speaker on the project management circuit. She is the Certificate Lead Developer for the Business Information Technology Management (BITM) certificate course at the School of Continuing Studies at University of Toronto. She teaches courses ranging from foundations of project management to advanced programme and portfolio management. She brings a wealth of industry experience in addition to her academic accreditations and experience.

Halvard Kilde is the CEO of Metier. He was the programme director for PS2000, which was Europe's largest research programme in project management, and he has 20 years' experience in the practical application of project management within large project-oriented companies. He has lectured in project management and participated in R&D project management programmes throughout his working career. He has been an advisor to many large project-oriented companies on how to improve their project success rate. He is a member of honour of the Norwegian Association for Project Management.

Laurence Lecoeuvre was formerly an International Director within the industrial sector and car industry (1984–2001). She integrated SKEMA in 2001. After a few years as Business Programs Director, she is today Director of Project Management Department and Director of the PhD in Programme & Project Management programme. She mainly teaches project management fundamentals and research methodology. Her PhD focused on the links between project marketing and project management; she continues to develop her research on this topic but also on governance.

Geneviève Poulingue teaches project management at SKEMA business school. She is responsible for the academic Grande Ecole Programme on the Paris campus.

She gained her PhD in 2009 with 'The Historigraphy of a Community of Experts in Project Management: The Club of Montreal', and a few days after its defence it was adopted by the Club of Montreal. She usually works on research topics within this community.

Sarah Ross is a Lecturer and Trainer in Project Management with over 25 years' experience in the service sector (health, telecommunications and tertiary education), primarily in the delivery of transformational projects, whilst involved in general management activities in New Zealand, Australia, UK and France. She is currently completing her PhD at SKEMA Business School, focusing on assurance of public sector project capability. She is also a PMP®, PRINCE2™ and MSP™ Trainer. She resides 'down under' in New Zealand and 'up over' in France, moving between the two for teaching and research-related activities.

Philippe Scotto was formerly a Nuclear Physicist and an IT project manager within the marine environmental sector at the IAEA. He is today the head of La Taureau Corporation (a consulting company specialized in the field of Strategic Management and Leadership). Since 1999 he has been a Visiting Professor at SKEMA teaching Project Management Fundamentals and Statistics/Mathematics. His PhD formed the basis of a Total Quality Control Managerial System based on methodologies coming from management and information sciences, and cybernetics. He still works on his researches but also on leadership. He received through and with the IAEA the Nobel Peace Prize 2005.

Rodney Turner is Managing Consultant at EuroProjex Ltd and Professor at SKEMA Business School, where he is Scientific Director for the PhD in Project and Programme Management. He is Adjunct Professor at the University of Technology Sydney and the Kemmy Business School, Limerick. He was educated at Auckland University where he did a Bachelor of Engineering, and Oxford University where he received an MSc in Industrial mathematics and a DPhil in Engineering Science. He was introduced to project management whilst working for ICI as a mechanical engineer and project manager in the petrochemical industry. He then worked for Coopers and Lybrand as a management consultant, working in shipbuilding, manufacturing, telecommunications, computing, finance, government and other areas. He is the author or editor of 16 books, including *The Handbook of Project-based Management*, the bestselling book published by McGraw-Hill, and the *Gower Handbook of Project Management*. He is editor of *The International Journal of Project Management* and lectures on project management worldwide. His research areas cover project management in small to medium enterprises, the management of complex projects, the governance of project management, including ethics and trust, project leadership and human resource management in the project-oriented firm. He is Vice President, Honorary Fellow and former Chairman of the UK's Association for Project Management, and former President and Chairman of the IPMA. From 1997 to 2005, he returned to the process plant industry as Operations Director of the Benelux Region of the European Construction Institute. He is a member of the Institute of Directors and Fellow of the Institution of Mechanical Engineers.

Murial Walas holds a degree in management (CAAE IAE Aix en Provence), a PhD in Computer Sciences and is a Consultant in Project Management and author of case studies in Statistics and Project Management. She is Scientific Director of the MSc Web-Marketing and International Project Management at SKEMA business school where she is also head of courses in Project Management and Statistics.

Sandra Walker is a training consultant with over 25 years' of experience in Europe, the Middle East and North America. She trains academia and corporate customers on intercultural project team leadership. She has been an adjunct lecturer at the SKEMA business school since 1998 and also works in the European Training Center, where her responsibilities include international business development and the creation of tailor-made workshops. She conducts doctoral research into optimal approaches to leadership of multicultural virtual project teams.

Foreword

Ralf Müller

It does not happen very often that I have dinner with a former State President, Special Envoy of the United Nations, or Director-General of the World Health Organization. Notably, it happened all at the same time, one evening in June 2012 in Shanghai, when I was invited to a dinner with Gro Harlem Brundtland.

There she was – the creator of the influential Brundtland Report and the author of the frequently cited definition of sustainability as being the meeting of today's goals while protecting future resources (Brundtland, 1987). During her dinner speech she gave a short overview of her work, told some anecdotes and reported on some of her experiences. It was certainly a story of an impressive career. However, what impressed me most was the final sentence of her speech, when she reflected back on her life and said, 'If there is one thing that I learned in my life, then it is that all things hang together.'

All things hang together – when reading through the present book there is probably no better way to summarize it. The book comes at a time when public awareness about the severity of interdependencies is growing, exemplified by the financial and other crises, which showed how fragile and interdependent things are, and how right Gro Brundtland is with her life reflection. To that end the book touches the *Zeitgeist* of society, which is an important criteria for long-lasting theoretical contributions (Müller and Shao, 2013), by describing interdependencies in the practical realm of projects and their management.

In line with that we see that after years of increasingly more detailed and focussed publications in project management literature, the time is ripe for a logical next step which links these details together. Which shows how *things hang together.* New concepts have been developed in many different fields, like *project networks* from an organization theory perspective, or *agile methods* from a project management perspective. However, little has been done yet to relate these newer concepts to each other with the aim of finding out about their combined contribution to better project performance within the constraints of careful use of resources, thus sustainability.

The present book fills this gap. It does it in many respects. For example by addressing not only projects per se in terms of methods, techniques and teams, but also project contexts in terms of governance or project management standards, or the different meanings of sustainability in the context of projects, as well as the differences when it comes to permanent and temporary organizations. In all these perspectives, the authors link relatively new concepts together for the benefit of project performance and sustainability. Examples include the integration of projects in the supply chain through project risk management practices, or the development of sustainable innovation projects, or the integration of project management baselining, project management training and process improvement into sustainable project management.

Of course, there are countless concepts and relationships between those concepts and only a fraction of them can be addressed in a book like this. This is where the authors' focus on project performance and sustainability ensures that *things hang together*. It helps in defining a cohesive framework of appropriate scope and sufficient depth, which is relevant for a broad readership. Academics will find a rich source of new ideas about concepts, relationships between concepts and their resulting effects on project performance, students will learn about some of the latest insights that research on project management has to provide, and reflective practitioners will be able to search for better understanding and, ultimately, hints for better performance of their projects.

The majority of contributions to this book are written by the faculty members of SKEMA Business School in France, who can be seen as *hanging together* in what is often called a permanent organization, in this case the faculty of a business school, to write about phenomena in temporary organizations – another example of interaction and interdependency. The contributions by these authors, together with some of their colleagues from other institutions, show how important it is to keep the big picture in mind while trying to understand what is going on at the detailed level.

This book makes a significant contribution to the development of new insights in project management and its related research, by showing that it is not enough to find the different concepts that influence project performance, but to understand their interactions and combined effects for the good or bad of a project and its management. Project managers and researchers may not realize it, but the most important aspects of what they manage and search for are the combined effects of several factors, because all *things hang together*.

References

Brundtland, G. H. (1987). *Our Common Future: Report of the World Commission on Environment and Development*. New York, NY: United Nations.

Müller, R., and Shao, J. (2013). A Model of the Dynamics in Theory Development. In N. Drouin, R. Müller, and S. Sankaran (Eds), *Novel Approaches to Organizational Project Management Research: Translational and Transformational*. Copenhagen, Denmark: Copenhagen Business School Press.

Preface

Laurence Lecoeuvre

When I prepared the general introduction, the issue for me was to decide either to describe the contents of the different chapters, which correspond to our main target to contribute to the development of the knowledge in project management, or to explain the adventure; not only my journey as director and coordinator of the book, but also our common story that led to this book. I finally decided to present both. Thus the first part of the general introduction focuses on the 'biological' development of the book, while the second part relates to the substance of the different parts.

The Essence of our Collective Book

The birth of a collective book often arises from a desire to work together or from a specific request of a publisher regarding a topic, but it may be due also to a less rational event. In our case, the origin of the collective work comes from the conclusion of a team building. Indeed I, as director of department, organized a seminar for our department project management where the main issue was to know how to promote our department inside our organization and internationally.

My first objective for this team building was to find a way to work closer together, and, as the name tells it, to build a factual team, engaged, motivated and able to share and contribute together to a common work.

We organized a brainstorming close to the Delphi method. As a result, we decided to develop a common strategy to clearly contribute to the development of the knowledge in project management, and to promote the faculty dedicated to project management, and their expertise, internal and external. Then we studied the best way to achieve this goal; the study was done using a weighting of votes: the first outcome was to launch a collective book. At that time, a decision to take action was made unanimously. To my great satisfaction, but not surprise, the team immediately showed enthusiasm.

Of course the subject of our book should focus on 'project management', but how could we be specific, different, even original in this topic when a lot of manuals and books already exist? How could we show our expertise within our organization and outside, where so many highly qualified researchers and practitioners deliver papers and books on our preferred area? Consequently we focused the following meetings on this issue.

The DNA of our organization SKEMA helped us: knowledge economy, international sustainability and performance. We all agreed on that point; we had to contribute to the knowledge area of project management, but also to reflect the 'genetic' developments of our organization.

At that point we discussed the way of working in this line. Indeed we could 'use' our different experiences, origins and expertise, and build a balance between practitioners and researchers of our team. It sounded obvious: our expertise and histories were complementary; our topics of research and development suited to the DNA of the organization. Therefore we could combine experiences related to research and professional experiences in projects.

Thus in this book we present diverse, but harmonizing, perspectives and currents of thought. This is certainly the major competitive advantage of our manuscript. The second difference with the existing volumes in project management is that we don't structure the book as a manual or a guideline; however, each chapter of the book is made as a paper of a journal. Each chapter has his own subject, of course linked with the main topic of the book, indeed it points out one key element; each chapter has an introduction, an abstract, a literature review, a methodology or case study, a discussion and conclusion and finally presents references.

In this way the reading is dynamic; furthermore all chapters are very pragmatic (case, research papers, viewpoints and so on) and definitively contribute to knowledge.

Contents and Development

Of course I managed the collective manuscript as a project. And I can say now that it was a complex project with multiple stakeholders and personalities who are engaged in other different projects and responsibilities, whose majority consequently found it difficult to meet deadlines. It is itself a case study! I must admit that in the middle of our project life I said to the team that I would never again pilot such a project . . . But today the satisfaction of this common adventure and outcome prevails.

We firstly thought about three main perspectives to cover the subject. To go forward, I asked for proposals, i.e. first tracks with title and abstracts. After a discussion of our expertise and synergies, also bearing in mind that is always more difficult to work alone and meet deadlines, the majority decided to write joint papers. Based on the abstracts delivered, we began to study the golden thread and to structure the parts. This first step was very encouraging, but we acknowledged that our first proposal wasn't sufficient in terms of contents and coverage of the theme. I therefore discussed this project with our director of research, who acknowledged the project but advised we ask, to help us to cover all the main topics, and to enhance the book to some external writers to contribute a larger target and appeal to gain visibility outside our organization.

Then each of us contacted a friend, a usual co-author, a colleague from another institution, an expert of his network and so on to contribute to our collective book. Of course we also paid attention to keep the balance between researchers and practitioners. As a result the team was completed and balanced.

The next step was to provide first tracks of chapters. A few months later, a consolidation of these chapters allowed me to contact publishers; and we had the honour and pleasure to be accepted by Gower Publishing. We of course worked a lot with them, we developed greatly thanks to their support to get this final issue.

Therefore the manuscript is based on project situations linked with sustainable performance of companies and/or of projects that are an important issue today. As explained before, we thought originally about three main parts to cover the topic, but after more contributions and the development of the different chapters, four main parts were formed, that correspond better to the subject that developed.

The issue today for companies and organizations is not only to perform but to achieve sustainable benefits; this competence is required at different levels, such as investment and resourcing, stakeholder management, project management or governance. This corresponds to the capability to manage change in the current world. But each change requirement is often linked to project management and, as change is a major source of risk, risk must be managed. By the way, the authors point out that project performance can be improved by risk management, in particular in situations of complex project that are a source of strong uncertainty. This question will be notably developed in the first part: (I) Project Risk Management and Sustainable Performance.

Moreover, sustainable performance of projects also depends on the organizational project management maturity and on the organization designed for managing projects. Besides, some form of governance, formal or informal, has to be present for an organization to exist and operate in the best way. Thus governance of project and corporate governance, and their environments, are questioned in the second part of the book: (II) Project Governance and Sustainable Performance.

In the context of the development of global mergers between organizations and of virtual relationships, managing projects becomes more complex, especially because of the difficulty of creating cross-relationships and processes within organizations, and also within stakeholders and project teams. Consequently, the need to generate innovative projects increases in line with the emergence of a unified role of business intelligence and knowledge, consistent with an updated managing of people for a long-term performance; this will be especially examined in the third part: (III) Project Teams and Sustainable Performance.

Finally, sustainable project management can be assured by a progressive, systemic approach that an organization will develop, based on the three keys of the project management: people, process and tools. Indeed, standards, baselines, methods and tools exist also to improve the performance of companies; that matter will be studied in the last part: (IV) Project Standards and Sustainable Performance.

Conclusion and Acknowledgement

To conclude on this general introduction, I would like to add that this work is not only the result of a year's work, but it is somehow an outcome of the professional and personal development of each of us, and of our team. That is the reason why I chose the quotation of W. A. Mozart that really illustrates our present job, and that corresponds to project management.

This book is intended for anyone interested in performance and/or in project; it can be read by senior managers, managers, project and programme managers, and by postgraduate students.

To finish, the authors would like to thank Alice Guilhon, Dean of SKEMA, who gave us the chance to develop our topic in line with the DNA of SKEMA, in piloting the strategy of our organization. We express gratitude to Pascal Grandin, Director of Research, whose idea to invite external contributors allowed an increased quality of the manuscript. We also acknowledge the companies, listed or not, without which the cases would not have existed. And thank you to Jonathan Norman and Darren Dalcher of Gower Publishing for their time, availability and advice, which helped us to produce a highly qualified book.

I personally would like to express thanks to all the contributors, my dear friends, for this job and wonderful adventure.

Part I

Project Risk Management and Sustainable Performance

Le véritable voyage de découverte ne consiste pas à chercher de nouveaux paysages mais à avoir de nouveaux yeux.

The real voyage of discovery consists not in seeking new landscapes but in having new eyes.

Marcel Proust (1871–1922)

Project Risk Management and Sustainable Performance

Chapter 1

Vision—Implementation—Organization

The VIO Approach for Complex Projects and Programs[1]

Pierre Daniel and Rodney Turner

Introduction

For 25 years, leading writers in the field of project management have been suggesting that before the project team start planning a project, they should develop a strategy for how they plan to implement it (Morris and Hough, 1987; Turner, 2009, first edition 1993). Project managers have a tendency when they have a project to plan just to start by stuffing activities into Microsoft Project, without first thinking about the key elements of the project and how they should be addressed. It is important on all projects to start by developing a basic strategy for how the project should be undertaken, but it is particularly important on complex project. On complex projects, a small change in input conditions can lead to a very large change in output conditions. So it is important to think first about what the desired end point is and work back to defining the input conditions for the project.

Rodney Turner (2009) defines project management as the process of converting vision into reality. Graham Winch (2010) defines it as the process of converting desire into memory. For all projects, we need to start with a clear vision, desire, of what we want the project to do, and then define the process of how to realize that vision, and by undertaking the process convert it into memory. That is particularly important on complex projects.

In this chapter we describe the Vision—Implementation—Organization (VIO) approach to the management of complex projects and programs. Eweje, Turner and Müller (2012) say that complex mega-projects are in fact more like programs than projects. In this chapter we are talking about the management of complex projects or programs, but for simplicity we will use the word "project" throughout, but it can mean project or program. In the next section we describe how to develop a project strategy. Then we describe the three elements of the VIO approach, Vision, Implementation and Organization.

Strategy

Turner, Huemann, Anbari and Bredillet (2010) suggest a four-step process for defining project strategy:

---

1 This chapter is partially inspired by a book that one of the authors co-authored with Emeline Hassenforder and Benjamin Noury (2012), towards who we express our gratitude.

1   develop corporate strategy;
2   define the project requirements including the business plan;
3   identify the project success criteria and success factors;
4   design the project model.

Corporate Strategy

To develop a corporate strategy, there are three steps, each of which has three components:

1   position;
2   strategic choices;
3   implementation.

Position

To identify the organization's current position, we need to investigate its context, its capabilities and its stakeholders. There are several tools for analyzing the position. One is PESTLE analysis. This investigates the pressures on a firm from several sources:

* political;
* economic;
* social;
* technical;
* legal;
* environmental.

Another tool is Michael Porter's Five Forces (Porter, 1980). This investigates five forces that act on a company from within the industry it operates in. They are:

* buyers;
* suppliers;
* new entrants;
* substitutes;
* rivals.

The analysis of the position identifies opportunities and threats the firm faces. Its capability tells us what strengths and weaknesses it has to deal with those opportunities and threats. Its capabilities include:

* competence of its staff;
* technology;
* management processes;
* organization;
* supply chain.

An analysis of the context and capabilities together can be done as a SWOT analysis, looking at strengths, weaknesses, opportunities and threats.

The third element of the position is the stakeholders. A narrow view of stakeholders says there is just one important stakeholder, the owners of the business or shareholders. The wider view says there are other important stakeholders, including:

- the board, management and staff;
- customers;
- the local community;
- suppliers.

The stakeholders will have a view on what the organization should be doing and so will influence strategy.

Strategic Choices

Having identified its position, the firm is then able to make strategic choices. It makes strategic choices at three levels:

1   company;
2   business unit;
3   operations.

The cascade is usually down: company to business unit to operations. This corresponds with the cascade portfolio to program to project, Figure 1.1. However, you must be careful, a project may sometimes influence corporate strategy under emergent strategy. A product development project may for instance show which new products will be both feasible and profitable, and so influence what business units the firm needs and its future strategic direction.

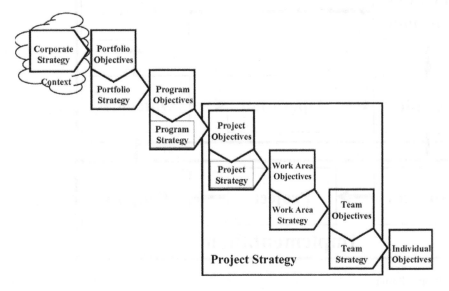

Figure 1.1 Cascade from Corporate Strategy to Project Strategy

Implementation

The strategic choices will identify the need for projects, programs and projects, Figure 1.1, and so we are now ready to start defining the requirements of projects.

Requirements

The requirements can exist in several dimensions. We need to define the results or objectives we want the project to deliver, the specification of one of those results, the output, and we need to develop the business plan.

Results

First we need to define the objectives of the project, the results we expect it to deliver. Figure 1.2 illustrates that there are (at least) three levels of results on projects. The result that is traditionally focused on is the project output. This is the project deliverable, the new asset it is expected to deliver. Success is judged by whether the new asset performs as expected and is delivered to cost and time. This judgement is made on the last day of the project, and is associated with the project and the operational level.

However, we do not want the project's output for its own sake. We undertake the project to solve some problem or exploit some opportunity to obtain benefit. In order to do that we need new competencies, we need to be able to do new things, and the operation of the new asset provides those new competencies. We call this the project's outcome. The operation of the outcome solves the problem or exploits the

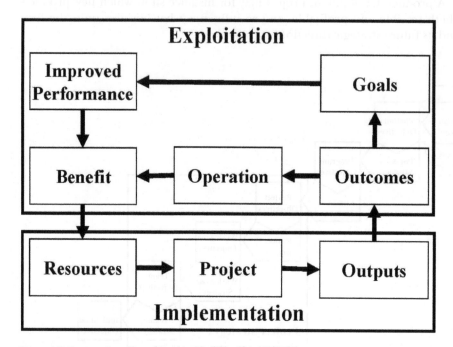

Figure 1.2 Project Results

opportunity and provides the benefit. We judge success by whether we are able to solve the problem or exploit the opportunity, and whether we obtain the desired benefit. We are able to judge this in the months following the project and it is associated with the program and the business unit.

With time, the project's output will enable us to achieve higher levels of performance improvement, which we call the impact. Success is judged by whether we achieve the higher levels of performance improvement. It is judged in the years following the project, and is associated with the portfolio and the company.

As an example, the Chinese government built a bridge across the Yangtze river just north of Shanghai. Why did they want the bridge? The reason was that whereas the area around Shanghai is the most economically developed part of mainland China, the area on the north side of the river was less developed. The reason why people were not building their factories on the north side of the river was because transport across the river was poor, so it was difficult to get their products to Shanghai for them to be shipped out. So the desired impact was economic development on the north side of the river, and the required new competencies, the project outcome, was better traffic flows across the river. The project output to achieve this was a bridge.

Again, the normal cascade is the desired impact defines the desired project outcome and that defines the required output. However, sometimes a project will result in unexpected but beneficial outcomes that will define new businesses for the organization, which with time will lead to new impacts and changes to the organization itself.

Above we define three levels of results. Later we define a fourth level, intermediary deliverables, produced during the project to deliver components of the project output. The intermediary deliverables are associated with packages of work undertaken during the project.

Specification

The second dimension of requirements is the specification of the project's output, the definition of the performance it is required to deliver, and the functionality we desire of it in order to produce the outcome (Dalcher, 2013). Additional elements include the scope of work to be done, the technology to be used and the required resources.

Business Plans

Another necessary element not created in the strategy for many projects is the business plan. Every project should have a business plan, detailing in particular how much the project is expected to cost and what the expected benefits are, and performing an investment appraisal to justify the project. The contents of a business plan should include:

- strategic objectives reflecting vision statement;
- expected benefits;
- overall risk profile;
- assumptions;
- estimated costs and timescales;
- investment appraisal.

The timescale is necessary to perform the investment appraisal. The time at which the benefits are obtained will affect the profitability of the project.

Success

The next step is to identify the success criteria and success factors for the project. The success criteria are the measures against which we will judge the success of the project. They will be defined by the strategic choices of the parent organization, the requirements and the business plan for the project. The success criteria are those elements of the project we can influence to increase the chance of achieving the success criteria. Well-known lists of success factors are published (Pinto and Slevin, 1987). However, every project is different and so will have different success factors, (Turner, Huemann, Anbari and Bredillet, 2010). In fact the success criteria will suggest what the success factors might be (Khan, Turner and Maqsood, 2013; Wateridge, 1995, 1998). If acceptance by the stakeholders is an important success criterion, then communication will be an important success factor; if making a profit is an important success criterion, then managing the cost and time will be important success factors; if opening the sporting event on a specific date is a key requirement, then managing the timescale will again be an important success factor. We focus on certain success factors depending on what the key success criteria are for our project.

Model

We are now in a position to design the project model. The three main components of the project model are the planning and control systems, the people and resources we need to undertake the work, and the organization of them into a project team.

Figure 1.3 illustrates the seven project forces model developed by Rodney Turner (2009). He suggests that there are seven forces acting on a project, four external to the project, and three internal drivers. Of the four external forces he suggests two are resisting the project, the context and the attitudes of stakeholders, and two are driving the project, sponsorship and the definition of the project. In the context of the discussion above, we can relate the seven forces to all the elements we have identified.

- *Context*: In fact we would now say that this is the strategic position of the parent organization, the context, its capabilities and the stakeholders of the parent organization.
- *Sponsorship*: These are the strategic choices made by the parent organization and the business case for the project.
- *Definition*: These are the requirements for the project.
- *Attitudes*: These are the attitudes of the stakeholders of the project, which we have not discussed above, but which is a key part of the VIO approach. The stakeholders of the project will include the stakeholders of the parent organization.
- *Project drivers*: These are the three specific elements of the project model which follow on from the success factors: the planning and control of the project; the people and resources we need to undertake the project; and the organization of them into a project organization.

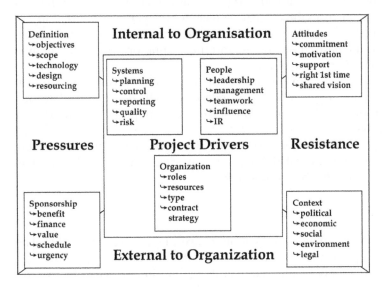

Figure 1.3 Seven Forces Model

The VIO Approach

For the remainder of this chapter we will describe the VIO approach for managing complex projects and programs. The approach is illustrated in Figure 1.4. It covers key elements of the project strategy:

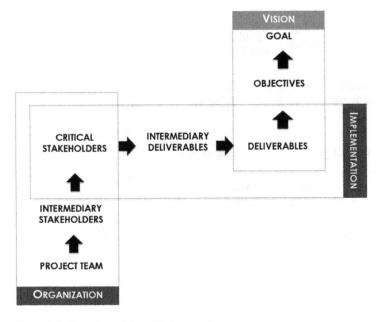

Figure 1.4 Overview of the VIO Approach

Vision: First we define the vision for the project. This primarily consists of the project results, but also encompasses the strategic choices for the parent organization and the business plan for the project. We identify the three levels of results in Figure 1.2, the impact of the project, the desired outcomes, and the output, or project deliverables required to help us achieve the outcomes.

Implementation: We then develop the project plan. The plan is based on a fourth level of results, intermediary deliverables required to create the deliverables that comprise the project output. We also identify the stakeholders required to produce the intermediary deliverables.

Organization: We create the project team, and identify responsibilities of project team members for managing the stakeholders and ensuring they deliver the intermediary deliverables for which they are responsible.

Project Vision

We said above that project management is about converting a vision into reality. The first step of the VIO approach is to set a clear vision for the project. Then through the second and third steps of implementation and organization we define how we are going to convert that vision into reality. Figure 1.5 illustrates the setting of the vision.

Figure 1.5 Setting the Vision

The vision is initiated with a clear and verifiable goal, the impact in Figure 1.2. We then identify various important dimensions of the project, and objectives associated with each dimension. From the objectives we identify final deliverables required to achieve each one.

Goal

In order to initiate the vision, we need to define a clear and verifiable goal, Figure 1.2. The goal is the desired future state we would like our organization to achieve, the impact of the project: economic development on the north side of the Yangtze river; greater profitability for our business.

A Goal Is a Way of Explaining Long-Term Ambition

The project vision must be clearly defined through a global and comprehensive goal stated as a long-term outcome for people benefiting from the project's results. Setting a goal is at the core of the VIO approach (Giard and Midler, 1996). The goal is our project development objective, and describes the desired future state of our organization that the project is expected to contribute to, or how the present situation will be changed as a result of the project's achievement. The goal defines the ideal we are aiming for, not the actions to realize it. It guides the stakeholders of the project by providing them with a direction for their actions. If at any point of the project there is uncertainty about what they are doing, the goal should provide them with the answer. Therefore, the expression of a unique goal is essential. Multiple goals weaken the design and diffuse project efforts.

The Goal Must Be Measurable

The project vision has to be discussed, challenged and evaluated through quantifiable and verifiable indicators. How we are going to measure the medium and long-term success of a project must be defined and debated in the early stages. The quantifiable measures of the expected future performance of our organization are a central element for discussions, negotiations when the project is being designed. Defining the expected long-term performance with objectively verifiable indicators is a way of focusing everybody's energy on practical and verifiable questions. Objectively verifiable goal indicators, which measure the end of project impact (EOPI), show the important characteristics of the goal and the performance standard expected to be reached in terms of quantity, quality, time frame and location. The word "objectively" implies that indicators should be specified in a way that is independent of possible bias of the observer.

Since it is a difficult exercise, indicators at the strategic level of the project (goal and objectives) do not always exist or are not precisely targeted in terms of quantity, quality and time. Yet, it is a necessary effort in order to be able to evaluate the success of the project. Indicators that are too vague facilitate the final evaluation to grade the project as a success but do not pledge for sustainable changes. Normally goal indicators should be measured several years after the end of the project in order to assess the sustainability of the project efforts. Unfortunately, the question of who should fund this post evaluation remains an unanswered issue in most cases. Setting clear goal indicators makes it easier to set indicators at objectives and deliverables level.

A Goal Is an Opportunity to Reveal Contradictions

The project vision is a mix of multiple interests coming from various stakeholders. They must be combined in a comprehensive vision. Ideally, the goal must be consensual and acceptable for all the key groups of stakeholders. Rodney Turner (2009) suggests that getting agreement of the stakeholders to the goal is a necessary condition for projects success. The project team and the local stakeholders must take a leading role in the definition of the goal to help ensuring ownership and commitment. Goal definition is the opportunity for the stakeholders who are involved in the project to be gathered together to express their interests. It provides an opportunity for the stakeholders to meet, share their experiences and views, and be aware of their respective interests and potential contradictions.

Each stakeholder can have interests that do not necessarily concur with another stakeholder (Cleland and Ireland, 2002). These potentially conflicting views need to be formulated and considered to establish the clear goal of the project. The goal should not hide the contradictions among the stakeholders but rather highlight them. Setting the goal is the occasion for revealing conflicting interests early in the project to prevent them popping up later during the implementation with potential broader negative impacts.

Dimensions and Objectives

Next we identify the project's objectives, but we acknowledge that the objectives may fall in one of several dimensions.

The Project Vision Comprises Multiple Dimensions

The project vision can be detailed through various dimensions that help us achieve coherence. Acknowledging the existence of the dimensions is a significant step in designing the project vision, and helps build an integrated, comprehensive and sustainable framework. Figure 1.5 suggests that the dimensions may include the following components:

- political;
- economic;
- social;
- technical;
- scientific;
- legal;
- financial;
- media.

Objectives Are Long-Term Outcomes that Contribute to the Overall Goal

The overall goal of the project vision must be broken into objectives that represent each key dimension. The objectives describe an achievement we aim to realize at some point in the future in order to be able to achieve the goal. They represent the outcomes in Figure 1.2. As for the goal, the objectives must be formulated as an expression of a desire for a future end state. Objectives are much more specific than the goal and must be stated in terms of a particular result to be expected, a future completed action (Cleland and Ireland, 2002). They should not either be formulated as a means or a process (Andersen, Grude and Haug, 2009). They are the end state we wish to achieve, not the method of getting there.

The Objectives Are Very Sensitive to Stakeholders' Interests

The objectives help reveal the interests of stakeholders and how they are impacted by future outcomes of the project. Behind each dimension, there are stakeholders. The objectives formulated for each dimension must reflect the interests of the stakeholders of this dimension. At this, the design stage of the project, the main stakeholders can be identified and assigned in each dimension according to their scope of activities and interests. This can be done through a stakeholders' analysis (Huemann and Eskerod, 2013; Turner, 2009). Several stakeholders and groups of stakeholders are often recurrent in complex water projects:

This representation is not comprehensive. The idea is to list the various stakeholders who could be involved in or impacted by the project. The identification dimensions of the project help us not to forget any major group of stakeholders. Each dimension represents a specific interest, and is a source of impact and influence from groups of stakeholders.

Objectives can change in the course of the project under the pressure of various stakeholders with opposite interests. Events might occur that require modifications or changes to the project objectives. The context can lead to rephrasing of the issue and gets the targeted objectives to evolve (Giard and Midler, 1996).

Final Deliverables

To complete the defining of the vision we identify the deliverables of the project. These describe the project output, Figure 1.2.

Final Deliverables Are New Strategic Resources

In order to achieve the goal and objectives, the organization needs to develop new strategic resources. These are the deliverables from the project and must be clearly identified as part of the vision. The final deliverables are required products or services that must be produced during the project's development phase and are delivered by the project stakeholders. The final deliverables must be tangible and can be of four different types:

Money: subventions, loans, transfers, basket funding . . .

Information: documents, treaties, agreements, training, website, information systems . . .

People: country coordinator, interministerial committee, social groups . . .

Equipment: Offices, craft center, monitoring equipment, dams, wells . . .

Final Deliverables Are Sources of Sustainable Operational Performance

The final deliverables must be defined as sustainable resources that will generate the operational performance required to achieve the objectives defined by stakeholders. They should be long-term oriented, meaning that the deliverables themselves, or their benefits, must last after the end of the project. They are future resources, expected results that will be used in the long run.

Formulating the final deliverables as long-term oriented tangible results forces the project team to consider how these deliverables will be maintained after the end of the project. Who will be in charge of them? Who will pay for them? This exercise strengthens the sustainability potential of the project. Yet, our analysis of ten transboundary water projects revealed that the design of complex water projects is often very weak in this respect (Hassenforder, Daniel and Nouray, 2012). Many deliverables considered as final are not actually sustainable. Therefore, once the project ends, they are not maintained.

Far too often as well deliverables are identified which don't fully deliver the project's observes. When all deliverables of a dimension taken together are not sufficient to achieve the objective of that dimension, it means that the list of deliverables is not comprehensive and one or more need to be identified.

The Final Deliverables Must Be Specific

Knowing what to do does not mean you are absolutely sure of the outcome. Deliverables must be clear and limited to a small number, in order to facilitate discussions, negotiations and arrangements between beneficiaries and stakeholders in charge of the implementation of the project. A common problem in the problem analysis and objective setting phase of the projects is an inappropriate level of detail, too much or too little. We suggest to restrict the number of key final deliverables to five per dimension, which makes a total of 40 maximum. Even in large projects, key final deliverables rarely exceed this number. This exercise helps to keep a systemic vision on the project and setting priorities. When the project design is too detailed, project stakeholders often get confused and miss a clear global picture on the project and on what they need to produce. The choice of the indicator must rely on the value the deliverable will bring to achieving the objective. Deliverable indicators must be tailored according to what needs to be implemented in order to reach the objective. The choice of an indicator will impact on the implementation of the deliverable. The process of defining and targeting such indicators will help to shape the synergy among the deliverables and opportunities for integration. Indicators on deliverables are usually poorly defined, and many projects suffer from a lack of verifiable indicators of success for deliverables. Project stakeholders tend to use binary indicators, which measure the completion of the deliverable with no emphasis, placed on functional and quantified expectations.

Project Implementation

Having defined the project vision we must now determine how it will be achieved; the means by which we deliver the vision is project implementation.

Converting Vision to Reality

The Project Vision Is Dependent on a Causal Structure of Implementation

The project vision is not static. All the final deliverables that are listed in the strategic wheel as required for the achievement of the project vision must be produced in the project development, or implementation, phase. However, these final deliverables have interdependencies; they are partly intertwined and cannot be implemented separately, Figure 1.6. The production of one of them can have impacts on the production on others. The consequence is that their production process is dynamic; changes in the implementation of a one deliverable may generate changes in the implementation of another. Developing all of them in the project implementation phase may become very complex, unstable and uncertain. Eventually, because every deliverable is a piece of the future operational performance, if one key deliverable does not reach the expected performance or is not implemented, it raises doubt about the future performance and sustainability of the whole system. Hence, the project development phase is at the center of the future operational performance.

In such conditions, managing the project performance means managing the risks of production for every final deliverable, as well as the interdependencies in between final deliverables processes of development. We focus on implementation risks considered as dynamic changes able to modify the final project vision: if some final deliverables are not delivered in conformity with the design of the vision, it naturally influences our capacity to achieve the specific objectives, and, as a consequence it impacts the capacity to achieve the overall goal, Figure 1.7.

Dependency links need to be established among the key deliverables of the various dimensions. Hence, a *causal structure* of the project can be established, Figure 1.6. These links represent the influences and connections in between the key deliverables.

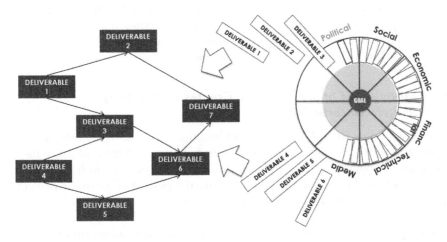

Figure 1.6 Causal Structure of the Deliverables

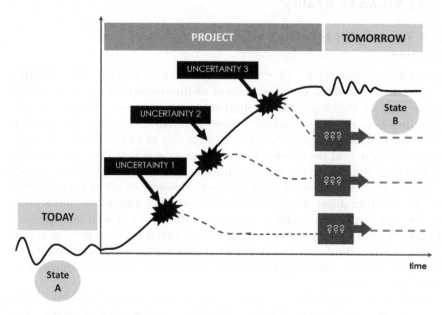

Figure 1.7 Implementation Risks

A link can be established between two deliverables A and B if the following assertion is affirmative:

> IF key deliverable A does not reach the expected performance, THEN key deliverable B will be impacted in its capacity to reach its own performance.

Trying to establish relations between too many key deliverables risks our getting mired in complexity at the expense of effectiveness. That is why we suggest you should not focus on four to eight key deliverables maximum per dimension. The fact that the key deliverables of the various dimensions are linked one to another, and therefore that the various dimensions are linked one to another, naturally generates *transversality* inside the project. It is a characteristic of complex projects.

The Causal Structure of Implementation Creates a Trajectory Sensitive to Project Uncertainties

During the project, key final deliverables will be implemented. The multiple processes to produce the final deliverables, and the links between deliverables and then processes creates a dynamic *trajectory*. During the project, events will happen that will modify the deliverables trajectory and therefore the performance of the project. The trajectory generates high degrees of complexity for stakeholders involved in the project.

Projects are prone to uncertainty, Figure 1.7. Projects teams cannot precisely predict the project results but they can anticipate their impacts by modeling the deliverables trajectory. The trajectory of implementation is based on the multiple actions that are done by stakeholders in the project. Some actions tend to generate stability; others will lead to trouble and contradictions. All these actions lead to the production of *intermediary deliverables* (results), Figure 1.8, that are required in order to produce final deliverables. These intermediary deliverables are like events that can modify the project trajectory and affect the final performance defined in the project vision. The project team will have to be adaptive and flexible during the project implementation in order to integrate them. These uncertain "events" can come from:

- *Outside the project* (exogenous events): events occurring in the project environment that will impact the project; a flood for instance.
- *Inside the project* (endogenous events): deliverables or stakeholders of the project that will impact other deliverables or stakeholders of the project. These modifications will occur in multiple dimensions: a technical deliverable is not necessarily impacted by a technical problem; it can also be impacted by a legal or financial problem for instance.

Intermediary Deliverables

Intermediary Deliverables Are Temporary Actions Generating Final Deliverables

The actions required to produce intermediary deliverables must be clearly defined and discussed during the project trajectory, as they are the way to generate the final deliverables. The intermediary deliverables are the results of actions that need to be implemented in order to produce final deliverables. Formulating intermediary

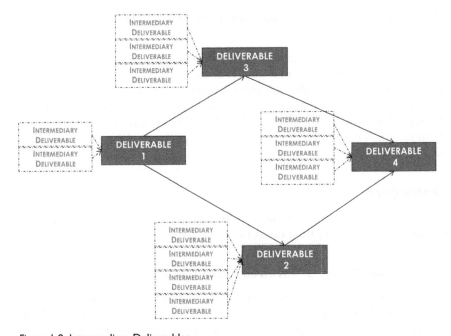

Figure 1.8 Intermediary Deliverables

deliverables rather than activities allows a simple and clear representation of what needs to be done during project implementation (Andersen, Grude and Haug, 2009).

Intermediary deliverables are temporary. They are only implemented as an intermediary action leading to the results: the final deliverables. At the end of the project development phase, these intermediary deliverables are not useful anymore. They are elements that are used for the project implementation sake. Once final deliverables are produced, intermediary deliverables become obsolete. Examples of intermediary deliverables include meetings, feasibility study, project budget, financial management system, preliminary report, financial audit, proposals, contracts for project implementation, field visits, and so on.

Intermediary Deliverables Are Tactics of Experimentation

The selection of intermediary deliverables that are highlighted and implemented in a project constitutes the practical tactics that are chosen in order to deliver the project final deliverables. These intermediary deliverables are chosen by project stakeholders as good solutions to produce the final deliverables. However, they are just one way of going to the final result, which is the final deliverable. The set of intermediary deliverables can evolve considerably during the project life cycle. Implementing a project means testing certain actions. During project implementation, the intermediary deliverables initially identified might not provide the expected results, thereby impacting the final key deliverable. The project design must be adjusted to take into account these alterations. This unpredictability creates new opportunities that need to be caught by the project team in order to adapt the project to evolving conditions. It is an *experimentation* principle.

Intermediary Deliverables Have Transversal Impacts on the Project Trajectory

The intermediary deliverables that are selected must be described and studied regarding the collateral impacts that they may generate on the project's long-term performance. An intermediary deliverable of one dimension can impact one or several final deliverables of another dimension. Projects are not made of separated fields of action. All dimensions can potentially be interrelated. Therefore, any modifications of a social intermediary deliverable for instance can impact technical or political final deliverables.

Key Stakeholders

It is important to clearly define the stakeholders who are going to play a key role in the implementation of each key final deliverable, Figure 1.9.

Key Stakeholders Are "Players" Involved in the Deliverables "Game"

All final and intermediary deliverables are implemented by key stakeholders. A *stakeholder* is an individual or institution that may – directly or indirectly, positively or negatively – be affected by or affect a deliverable (Huemann and Eskerod, 2013).

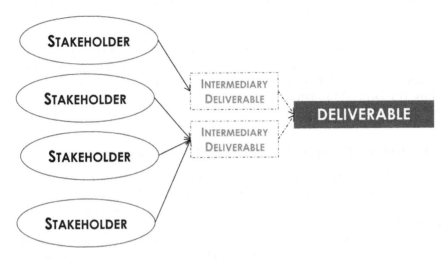

Figure 1.9 Key Stakeholders

If intermediary deliverables are sources of slowdown, acceleration, opposition or synergy, it is because the stakeholders related to these deliverables are themselves facing problems or oppositions. All stakeholders must be clearly identified. For each key final and intermediary deliverables, several questions can be raised:

- Who are the stakeholders in charge of its implementation?
- Who are the beneficiaries? *Beneficiaries* are stakeholders who benefit in whatever way from the implementation of the project. Distinction may be made between:

  1   *Target groups*: The group or entity who will be directly positively affected by the project at the Project level. This may include the stakeholders in charge of its implementation.
  2   *Final beneficiaries*: Those who benefit from the project in the long term at the level of the society or sector at large.

- Who else could affect the deliverable, directly or indirectly? These stakeholders can be internal or external to the project.

Stakeholder identification is a continuous process and can be difficult. Thinking in terms of dimensions will help not to forget any stakeholder.

Key Stakeholders Have Their Own Interests and Behaviors

It is important to analyze and understand the interests that are going to drive the behaviors of stakeholders in the project trajectory. The identification of the various stakeholders and their link with the project deliverables is followed by the detection of their interests (Huemann and Eskerod, 2013; Turner, 2009). The *interest* of a stakeholder in a project is the expectations the stakeholder has towards the project. The interest is relative depending on the stakeholder. The stakeholders can be placed in the various dimensions of the wheel according to the deliverables they are involved with, Figure 1.10.

In complex water projects, key stakeholders have various and sometimes contradictory interests (Hassenforder, Daniel and Noury, 2012). Each stakeholder can have interests that do not necessarily agree with another stakeholder. These potentially conflicting views can result in one person calling a project a success and another calling it a failure (Cleland and Ireland, 2002). Moreover, these conflicting interests can have adverse impacts on the project.

Key Stakeholders Are Potential Sources of Positive or Negative Impact

The stakeholders behave in a positive or a negative way for the implementation of the project; their actions must be anticipated and prioritized. A common misconception is the idea that problems on strategic deliverables come from stakeholders at the strategic level. The stakeholders' analysis is often made based on hierarchical organization perspectives. This leads to the attention being focused on people working in organizations and institutions at the strategic level. However, impacts on the project performance can come from stakeholders involved in the deliverables' production processes. Very frequently, these stakeholders are not in strategic positions.

Risks

The final performance of the project depends on problems on intermediary deliverables which themselves comes from the stakeholders involved in their implementation, Figure 1.11. In order to manage the implementation of the project, it is necessary to anticipate the risks that might impact the expected performance of the project. *Risks* are key factors, which have the potential to impact negatively on the project. Evaluating the risks linked to intermediary deliverables and key stakeholders will allow explanation of the potential causes of problems and modifications that might happen on key final deliverables. It is not possible for the project team to

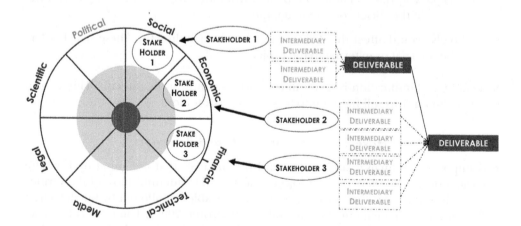

Figure 1.10 Areas of Interest of the Stakeholders

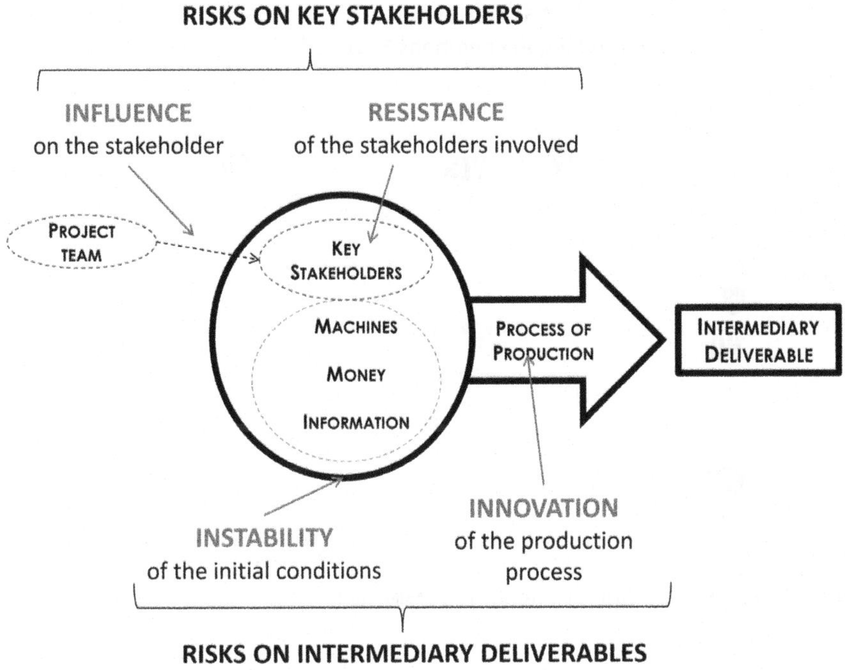

RISKS ON KEY STAKEHOLDERS

INFLUENCE
on the stakeholder

RESISTANCE
of the stakeholders involved

PROJECT
TEAM

KEY
STAKEHOLDERS

MACHINES

PROCESS OF
PRODUCTION

INTERMEDIARY
DELIVERABLE

MONEY

INFORMATION

INSTABILITY
of the initial conditions

INNOVATION
of the production
process

RISKS ON INTERMEDIARY DELIVERABLES

Figure 1.11 Risks on Intermediary Deliverables and Key Stakeholders

monitor all stakeholders and deliverables. It is therefore necessary to identify critical ones, which will need particular attention.

Risks on Intermediary Deliverables

The key deliverables of the project may not be traditional for the stakeholders who will be in charge of producing them. This is a source of lack of performance that must be identified. For each intermediary deliverable, a first question that must be answered is: Have key stakeholders in charge of the implementation of this intermediary deliverable already implemented the same deliverable successfully before?

- *NO*: The process to produce this deliverable, the tasks and methods that needs to be employed are totally or partially new to the stakeholders: the process is innovative.
- *YES*: The stakeholders are used to such tasks and methods: the process is traditional.

This question measures the degree of innovation of the project process, Figure 1.12, title of rows.

The key deliverables of the project may be produced in conditions of implementation that are not traditional for the stakeholders who are in charge of delivering them. This is a source of lack of performance that must be identified. For each intermediary

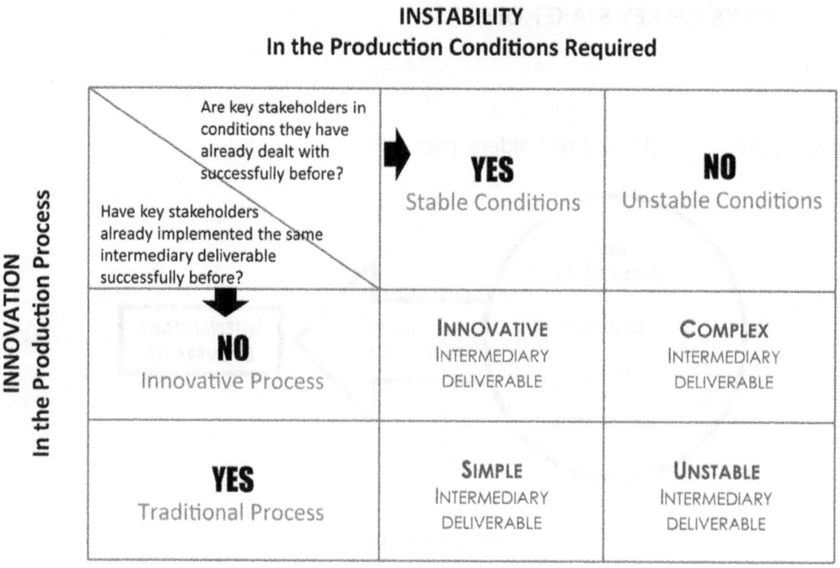

INSTABILITY
In the Production Conditions Required

		YES Stable Conditions	NO Unstable Conditions
Are key stakeholders in conditions they have already dealt with successfully before? Have key stakeholders already implemented the same intermediary deliverable successfully before?	**NO** Innovative Process	**INNOVATIVE** INTERMEDIARY DELIVERABLE	**COMPLEX** INTERMEDIARY DELIVERABLE
INNOVATION In the Production Process	**YES** Traditional Process	**SIMPLE** INTERMEDIARY DELIVERABLE	**UNSTABLE** INTERMEDIARY DELIVERABLE

Figure 1.12 Risks Associated with Critical Intermediary Deliverables

deliverable, a second question that must be answered is: Are key stakeholders in conditions they have already dealt with successfully before?

- *NO*: the conditions can be of two types:
  1 *Human*: The stakeholders have never worked with these other stakeholders before; and
  2 *Technical*: The stakeholders will use technical resources (materials, information, money) that are new to them. The conditions are new, the environment is *unstable*.
- *YES*: the stakeholder has already worked in those conditions, in that geographical area, with the other stakeholders of the project, with those materials, under the same budget constraints: the conditions are traditional, the environment is *stable*.

This question measures the degree of instability of the project conditions, Figure 1.12, title of columns.

An intermediary deliverable produced with both an innovative process and in unstable conditions *critical*, Figure 1.12. On very large projects, assessing risks on all intermediary deliverables can appear to be a long and tedious process. In that case, it is possible either:

- To assess risks on key final deliverables in order to identify zones of risks. For key final deliverables that appear to be a critical, a more thorough analysis on intermediary deliverables can then be led.
- To identify key final deliverables that are potentially risky based on knowledge and experience and assess the risks on intermediary deliverables for those key final deliverables only.

Risks on Stakeholders

The stakeholders involved in the implementation of key deliverables may be a source of lack of performance for reasons of personal interest competence or means. This must be identified. For intermediary deliverables that were identified as critical, a deeper analysis of the risks linked to the stakeholders in charge of their implementation can be done. A first question that must be answered is: Does the stakeholders have a positive behavior towards the project?

- *NO*: the stakeholders are not favorable to the project. The resistance can be of three types:

  1 *Lack of will*: they do not show interest in the project because it is not a priority; they do not come to meetings;
  2 *Lack of skills*: they are insufficiently trained, they do not have the skills to do what they have to do;
  3 *Lack of means*: they do not have time, or the money or the material to do what they have to.

  The stakeholders are *resisting*.

- *YES*: the stakeholders have the will, skills and means to do what they are there to do: they are capable, show good will towards the project and have the means to undertake their work. The stakeholders are *supportive*.

Several *mitigation strategies* exist in order to lessen the degrees of resistance of the stakeholders. Many well-documented books and publications identify solutions to face these risks. Common and simple solutions include:

Lack of will: In the water projects (Hassenforder, Daniel and Nouray, 2012), the analysis of the ten projects allowed us to identify solutions to reduce the lack of political will. These included:

- requiring a financial involvement of the countries in order to increase their ownership of project activities;
- the use of international media to increase their visibility on the international scene, lobby of non-governmental organizations (NGOs).

Many solutions are drawn from public participation. Another solution encompasses establishing a global strategy but leaving room at the national and local level for stakeholders to decide of their actions.

Lack of skills: Mitigation actions to increase skills of the stakeholders include capacity-building training, study tours and training in other countries and hiring of consultants.

Lack of means: In the water projects (Hassenforder, Daniel and Nouray, 2012), several countries supported stakeholders who lacked of means by providing them with assistance that would help them to catch up with other stakeholders.

The stakeholders involved in the key deliverables implementation may be out of the influence of the project management team. It potentially amplifies problems in the project, and must be identified. For each key stakeholder in charge of implementing a critical intermediary deliverable, a second question must be answered: Does the project team have a direct influence over the stakeholder?

- *NO*: There is no such linkage between one or several members of the project team and the stakeholder: the stakeholder is out of influence.
- *YES*: The influence can be of two types:

  1 *There is a power relation towards this stakeholder*: members of the project team are hierarchically superior, they have signed a contract with the stakeholder, they pay him or her for his or her activities, they have a legal power that allows them to give him or her orders.
  2 *There is an emotional relation towards this stakeholder*: they are friends or of the same family, they come from the same village, the stakeholder admires them. The stakeholder is under influence.

A key stakeholder who is both resisting and out of influence is *critical*, Figure 1.13. Conversely, a stakeholder who is both supportive and under influence is *positive*.

Risks must be identified at the beginning of the project. Mitigation strategies have two advantages:

1 They allow anticipating problems by managing their sources. The degrees of risk on intermediary deliverables and stakeholders can be reduced.
2 They allow more reactive responses when problems appear.

So far, mitigation strategies have been used to decrease the levels of innovation, instability and resistance but not to increase the influence of the project team on critical

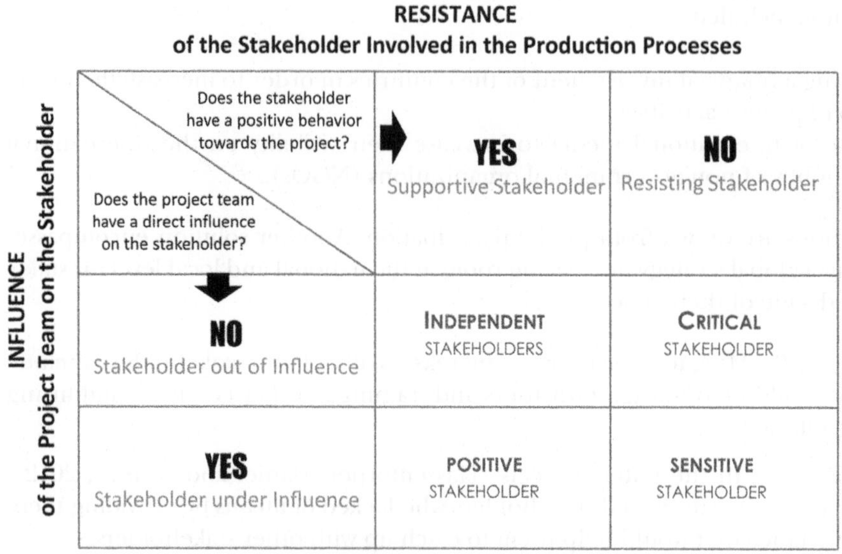

Figure 1.13 Risks Associated with Critical Stakeholders

stakeholders. Yet, if successful mitigation strategies must be implemented, it has to be by a positive stakeholder. Assessing the risks will allow anticipating potential difficulties that might happen during the implementation of key deliverables and that might threaten the final performance of the project. Assessing the risks on intermediary deliverables and key stakeholders is a good exercise to question the project implementation arrangements and make sure of its strength. Then, formulating mitigation strategies is a good way to decrease the level of risk on critical deliverables and stakeholders. Assessing the risks during the project or at the end can also help identify where the problem comes from. Two theoretical principles are linked to risks.

Risk levels change constantly; this is *unpredictability*. Risks linked to intermediary deliverables and key stakeholders evolve during the project life cycle. When taking a mitigation action, do not expect the level of risk to disappear completely, it might also move from one deliverable to another. Risks need to be constantly monitored and project design adjusted in response to those changes.

When you want to set up a monitoring and evaluation mechanism, you will monitor with particular attention key final deliverables that depend on intermediary deliverables and stakeholders that were identified as critical.

Globally, there are two major mitigation strategies to mitigate a risk:

1   create positive intermediary deliverables in order to decrease the degree of risk on the final deliverable (for example, training, communication and so on);
2   put critical stakeholders under influence.

Project Organization

We consider three elements of the project organization:

1   critical stakeholders;
2   intermediary stakeholders;
3   the project team.

Critical Stakeholders

Critical stakeholders are sources of problems: they can impact the final performance of the project. Very often complex projects deal with risks linked to deliverables but the project team do not plan mitigation strategies for stakeholders. It is essential to organize and structure the stakeholders. It is the role of the project team. In complex water projects (Hassenforder, Daniel and Nouray, 2012), the difficulty comes from the fact that the stakeholders involved are numerous. The project team cannot keep an eye on everyone. It will have to focus on critical stakeholders.

By definition, critical stakeholders are not under the direct influence of the project team. The project team will need to find a way to influence them indirectly. In simple projects, this indirect influence can go through hierarchical links. The hierarchical model corresponds perfectly to routine and organized structures. But when it comes to complex projects, organizations and institutions are multiple and not ruled by clear power liaisons. The hierarchical model seems inappropriate. The project team will have to use other influence linkages: intermediary stakeholders.

The issue of how to depict stakeholders' organizations is often controversial in complex projects. Out of habit and easiness, projects' organization charts are still often depicted as hierarchical structures. But it displeases many stakeholders who think that hierarchical structures do not represent adequately the links of influence between the stakeholders. Finding a consensual chart is often a difficult process, which is why projects often end up with traditional hierarchical structures.

Critical Stakeholders Are Sources of Long-Term Lack of Performance

It is important to clearly identify the stakeholders that are assumed to be able to impact significantly the production of final deliverables, and thus the project vision. Among all the stakeholders that are evaluated as "critical," some may have a direct or indirect influence on the final deliverables that will be the source of long-term performance. These very special critical stakeholders are more than "critical" through the people point of view, they are also "critical" through the "project outcome" point of view. These stakeholders are directly in line with the expected performance of the project vision. They must be identified, classified and influenced by the project team.

Critical Stakeholders Are Assigned to Key Project Dimensions

It is important to assign each critical stakeholder to the one and only dimension that is in line with the function/job of the stakeholder. The project team must identify clearly all the project dimensions in which critical stakeholders might intervene, Figure 1.10. All critical stakeholders that might impact the project must be known and clearly identified. The project team is often unable to identify or influence certain critical stakeholders.

Critical Stakeholders Can Influence Deliverables in Multiple Dimensions

It is important to identify the stakeholders who can influence more than one dimension, impacting multiple key final deliverables assigned to various dimensions of the project. Critical stakeholders can be assigned to a specific dimension regarding their traditional professional interactions and networks. However, it does not mean that their capacity to influence the project deliverables and objectives is limited to this dimension. A political stakeholder (a cabinet minister) can have direct or indirect impacts on political deliverables (votes on laws and regulations) but also on social deliverables (communication campaign on a specific issue). There is no segmentation of the potential impact of stakeholders on the operational dimensions of the project.

Intermediary Stakeholders

The capacity for the project team to work with indirect networks of control is a key element for the project performance.

Intermediary Stakeholders Are Positive Interfaces towards Critical Stakeholders

It is important to clearly identify (for each project dimension) intermediary stakeholders who are positive towards the project, and who could play a role of interface to promote the project. As the project team does not have a direct influence on some critical stakeholders, they will need to find intermediary stakeholders who have a direct influence on critical ones. These people must be *positive* stakeholders. Positive stakeholders are people who are both supportive towards the project and under the influence of the project team. They could be identified when assessing the risks linked to key stakeholders. If the intermediary stakeholder is not positive, they might not be able to decrease the risk linked to critical stakeholders and might even increase the negative impact of that stakeholder on the project performance.

Intermediary Stakeholders Are Canals of Coordination towards Critical Stakeholders

In order to cope with the behaviors of critical stakeholders, it is necessary to work with positive intermediary stakeholders who can create and maintain a coordination contact thanks to linkages of influence. An *intermediary stakeholder* is a stakeholder or a group of stakeholders who is able to influence critical stakeholders and is under the influence of the project team. As a reminder, there are two types of influence:

1   *Power.* Hierarchy, contract, legal authority;
2   *Emotion.* Friends, family, same background, admiration.

Intermediary stakeholders motivate and mobilize critical stakeholders by using their influence. They orient critical stakeholders towards a supportive and favorable behavior towards the project. Apart from this influence link, intermediary stakeholders also have two major roles:

1   *Coordination.* They make sure that actions are followed-up by key stakeholders at the national and local level;
2   *Communication.* They convey information from the project team down to the implementation level and the other way round.

Intermediary Stakeholders Are Efficient Networks of Influence towards Critical Stakeholders

In order to cope with the behaviors of critical stakeholders, it is necessary to work with positive intermediary stakeholders who are real sources of influential control over the critical stakeholder that are not under the natural hierarchical control of the project management team. Sometimes intermediary stakeholders are identified but they do not have the real capacity to influence critical stakeholders or their influence is too weak. In that case, two possibilities exist:

1   *Strengthening the influence of the intermediary stakeholder.* Organizing meetings or seminars between intermediary and critical stakeholders, signing bidding contracts, memorandums of agreement, can do this.
2   *Increase the number of intermediary stakeholders.* As indirect influence exerted by intermediary stakeholders on critical stakeholders is weaker than direct influence of the project team, it is possible to build stronger influence in a cumulative way, that is by combining several intermediary stakeholders in order to achieve a critical size of influence and a coercive effect.

It is possible for an intermediary stakeholder of one dimension to put under influence a critical stakeholder of another dimension.

Project Team

To achieve a successful outcome the project manager and project team must influence the critical stakeholders with respect to the project outcomes, Figure 1.14.

Project Team Members Are Responsible for Zones of Influence

Each and every dimension of the project network of intermediary and critical stakeholders must be assigned to the responsibility of project team members who are clearly aware of the network they have to manage. A member of the project team must be clearly assigned as responsible for the critical stakeholders of that dimension. It becomes now commonly agreed that a member of the project team must be responsible for all key deliverable. But it is not yet accepted that a member of the project team must be responsible for all critical stakeholders.

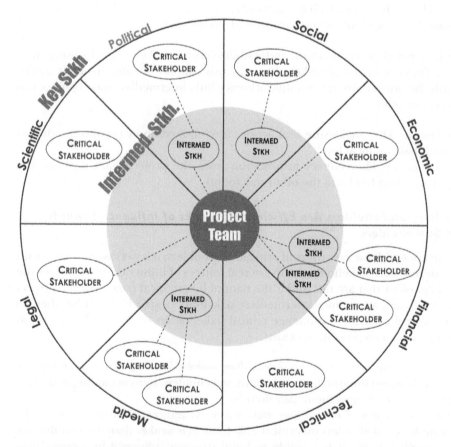

Figure 1.14 The Project Manager Influences of the Stakeholders in Relation to the Project
    Requirements

Project Team Members Must Activate Their Zones of Influence

It is necessary to make sure that each project team member creates actions, behaviors and real coordination in the network zone they are in charge. When a direct influence link does not exist, the project team must identify an intermediary stakeholder in order to put critical stakeholders under influence. Apart from this influence role, another major role of the project team is to inform and communicate: the project team must select relevant information, understand it, prioritize it and share it. As a matter of fact, a zone of influence should never remain static. The role of the project team member is to use the channels of influence that exist in order to implement actions that will make the network alive, useful and efficient. These actions, communications, messages, meetings and events are the vital energy required by the network of influence in order to be effective.

Project Team Members Must Communicate about Zones of Influence

All the project team members who are in charge of managing network zones must ensure a full sharing of what they know about the project with the other project team members. This is the only way to ensure a high capacity to manage the project transversally and to adapt to changes. The project team, or project management team, is a group of people that takes the responsibility for planning, implementing, monitoring and improving the project. They are at the core of the project network, which they have the responsibility to coordinate. They make the link between decision and policy makers at the strategic level (Hassenforder, Daniel and Nouray, 2012), and implementation stakeholders at the regional, national and local level.

In order to do so, the project team should not be too small or too big. If it is too small then its members will have difficulties activating their networks. They will not be able to manage all dimensions. If it is too big, it leads to major structural costs and inertia and the level of communication is not maintained. That is why in many projects a team is constituted for the project time-being only. It allows selection of people who already have existing networks and can be flexible and adaptive in order to be able to respond to lessons learned and changing circumstances on the ground.

References

Andersen, E.S., Grude, K.V. and Haug, T., 2009. *Goal Directed Project Management*. London: Kogan Page.

Cleland, D.I. and Ireland, L.R., 2002. *Project Management: Strategic Design and Implementation*, 4th edition. New York: McGraw Hill.

Dalcher, D., 2013. Requirements Management, in Turner, J.R., *The Gower Handbook of Project Management*, 5th edition. Farnham: Gower.

Eweje, J.A., Turner, J.R. and Müller, R., 2012. Maximising Strategic Value from Megaprojects: The Influence of Information-Feed on Decision-making by the Project Manager, *International Journal of Project Management, 30*(6), 639–651.

Giard, V. and Midler, C., 1996. Management et gestion de projet: bilan et perspectives. *Cahiers de recherche IAE*, Paris-Gregor, n°11.

Hassenforder, E., Daniel, P. and Noury, B., 2012. *New Perspectives for the Management of Water Projects*. Roubaix: La guilde des créateurs de mondes.

Huemann, M. and Eskerod, P., 2013. Managing for Stakeholders, in Turner, J.R., *The Gower Handbook of Project Management*, 5th edition. Farnham: Gower.

Khan, K., Turner, J.R. and Maqsood, T., 2013. "Factors that influence the success of public sector projects in Pakistan," in *Proceedings of IRNOP XI: The Eleventh Conference of the International Research Network for Organizing by Projects, Oslo, June*, ed. J. Söderlund and R. Müller, BI, the Norwegian Business School, Oslo.

Morris, P.W.G. and Hough, G.H., 1997. *The Anatomy of Major Projects: A Study of the Reality of Project Management*. Chichester: Wiley.

Morris, P.W.G. and Jamieson, A., 2003. *Translating Corporate Strategy Into Project Strategy: Realizing Corporate Strategy Through Project Management*. Newtown Square, PA: Project Management Institute.

Pinto, J.K. and Slevin, D.P., 1987. Critical Factors in Successful Project Implementation, *IEEE Transactions on Engineering Management*, 34(1), 22–27.

Porter, M.E., 1980. *Competitive Advantage*. New York: Free Press.

Turner, J.R., 2009. *The Handbook of Project-based Management*. New York: McGraw-Hill.

Turner, J.R., Huemann, M., Anbari, F.T. and Bredillet, C.N., 2010. *Perspectives on Projects*. New York: Routledge.

Wateridge, J.F., 1995. IT Projects: A Basis for Success, *International Journal of Project Management*, 13(3), 169–172

Wateridge, J.F., 1998. How Can IS/IT Projects be Measured for Success? *International Journal of Project Management*, 16(1), 59–63.

Winch, G.M., 2010. *Managing Construction Projects*, 2nd edition. Chichester: Wiley-Blackwell.

Chapter 2

Integrating Change, Process, and Project Management as Well as Business Analysis to Assure the Sustainable Development of Companies

Roland Gareis and Lorenz Gareis

Introduction

In many organizations there exist competing governing structures for the management of changes, processes, and projects. On the one hand these different management approaches provide specific solutions. On the other hand the approaches need to be combined in the development of organizations, in order to achieve holistic solutions.

In this chapter, we present ONEmanagement as an integrated perspective on management approaches. We identify a common basis for the application of change, process, and project management and describe the relationships between these management approaches. The ONEmanagement concept should improve the management quality of organizations and reduce their management complexity. Eliminating redundancies and competitions between management approaches contributes to the sustainable development of organizations.

We open the chapter with short descriptions of the different management approaches before developing the integrative perspective of ONEmanagement. Finally, we analyze the organizational as well as the personnel-related consequences of ONEmanagement.

Change Management and Its Relationships to Process and Project Management

Lewin defines a change as transforming an existing dynamic balance of an organization into a new one (Lewin, 1947). Levy and Merry define change as a continuous (first order change) or a discontinuous development (second order change) of an organization (Levy and Merry, 1986). In an organizational change some or all dimensions of an organization's identity, i.e. its services, markets, organizational structures, processes, cultures, personnel, infrastructures, budget, and stakeholder relationships, are affected. In a second order change all of these dimensions are affected, which results in a new identity of the changed organization. The change types "organizational learning," "further developing," "transforming," and "radical new-positioning," which require different change management approaches, can be differentiated (Gareis, 2010).

Change management can be defined as planning, organizing, controlling, and communicating a change. Therefore change management is more than just change communication. It focuses on the management of a change and does not include content-related work, such as develop new services, adapt the organizational structures and

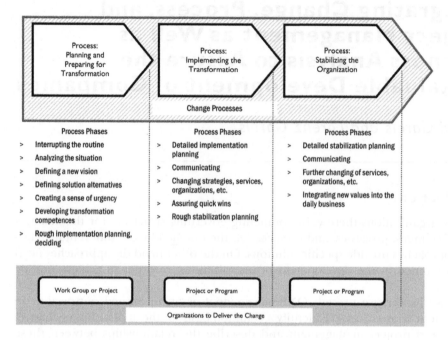

Figure 2.1 Chain of Processes for Transforming an Organization

processes, train the personnel. As examples for a change and for change management as well as for the relationships between change management and process and project management the change "transforming" is shown in Figure 2.1.

Reasons for transforming an organization are signals about future threats or potentials for the organization. Also, acquisitions or mergers often lead to transformations. A transformation does not come by surprise, it can be planned and prepared for. This is not so for the change "radical new-positioning," required in a crisis situation of an organization, asking for ad-hoc decisions, for operational involvement of top management, etc.

The change "transforming" involves the processes of planning and preparing for the transformation, implementing the transformation, and stabilizing the organization. Change management functions to be performed in this change are interrupting the routine, defining a change vision, assuring a sense of urgency of important stakeholders, planning the organizational structures to deliver the change, planning the change communication, dealing with resistance, and planning for quick wins. For performing these change management functions specific roles such as change sponsor, change manager, and change agents are required.

Different temporary organizations, namely a working group or a project or a program, can be applied in order to perform the different change processes. The process of planning and preparing for a transformation can either be performed by a working group or a project; the process of implementing a transformation requires usually a program of projects. The process of stabilizing an organization might require either a project or a program, depending on the scope of work. Therefore to deliver the change, "transforming" a chain of projects and/or programs results. Change management provides the integrative function across the projects and programs of this chain. The benefits of change management are efficient change processes and sustainable change results.

Process Management and Its Relationships to Change and Project Management

A process can be defined as a sequence of tasks with defined objectives and a defined start and end event. Its performance requires the cooperation of several roles from one or several organizations, it is cross-organizational. Process management focuses on the management of process portfolios and of single processes.

Process management can be differentiated into macro and micro-process management. Macro-process management is concerned with the company's process portfolio, process types, and the relationships between processes. Macro-process management tasks include the identification of processes, the structuring of the process portfolio, the assignment of process managers, the definition of process management standards, and the qualification of process management personnel. Macro-process management methods are e.g. process maps, chains of processes, networks of processes, and process portfolio reports. Micro-process management considers single processes, their phases and tasks. Micro-process management includes planning, controlling, and optimizing a process. Micro-process management methods are e.g. process description, process work break-down structure, process flow chart, process responsibility chart, process key performance indicators, and process progress report.

The roles for micro-process management are the process manager and the process management team. The process manager is responsible for modeling, controlling, and optimizing of a process. He/she also takes care of the appropriate communication of the process. The process manager might be supported by a process management team, consisting of experts with specific knowledge about a process. The roles of the process manager as well as of the process team members are taken on by experts as job-enlargements. These add-on functions are not continuous functions but are performed only periodically, whenever e.g. an existing process requires optimization.

The Process Management Office is responsible for macro-process management. This role might be combined with other office functions, such as quality management or project management. Companies like the Vienna Hospital Association or the Austrian Airlines have a combined Project and Process Management Office. All mentioned process management roles are to be differentiated from the roles required for performing processes (Gareis and Stummer, 2008).

The benefits of process management are to ensure organizational efficiency and to support organizational and individual learning. Organizational efficiency can be measured in terms of the quality of the process results, the use of resources, the costs, and the throughput time. Organizational and individual learning is supported by documenting and by communicating processes.

In Figure 2.1 the chain of processes for performing the change "transforming" and the phases of each process are shown. For the performance of relatively unique processes of medium to large scope, such as the change "transforming," temporary organizations, namely working groups, projects or programs are applied.

Project Management and Its Relationship to Change and Process Management

A project is a temporary organization for the performance of a relatively unique, strategically important business process of medium or large scope and short to medium duration. A program is a temporary organization for the performance of a relatively unique, strategically important process of large scope and medium duration. The projects that make up a program are coupled by common objectives, strategies and processes. Projects and programs deliver changes. In addition to other applications, such as performing a comprehensive client contract, projects are applied for the performance of change processes.

Project management is a business process which includes the sub-processes project starting, project coordinating, project controlling, and project closing as well as project transforming or project new-positioning. In these project management sub-processes not only the project scope, schedule and costs but also the project objectives, the project organization and culture, the project personnel, the project infrastructure, the project risks, and the project contexts are considered. Project contexts include the project stakeholders, the investment implemented by the project, the strategies of the organizations performing the projects, and the relationship of the project to other projects and programs. Project management methods are e.g. the project objectives plan, the work break-down structure, project schedules, the project budget, the project risk analysis, the project organization chart, the project stakeholder analysis, etc.

The project management process is shown in Figure 2.2 and is described in Figure 2.3.

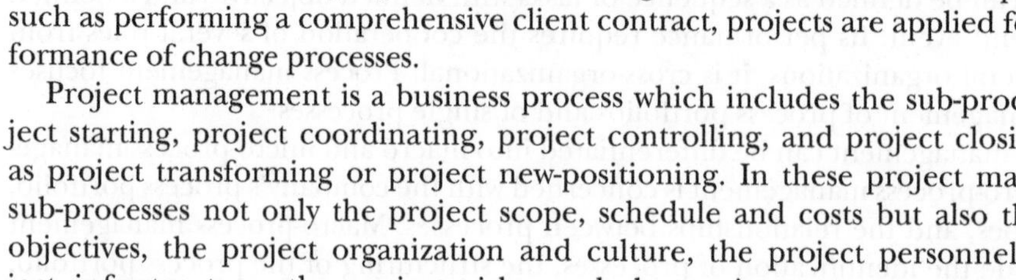

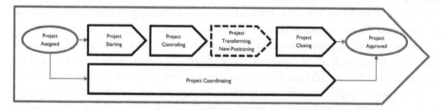

Figure 2.2 Graphical Presentation of the Project Management Process

Process Start		Project assigned by the project sponsor to the project manager	Process End		Project approved by the project sponsor
Economic Objectives	>	Professional management of the project; efficient performance of the sub-processes project starting, project controlling, project coordinating, and project closing; possibly project transforming			
	>	Management of the project complexity, the project dynamics, and the relationships to project contexts			
	>	Optimizing the economic consequences of the investment implemented by the project			
Ecologic Objectives	>	Considering the (local, regional, and global) ecologic consequences of the project			
	>	Optimizing the ecologic consequences of the investment implemented by the project			
Social Objectives	>	Considering the (local, regional, and global) social consequences of the project			
	>	Assuring stakeholder participation in the project management process			
	>	Optimizing the social consequences of the investment implemented by the project			
Non-Objectives	>	Performing content-related processes (e.g. procurement, engineering)			

Figure 2.3 Description of the Project Management Process

Project starting as well as project closing are project management sub-processes, which are performed only once in a project. Project controlling is performed several times during the project performance, usually periodically. Therefore, project controlling is differentiated from the continuous project coordination function of the project manager. Project transforming or project new-positioning as change processes of projects are to be applied only if a project identity change is required, e.g. in the case of a project crisis.

The roles performed in projects are the project sponsor, the project manager, the project team members, and the project contributors as well as the project team. A success factor of projects is the management attention it gets. This can most of all be provided by the project sponsor, who needs to support the performance of the project management process by participating in progress meetings, making strategic decisions, providing context information, etc. An essential task of the project sponsor is to lead the project manager. A project manager has the right to leadership (Gareis, 2005). The project manager is the integration role of a project. He/she is the contact person for the members of the project organization and for stakeholders. In comparison to the project contributor, the project team member is not only responsible for project-related content work but also for contributing to project management and to project marketing. An "empowered" project team as a team role accepts an overall responsibility for the project success. The benefits of project management are efficient projects and sustainable project results.

In changes project roles are performed in addition to the change roles. The appropriate cooperation between these roles is to be assured, e.g. by assuring that the members of the project organization understand and accept the change vision, by defining some project results as quick wins of the change, by assuring that the project role players contribute to the change communication, etc.

Competing Management Approaches

Change, process, and project management are considered as specific management approaches, requiring specific methods, roles, and terms. Some of the methods, roles, and terms are similar but often described in a language that is specific to the approach.

These approaches are represented by different communities of practice and communities of research, and they are represented by different associations, such as the Association of Change Management Professionals (ACMP), the European Association of Business Process Management (EABPM), the International Project Management Association (IPMA), or the Project Management Institute (PMI). Management standards provided by different professional associations relating to the same management approach are similar but not consistent with each other. Major differences e.g. can be observed between the project management approach documented in the International Competence Baseline (ICB) of the IPMA and in the Project Management Body of Knowledge (PMBoK) of PMI. This has a practical impact because company-specific guidelines often are based on the international standards of professional associations.

On the one hand a clear differentiation between the mentioned management approaches provides orientation and allows for approach-specific solutions. On the other hand the approaches need to be combined in order to achieve holistic solutions.

In companies guidelines for change, process, and project management often exist in parallel. In some large companies organizational units such as a Project Management Office, a Process Management Office, possibly also a Change Management Office and a Quality Management Department are competing. The "costs" of partly redundant management approaches and competing organizational units are sub-optimal solutions. These result because:

- the relationships between the different management approaches are not managed appropriately;
- personnel is not broadly qualified, only specialists for the different management approaches exist;
- the relationships between the roles in changes, processes, projects, and programs are unclear;
- there exists a high resource demand due to parallel activities of the different organizational units;
- stakeholders are confused because of unclear terms and different concerns of the organizational units representing the different management approaches.

ONEmanagement

ONEmanagement is an integrated perspective of management approaches, not an approach itself. By defining a common basis for the application of change, process, and project management and by describing the relationships between these management approaches, the management quality of companies can be improved and complexity reduced. The integration of change, process, and project management is a corporate governance function.

A Common Management Basis

A common basis for the application of change, process, and project management has to include a common perception of organizations, common values, a common language, and commonly applied methods and tools.

Different perceptions of organizations, e.g. as trivial machines or as living organisms, make a difference in their management. According to the social systems theory and radical constructivism organizations can be perceived as social systems, which are characterized by self-organizing structures and not by linear cause and effect relationships. A common perception of organizations leads to consistent expectations regarding the demands and objectives for their development, the managerial behavior to be applied, the effects of interventions, etc.

A further basis for a successful application of change, process, and project management are common values, such as empowerment, teamwork, partnering, and sustainable development. Sustainable development can be perceived as a new management paradigm to cope with the complexity and dynamics of companies. The concept of sustainable development has acquired wide attention following the publication of the Brundtland Report by the World Commission for Environment and Development in 1987 (World Commission on Environment and Development, 1987, p. 41). Although many different definitions of sustainable development for companies can be found in the literature, some basic guiding principles can be identified. A generic definition of sustainable development considers the following principles: economic, ecologic, and social-oriented, short-term, mid-term, and long-term-oriented, local, regional, and global-oriented as well as values-based (Gareis et al., 2013). A commitment to sustainable development involves integrating sustainable development principles into services, products, and processes of a company implying a fundamental "re-thinking of the business." The consideration of the principles of sustainable development in change, process, and project management contributes to a common value basis.

Some terms, methods, and templates used by the different management approaches can be harmonized. A harmonization of terms, such as "sub-process" and "phase," or "task"; "work package" and "activity"; or "investment," "business case," and "life cycle;" or "responsibility chart," "RACI matrix," and "swim lane," reduces management complexity and can reduce misunderstandings of stakeholders. Some methods, such as the work break-down structure, the stakeholder analysis, and the responsibility matrix can be applied not only in project management but also in change and process management.

Relationships between the Management Approaches

Change, process, and project management relate to each other. Figure 2.4 illustrates relevant correlations between these various approaches. The relationships between changes, processes, and projects are visualized in Figure 2.5.

- Relationships: Change management and process management

  - A change is performed by a chain of processes.
  - Different change types require different change management processes.
  - Business processes are affected by organizational changes.

- Relationships: Change management and project management

  - Projects (and programs) deliver changes of permanent organizations. Changes are managed "by projects." "External," client-related projects are contributing to changes of client organizations.
  - Change management methods can be applied in projects, even if no formal change is defined. Communicating the business benefits to stakeholders, dealing with resistance, assuring quick wins, the explicit planning of a stabilization phase after the end of a project are examples for that.
  - Projects (and programs) are themselves subject to change and may require change management. 2nd order changes of projects are project transforming and project new-positioning (Gareis, 2013).

- Relationships: Process management and project management

  - The process map provides the basis for identifying the project types of a company.
  - Relatively unique processes of large scope and mid-term duration get the required management attention by defining projects or programs for their performance.
  - Project initiation, project management, and program management are processes, i.e. that a process quality for these processes can be defined and controlled by key performance indicators.
  - Similar concepts (e.g. boundaries definition, stakeholder-orientation) and similar methods (e.g. break down structures, responsibility charts) are applied in process as well as in project management.

Figure 2.4 ONEmanagement—Relationships between Management Approaches

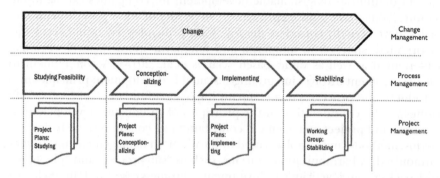

Figure 2.5 ONEmanagement—Relationships between a Change, Processes, and Projects

Different roles are required for change, process, and project management. The responsibilities of the required roles and their relationships are as follows:

- The change sponsor, the change manager, and the change agents are responsible for an overall change.
- The project sponsor, the project manager, and the project team member are responsible for the success of a project contributing to the delivery of a change.
- The process managers are responsible for modeling processes in the scope of a project. The process managers can be team members of projects.
- In order to reduce the management complexity multiple role assignments are suggested in changes. E.g. the change sponsor or the change manager can also be sponsors of projects, the change manager or a change agent can also be project managers.

ONEmanagement: Organizational and Personnel-Related Provisions

To assure the benefits of ONEmanagement both personnel and organizational measures are required. The following organizational provisions support the integrated management perception of ONEmanagement:

- Establishing an integrated management office, to assure appropriate corporate governance for change, process, and project management.
- Developing a common basis for the application of change, process, and project management by assuring a common perception of organizations, developing common corporate values, assuring a common terminology, and aligning the applied methods and tools.
- Assuring a common understanding of the relationships between change, process, and project management.
- Assuring common communication forms such as team meetings and workshops for the different management approaches.
- Assuring a common understanding about the required cooperation of the different role players for changes, processes, and projects.

The following personnel-related provisions support the integrated management perception of ONEmanagement:

- Defining new job profiles for change sponsors, change managers, and change agents; process managers and process team members; project sponsors, project managers, and project team members.
- Aligning the career paths of change, process, and project managers.
- Developing and offering integrated education programs for the role players of change, process, and project management assuring the holistic competences required.
- Assuring the social competences of managers for cooperating in changes, processes, and projects.
- Assuring common values and a similar self-understanding of the different role players as a basis for their cooperation in changes, processes, and projects.

Conclusion

In order to reduce management complexity and to assure an appropriate management quality in organizations change, process, and project management can be integrated. ONEmanagement is an integrated perception of management approaches. It assures a common basis for the application of change, process, and project management and an understanding of the relationships between these management approaches. In order to assure ONEmanagement appropriate organizational and personnel-related provisions are required.

References

Baumgartner, R. J., and Ebner, D. (2010): Corporate sustainability strategies. Sustainability profiles and maturity levels, *Sustainable Development*, 18(2), 76–89. doi:10.1002/sd.447

Gareis, R. (2005): *Happy Projects!* Vienna: Manz Crossmedia.

Gareis, R. (2010): Changes of organizations by projects, *International Journal of Project Management*, 28(4), 304–320.

Gareis, R. (2013): Changes of Projects by Considering the Principles of Sustainable Development; in Silvius, G., Tharp, J. *Sustainability Integration for Effective Project Management*. Hershey, PA: IGI Global.

Gareis, R., and Stummer, M. (2008): *Processes and Projects*. Vienna: Manz Crossmedia.

Gareis, R., Huemann, M., Martinuzzi, A., Weninger, C., and Sedlacko, M. (2013): *Project Management & Sustainable Development Principles*. Newtown Square, PA: Project Management Institute.

Global Reporting Initiative (2011): *Sustainability Reporting Guidelines Version 3.1*. Amsterdam, The Netherlands: Global Reporting Initiative.

Levy, A., and Merry, U. (1986): *Organizational Transformation—Approaches, Strategies, and Theories*. New York: Greenwood Publishing Group.

Lewin, K. (1947): Frontiers in group dynamics, *Human Relations*, 1(1), 5–41.

Luhmann, N. (1995): *Funktionen und Folgen Formaler Organisation*. Berlin: Duncker und Humblot.

von Glasersfeld, E. (1995): *Radical Constructivism: A Way of Knowing and Learning*. London: The Falmer Press.

World Commission on Environment and Development (1987): *Our Common Future*. Oxford: Oxford University Press.

Chapter 3

Combining Supply Chain Risk Management and Project Risk Management to Improve the Sustainable Performance of a Company

Régis Delafenestre and Laurence Lecoeuvre

Introduction

Risk management based on anticipation is one of the main issues of project management (Cole et al., 2006; Loch et al., 2006). "Sustainability risk management requires holistic and systematic integration of ecological, socioeconomic, and corporate risk factors in the business management" (Yilmaz and Flouris, 2010), especially today in the current controversial economic context. Consequently many researches and models have been developed to manage risks, in the areas of project management (Scott and Vessey, 2002) and supply chain (Jüttner, 2005).

Indeed, over the years, the relationship between environmental organizations has become increasingly complex (Hillman, 2006). Supply Chain Management, which corresponds to the management of the flow of goods and information between members of a supply chain, is not an exception to this complexity. Partnerships have increased between companies and their suppliers/subcontractors and/or their distributors, notably because of the trend for outsourcing.

The consequences of poor control of the supply chain can be harmful. This lack of mastering is often illustrated by a lack of control from suppliers who are excluded from the scope of the business of the company. The goal is to ensure the continuity of the supply chain and implement an action plan to prevent or minimize the risk. But other risks of breaking the chain exist; floods, terrorism, strikes and natural disasters are also potential threats. In this context, the management of the supply chain (also known as Supply Chain Management or SCM) has become undoubtedly more risky.

Of course risk is an integral part of all human activity, and these effects disrupt production systems. Thus risk management is growing in management science, especially to reduce the probability of risk and their impacts; in particular in project management where standards established by the Project Management Institute (PMI) or APMG present models and processes to manage and reduce risks. All these developments are involved in both disciplines of supply chain and project management.

It is now a question of whether to use SCRM, which is both an intra-organizational (Lavastre and Spalanzani, 2010) and inter-organizational risk management tool. SCRM is the set of practices that an organization deploys with its partners to manage its risks: meetings, information sharing, collaboration, cross-functional processes, development of common processes etc.

In the same way, authors and practitioner in project activity point out that risk management based on anticipation is one of the main issues of project management

(Cole et al., 2006); i.e. uncertainty is a "central feature of effective project management" (Chapman and Ward, 2003). Projects induce change, with a variety of resources, constraints and objectives.

This chapter questions the possible alignment of the two main models relative to risk management that are developed today in both project management and SCM in order to improve the sustainable performance of companies. The first part, based on literature, presents the models and in the second part the authors illustrate their thoughts and proposals based on a case study.

The chapter presented here won't develop the measure of performance, but the authors agree on the fact that performance describes the quality of the result obtained after an investment by a company. Assessing the performance of a company implies that its results are regularly monitored. However, the indicator used to assess a company's performance gives a judgement based on a comparison of a measure toward a particular purpose, in order to help with piloting and acting on a given variable. The overview of these indicators on design and operation take into account the diversification of objectives and interactions between variables and associated performance indicators (Clivillé, 2004). Moreover "implementation of differentiation, operational, and quality strategies is associated with new project development outcomes in terms of schedule, quality, and innovation performance" (Yang, 2012). Thus we point out here the importance of piloting and managing risk to improve performance.

From Risks to Modeling

Michael Lant (2010) characterizes risks as follows:

- Risks are influencing factors that might adversely affect the outcome of a project.
- Risk is the direct result of uncertainty. If there is no uncertainty, it is not a risk—it is a certainty.
- Risk analysis is used to help a team understand uncertainty that could affect the outcome of the project.
- Risk management (sometimes called risk mitigation) is the plan that the team puts into place to pre-empt, contain or mitigate the effects of risk to a project.

The important thing to remember is that even in simple projects, things can and will go wrong, and that you need to make plans to minimize the impact of those events when they occur.

Indeed risk is a possible event which can have negative consequences for organizations or persons. Risk management is a process of which the goal is to control corporate risks. These methods of analysis are known in the industrial world but are relatively new in the field of management. Risk should be addressed in management activities such as production, marketing, strategy and project management. Yates and Stone (1992) define risk as having three elements: (1) its probability, (2) its importance and (3) its impact. Whereas Sitkin and Pablo (1992) consider risk as the uncertainty that a potential event occurs with more or less negative effects. Finally, the Business Continuity Institute (BCI) defines risk as the management of the continuity of the business and as a process of holistic management. This process identifies the potential impacts that threaten an organization and supplies a frame to build "resilience" (BCI, 2005), knowing that the "resilience" of a company means the extent to which it would be able to restart its activities after an interruption (Sheffi, 2005).

Managing the Risks in the Supply Chain

March and Shapira (1987) define the risk supply chain as "a variation in the distribution of possible Supply Chain outcomes, their likelihood, and their subjective values." According to Zsidisin (2003), the risk of supply is "a supply risk defined as the probability of an incident associated with inbound supply from individual supplier failure or the supply market occurring, in which its outcomes results in the inability of the purchasing to meet customer demand or cause threats to customer life and safety." Consequently, managing risk in the supply chain requires the identification, evaluation and systematic quantification of supply chain disturbances with the objective of controlling the exposure to risks or the reduction of their negative impact. Disturbances connected to the Supply Chain can alter and even prevent the flow of products, and can improve or reduce communication between the suppliers or customers and the company. The risks can be internal (for instance: insufficient quality, unreliable suppliers and machine breakdowns) or external (for instance: flood, terrorism, strikes and disasters). Mason-Jones and Towill (1998) have identified five categories of Supply Chain risks: environment, demand, supply, process and control.

In order to avoid Supply Chain risk, different tools are needed. SCOR® (Supply Chain Operations Reference) is a model which provides a unique framework that gathers business process, metrics, best practices and technology features into a unified structure to improve the effectiveness of supply chain activities. This reference source involves Supply Chain Risk methods with processes, best practices and key performance indicators to evaluate and minimize disruption caused by potential risks in the Supply Chain in order to reduce negative impacts.

According to the SCOR® model, the supply chain risks steps are:

1   Risk identification: The objective here is to create of a list potential events that could disrupt any aspect of supply chain's performance.
2   Risk evaluation: A qualitative and quantitative evaluation is made from the identified risks to estimate and prioritize the probability of occurrence for each risk and its potential impact on the company' Supply Chain. The evaluation can be made by tools such as Failure Modes Effects Analysis (FMEA) or by councils of experts. FMEA is a design tool used to analyze potential elements failures and identify the resultant effects on system operations. The analyst involves all consistent failures modes for each element in the system. A FMEA is used to structure risk reduction based on either effect reduction or based on decreasing the probability of failure or both. The FMEA is in principle an inductive analysis, however the failure probability can only be estimated or reduced by understanding the failure mechanism. Ideally, eliminating the causes will decrease this probability.
3   Implementation of the risk management plan: The plan is estimated in terms of risk cover, the cost-efficiency ratio and its ease of implementation. The plan includes risk mitigation actions, risk transfer and sharing, and improvement actions in internal processes in order to limit the breaks of chain.

4   Risk follow-up and control: All identified risks are measured, allowing for evaluation.
5   Project performance can also be improved by risk management (Kwak and Smith, 2009; Meng and Gallagher, 2012; Yang, 2012).

Managing the Risks in Project Management

According to the Project Management Body of Knowledge (PMBOK® Guide, 2013), "Project Risk Management includes the processes of conducting risk management planning, identification, analysis, response planning, and controlling risk on a project." These six processes are summarized as follows:

1   Plan risk management: planning of the risk management activities.
2   Identify risks: determination and characterization of the risks which could influence the project life.
3   Perform qualitative risk analysis: prioritization of risks and calculation of their likelihood of occurrence and influence.
4   Perform quantitative risk analysis: calculation of the consequence of identified risks.
5   Plan risk responses: development of actions to improve opportunities and decrease threats in line with project objectives.
6   Control risks: implementation of risk response plans and monitoring plans, evaluation of risk process efficiency and usefulness during project life.

The idea of process is very important in the PMBOK® model (2013); the process is defined as the "sequence of interdependent and linked procedures which, at every stage, consume one or more resources (employee time, energy, machines, money) to convert inputs (data, material, parts, etc.) into outputs. These outputs then serve as inputs for the next stage until a known goal or end result is reached."

Nevertheless, this model is not always ideal. As example, let us report the results of a focus group of experienced project leaders in the industrial sector. At the end of 2012 we interviewed a group of 11 top project managers from several subsidiaries of a large international company. The main concern was to define together which key element(s) of the activity of project management they would like to improve to assure a sustainable and performing activity of their company: the first response was the risk management. At first, nine out of eleven project managers suggested this, but after discussion the question was posed again and agreement on risk management was unanimous.

Many of the project managers highlighted that it was difficult to plan schedules for high-risk activities. Despite the internal model of risk management applied (comparable to PMBOK® Guide, and also Prince2®), they pointed out that risk begins in the very early phase of the project when estimating the cost and negotiating with the client. According to them, this phase is not developed enough. In the early "engagement phase," marketing and commercial teams must also manage the risk; for them it is the beginning of a "chain of risks." For instance, risk in the cost (sub-estimating), contract risk, risk in product definition etc. The risk must then be managed during the execution phase until the aftermarket. Respondents also thought that prioritization and control were difficult to adapt to these activities.

One of the proposals of the focus group was to develop a cost model based on the anticipated costs of the project, with input from project managers on each phase of the project lifecycle—from the start of the bid process, maybe even from the idea for the project. Closer collaboration between project managers and employees from all the teams involved is a requirement for this model.

As also defined by PRINCE2®, two main principles for managing risk are: (1) "understand the project's context" and (2) "involve stakeholders." In the same way, the last issue of the PMBOK® Guide deepens the stakeholder management in regard with the management of project. The other principles defined by APMG are: (3) "establish clear objectives"; (4) "develop the project risk management approach"; (5) "report on risks regularly"; (6) "define clear roles and responsibilities"; (7) "establish a support structure and a supportive culture for risk management"; (8) "monitor for early warning indicators"; and (9) "establish a review cycle and look for continual improvement."

Another example led us to think that SCRM and Project Management are not ideal: In an international sanitary firm, the department managing the European supply chain was aiming to reduce risk in the forecast issuing process. The objective of this process was to produce a monthly prediction of product quantity over an 18-month period. This prediction was used to plan the monthly cycle of operations of the 18-month period in order to produce sustainable performance and financial results. The negative consequences of a failed forecast issuing process could be a poor quality of service, dissatisfied customers and wrong figures for production planning. The potential failures of this process were multiple, e.g. an under- or over-evaluation of forecasts, forecasts which did not include new products or other costs (such as showroom an safety stock), and so on.

The reasons for these failures included inaccurate source data, incomplete product lines (new products or removed products); or changes in information such as the statistical model of forecast.

Comparison between the SCOR® Model and the PMI Model

As a first step the authors present in the following part of a comparison between the SCOR® model and the PMBOK® model.

The first step of the PMBOK® model, plan risk management, is not involved in the SCOR® model. Consequently, within the SCOR® model, degree (1), types

Table 3.1 Alignment of Models

PMI Model	SCOR® Model
Plan risk management	None
Identify risks	Supply chain risk identification
Perform qualitative risk analysis	Risk evaluation
Perform quantitative risk analysis	Risk evaluation
Plan risk responses	Implementation of the risk management plan
Control risks	Risk follow-up and control

(2) and visibility (3) of risk management are not in line with risks and the importance of the project within the organization. However, companies need to know these elements and they can be provided by project management plan. The project management plan describes a current state of risks within a project. It provides information about scope, schedule and cost (project's input). In addition, it supplies a project charter, which is an essential point of plan risk management. Indeed, it involves high-level risk evaluation, business requirements and constraints. Moreover stakeholders and enterprise environmental factors are key elements of the risk management plan.

Finally, to produce a risk management plan, the outputs, tools and techniques need to be defined.

Analysis and Recommendations

As we pointed out above, in the focus group study the project managers indicated that risk begins in the very early phase of the project when estimating the cost and negotiating with the client. They felt this phase was not formalized enough. In the early "engagement" phase, marketing and commercial teams also need to be managing the risk.

One of the proposals of the focus group was to develop a cost model based on the anticipation costs, with input from the project managers of in each phase of the project lifecycle.

PRINCE® defines the two main principles for managing risk as:

1   understand the project's context;
2   involve stakeholders.

The other principles are:

3   establish clear objectives;
4   develop the project risk management approach;
5   report on risks regularly;
6   define clear roles and responsibilities;
7   establish a support structure and a supportive culture for risk management;
8   monitor for early warning indicators;
9   establish a review cycle and look for continual improvement.

Consequently, the phases of the risk management plan should each be completed before the project begins. These phases include (1) the project's context and (2) stakeholders:

1   The project's context involves a field of cooperation, a network of actors, shared representations, and a system of co-accepted rules for managing the risk (Lecoeuvre et al., 2009). It is the beginning of a "chain of risks." For instance, risk in the cost (sub or over estimating), contract risk, risk in product definition etc. The risk assessment of the project is based on the overall project context.

2   Before the project begins it is essential to get support from stakeholders. According to R.E. Freeman (2010), stakeholder management allows enhancing the management of a business unit and the project's stakeholder community. Stakeholder management allows for:

- identification of the activity's stakeholders and understanding of their needs;
- prioritization of the stakeholder;
- mapping the stakeholder profile;
- developing a commitment strategy;
- monitoring of the communication plan.

Thus, we propose the following model (see Figure 3.1), which encompasses the project's context, stakeholder's definition and the re-evaluation of risks. We won't go into detail about the other elements as these are common knowledge.

Proposal for a New Model

The above model is differentiated as a result of the risks in the phase before the project begins being taken into consideration and also because of the feedback loop. Indeed, using the feedback loop to monitor risk follow-up and re-evaluation ensures all risks are under control. Whatever the implementation results are, the risks are re-evaluated and the different steps can be carried out again, providing a sustainable improvement process.

The following part of the chapter will illustrate the model through a case study.

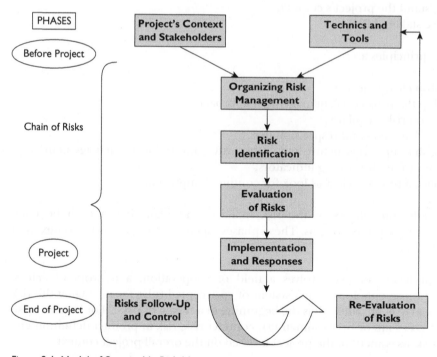

Figure 3.1 Model of Sustainable Risk Management

Case Study

This case study provides an illustration of how reducing Supply Chain risks affects the forecast issuing process. First, we will present the old process used by the company in the case study (Figure 3.2), followed by a review of the new process (Figure 3.3) defined in line with our model (Figure 3.1). Finally, we will define the case study.

Within the old model, the "Pull in previous month's actual market/SKU-level time-phased orders" and "Assess sales plan accuracy performance by market— product lines—model—SKU" stages constitute stages to gather historical data and monitor accuracy performance. The stages involve Supply Chain Risks methods, and the forecast manager manages all the steps alone. Any explanations and analysis are done. With the proposed new model, we involve different elements referring to the project's context such as the area economic trends and the market prices for explaining the level of monthly sales. Moreover, the stakeholders are associated to the history management as the marketing product manager, for understanding product and service requirements. The "History management: tools which identify

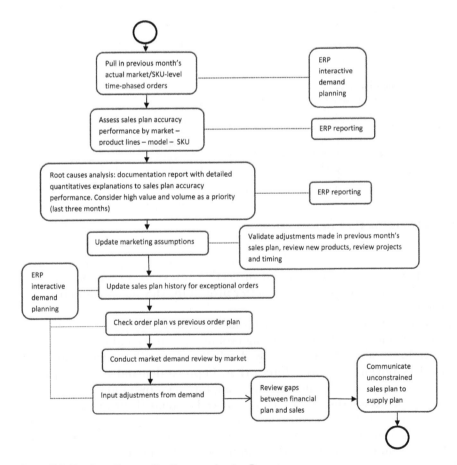

Figure 3.2 Previous Process for Forecast Issuing Process

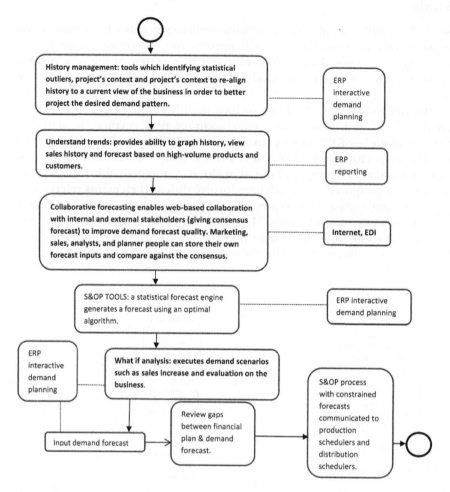

Figure 3.3 New Process for Forecast Issuing Process

statistical outliers, project's context and project's context to re-align history to a current view of the business in order to better project the desired demand pattern" stage is issued.

The steps described as: "Understand trends: provides ability to graph history, view sales history and forecast based on high-volume products and customers" and "Collaborative forecasting enables web-based collaboration with internal and external stakeholders (giving consensus forecast) to improve demand forecast quality. Marketing, sales, analysts, and planner people can store their own forecast inputs and compare against the consensus forecast" emphasize collaboration between stakeholders. According to forecasting's area, sales and marketing people can help the forecast manager to define the best time series (forecast). Consequently, sales and marketing people better understand the market and the associated target prices associated. Thus, they could:

- assess the level of sales for the future;
- ensure source data integrity;
- ensure new products are included and old products are removed.

The planner is able to forecast based on previous production as well. The financial team should provide the valuation and ensure the credibility of the data.

The "Collaborative forecasting enables web-based collaboration with internal and external stakeholders (giving consensus forecast) to improve demand forecast quality. Marketing, sales, analysts, and planner people can store their own forecast inputs and compare against the consensus forecast" stage allows for a very open discussion between all stakeholders. When the final times series consensus is issued, a "What if analysis: executes demand scenarios such as sales increase and evaluation on the business" stage is generated to elaborate some scenarios and choose the most relevant.

To conclude, the forecast manager becomes a project manager and manages the risk from the very beginning of the process to make sure all the necessary information is included in order to issue consistent forecasts at the end of the process (commercial and marketing information, macroeconomic information, etc.).

Conclusion

The aim of this research is to propose the imbricating of Supply Chain Risk Management and Project Risk Management to improve the sustainable performance of a company. Indeed, at an exploratory stage, we propose to adapt, even to combine, the Project Risk Management model(s) and the SCRM model(s) to anticipate risks and develop performance. The Project Risk Management model and the SCRM model have some shortcomings, which can lead to project failure. Therefore our model of sustainable Risk Management with the addition in particular of a phase before the project begins, allows the team's project members to take into account the project's context and its stakeholders.

This chapter provides a first contribution in developing a new model for the sustainable improvement of the company in order to facilitate the mutual contribution of both disciplines. We propose for future research to test its robustness in studying more cases in different sectors.

References

6° forum Suisse de la Logistique (2006) "Le management du risque dans la Supply Chain," Polytechnique Fédérale de Lausanne.

Boehm, B. and Turner, R. (2003) *Balancing Agility and Discipline: A Guide for the Perplexed.* Boston, MA: Addison-Wesley.

Business Continuity Institute (2005) The good practice guidelines, http://www.thebci.org/index.php/resources/the-good-practice-guidelines, accessed February 2016.

Chapman, S. and Ward, C. (2003) *Project Risk Management—Processes, Techniques and Insights,* Second Edition. Chichester: John Wiley & Sons.

Clivillé, V. (2004) "Approche systémique et méthode multicritère pour la définition d'un système d'indicateurs de performance" in Thèse de Doctorat, Ecole Supérieure d'Ingénieurs d'Annecy, Université de Savoie.

Cole, A. and Taylor, P.J. (2006) "Expecting the Unexpected: Anticipating and Managing Key Risks to Successful Projects," "Bones, Bombs and Bribes: Unique Construction Risks in International Contracting," American Bar Association Forum on the Construction Industry/TIPS Fidelity & Surety Law Committee, January 26, 2006, The Waldorf Astoria, New York, NY.

Freeman, R.E., Harrison, J.S., Wicks A.C., Parmar B.L. and de Colle Simone (2010) *Stakeholder Theory: The State of the Art.* Cambridge: Cambridge University Press.

Fu, Y., Minqiang, L. and Fuzan, C. (2012) "Impact Propagation and Risk Management of Requirement Changes for Software Development Projects Based on Design Structure Matrix," *International Journal of Project Management,* Vol. 30, No. 3, pp. 363–373.

Gomer, F. (2008) "Rappel massif, quand SCM rime avec gestion de crise," *Supply Chain magazine,* December, No. 30.

Halikas, J., Karvonen, I., Pulkkinen, U., Virolainen, V-M. and Traominen, M. (2004) "Risk Management Processes in Supplier Networks," *International Journal of Production Economics,* Vol. 90, pp. 47–58.

Harland, C., Brenchley, R. and Walker, H. (2003) "Risk in Supply Networks," *Journal of Purchasing and Supply Management,* Vol. 9 No. 2, pp. 51–62.

Hillman, M. (2006) "Strategies for Managing Supply Chain Risk," *Supply Chain Management Review.*

Jüttner, U. (2005) "Supply Chain Risk Management: Understanding the Business Requirements from a Practitioner Perspective," *International Journal of Logistics Management,* Vol. 16, pp. 120–141.

Kraljic, P. (1983) "Purchasing Must Become Supply Management," *Harvard Business Review,* Vol. 61, pp. 109–117.

Kwak, Y.H and Smith, B.M. (2009) "Managing Risks in Mega Defense Acquisition Projects: Performance, Policy, and Opportunities," *International Journal of Project Management,* Vol. 27, No. 8, pp. 812–820.

Lant, M. (2010) Five Simple Steps to Agile Risk Management (Blog), 4 June, http://michaellant.com/2010/06/04/five-simple-steps-to-agile-risk-management/, accessed January 2016.

Lavastre, O. and Spalanzani, A. (2010) "Comment gérer les risques liés à la chaîne logistique? Une réponse par les pratiques de SCRM (Supply Chain Risk Management)" AIMS 2010—Conférence Internationale de Management Stratégique—Luxembourg, 2–4 June, 2010.

Lecoeuvre, L., Deshayes, P. and Tikkanen, H. (2009) "Positioning of the Stakeholders in the Interaction Project Management—Project Marketing: A Case of a Co-constructed Industrial Project," *Project Management Journal,* Vol. 40, No. 3.

Loch C.H., DeMeyer A. and Pich M.T. (2006) *Managing the Unknown. A New Approach in Managing Uncertainty and Risk in Projects.* Hoboken, NJ: John Wiley & Sons.

March, J. and Shapira, Z. (1987) "Managerial Perspectives on Risk and Risk Taking," *Management Science,* Vol. 33, No. 11, pp. 1404–1418.

Mason-Jones, R. and Towill, D. (1998) "Shrinking the Supply Chain Uncertainty Cycle," *IOM Control Magazine,* pp. 17–22.

Meng, X. and Gallagher, B. (2012) "The Impact of Incentive Mechanisms on Project Performance," *International Journal of Project Management,* Vol. 30, No. 3, pp. 352–362.

Office of Government Commerce (2009) *Managing Successful Projects with PRINCE2,* Fifth Edition. London: TSO.

Project Management Institute (PMI) (2003) *A Guide to the Project Management Body of Knowledge* (PMBOK® Guide) Fifth Edition, Project Management Institute, http://www.businessdictionary.com/definition/process.html, accessed February 2016.

Project Management Institute (PMI) (2013) *The Standard for Program Management,* Third Edition. Philadelphia, PA: Project Management Institute.

Scott, J.E. and Vessey, I. (2002) "Managing Risks in Enterprise System Implementations," *Communications of the ACM,* Vol. 45, No. 4.

Sheffi, Y. (2005) *The Resilient Enterprise: Overcoming Vulnerability for Competitive Advantage*. Cambridge, MA: MIT Press.

Sitkin, S.B. and Pablo, A.L. (1992) "Reconceptualizing the Determinants of Risk Behavior," *Academy of Management Review*, Vol. 17, No. 1, pp. 9–38.

Yang, L-R. (2012) "Implementation of Project Strategy to Improve New Product Development Performance," *International Journal of Project Management*, Vol. 30, No. 7.

Yates, J.F. and Stone, E.R. (1992) "Risk appraisal" in J.F. Yates (Ed.), *Risk-Taking Behavior*. Chichester: John Wiley and Sons.

Yilmaz, A. and Flouris, T. (2010) "Managing Corporate Sustainability: Risk Management Process Based Perspective," *African Journal of Business Management*, Vol. 4, No. 2, pp. 162–171.

Zsidisin, G. (2003) "Managerial Perceptions of Supply Risk," *Journal of Supply Chain Management*, Vol. 39, pp. 14–26.

Project Governance and Sustainable Performance

Il n'y a pas de vent favorable pour celui qui ne sait où il va.

There is no favorable wind for the one who doesn't know where he goes.

Sénèque (65 after J.C.)

Chapter 4

Project Governance

Rodney Turner

Introduction

The governance of projects and project management continues to be a topic of interest (Turner and Keegan, 1999, 2001). These ideas built on work from the field of general management (Wiliamson, 1996), and it has now become an established field (Müller, 2009, 2011). Governance can be simply defined as (Stoker, 1998, p. 155):

> Governance is ultimately concerned with creating the conditions for ordered rule and collective action.

Governance is a form of regulation where the regulator is part of the system under regulation. The mechanism through which governance is executed is the governance structure, and includes formal procedures, processes, policies, roles, responsibilities and authorities (Müller et al., 2013).

In the project-oriented organization, there are three levels of governance (Turner, 2014) as seen in Figure 4.1:

1 at the level of the organization, where the board of directors takes an interest in the governance of projects, programs and portfolios being undertaken in the organization;
2 in the context of the organization, where the organization uses both programs and portfolios to link project objectives to corporate strategy and ensures it has in place the competencies and capability to undertake the projects it is doing;
3 at the level of the project, where the organization ensures that the right projects are done in the right way to deliver its corporate objectives.

Graham Winch (2014) recently introduced a model, Figure 4.2, were he suggests that there are three organizations involved in the management of projects: the investor, the contractor and the project itself. The relationship between all three organizations needs governing. The relationship between the project and each of the investor and contractor is governed through the three levels in Figure 4.1. The relationship between the contractor and investor is governed through the model introduced by Anne Keegan and myself (2001).

In this chapter I will describe the three levels of governance in Figure 4.1, and then the relationship between the investor and the contractor. I discuss first governance at the level of the project-oriented organization, then at the level of the project, and then the context connecting the two. I close by discussing the governance of the relationship between the contractor and the client.

Governance at the Level of the Project-Oriented Organization

We start at the highest level of governance, where the board of directors takes an interest in the (key, large) projects taking place within the organization. Traditionally, in client organizations, boards of directors and senior managers have ignored projects, taking a greater interest in routine operations. Projects were something taking place in the skunk works, managed by geeks. The geeks were sent off to the skunk works, and told to come back when they had a new operation to implement. But under modern compliance regimes boards are responsible for the performance of projects, and so they have to take an interest. The boards of directors of contractor organizations have always taken an interest, because that is their business. The United Kingdom's Association for Project Management (APM) has a special interest group (SIG) looking at the governance of project-based management, with specific focus on the overlap between the board and project management (Association for Project Management, 2004).

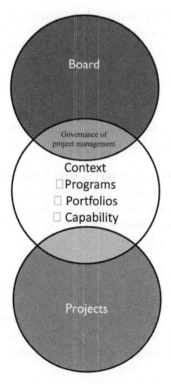

Figure 4.1 Three Levels of Governance in the Project-Oriented Organization

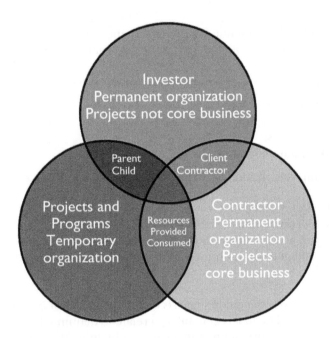

Figure 4.2 Three Organizations Involved in Projects

Thomas Clarke (2004) defines corporate governance using a definition developed by the Organization for Economic Cooperative Development (OECD):

> Corporate governance involves a set of relationships between a company's management, its Board (or management team), its shareholders, and other stakeholders. It provides the structure through which the objectives of the company are set, and the means of attaining those objectives and monitoring performance are determined.

There are two elements to this definition. The first says who governance is for, and the second says what governance is about: it is about defining the objectives of the organization, defining the means of obtaining those objectives, and then monitoring progress to ensure they are achieved. In order to achieve this, boards of directors should:

- ensure mechanisms are in pace within the organization to set objectives for projects, which link projects to corporate strategy;
- ensure people are competent and appropriately empowered and motivated to enact the projects;
- ensure appropriate controls are in place to ensure the projects achieve their objectives, both for the delivery of benefit and consumption of resources – the directors need to do this both to ensure the projects are profitable and from a compliance perspective to meet their responsibilities to their shareholders.

The APM Guide

The UK's APM (2004) has published a guide for the governance of project management. This guide suggests that the aims of good corporate governance are to ensure:

1   There is a clear link between corporate strategy and project objectives:

   - in the definition of projects;
   - in benefits delivered;
   - in project governance roles;
   - in portfolio and program management.

2   There is clear ownership and leadership from senior management to ensure projects are successful.
3   There is engagement with key stakeholders.
4   The organization has the appropriate capability to undertake its projects.
5   There is understanding of and contact with the supply industry at a senior level.
6   Project proposals are evaluated based on their value to the organization and not on capital cost alone.

In order to achieve these objectives, the guide suggests eleven principles of good governance of project management. The first is general, two relate to defining the objectives of projects in the organization, two define the means of obtaining the objectives and the rest refer to monitoring progress:

P1: The board of directors must assume overall responsibility for the governance of projects. They have a duty under modern compliance regimes to be able to predict future cash flows of the business, and this requires them to be able to predict outturn cost and future returns for all large projects, programs and portfolios.

Define the Objectives

P2: There must be a coherent and supportive relationship between the overall corporate strategy and the project portfolio to ensure project objectives are well defined through the project portfolio.

P3: The business case for all projects must be supported by sound and realistic data so decisions can be based on the knowledge that predictions are valid and the board can meet its duties under the compliance regimes.

Define the Means of Obtaining the Objectives

P4: Roles, responsibilities and performance criteria for the governance of projects (and programs and portfolios) must be clearly defined.

P5: Members of delegated authorization bodies have sufficient representation, authority, competence and resources to take the decisions for which they are responsible. Such authorization bodies include:

- project or program steering committees, including sponsor, owner, senior user, senior supplier and project manager;
- the portfolio selection committee.

Define the Means of Monitoring Progress

P6: Defined governance arrangements, supported by appropriate methods and controls, must be applied throughout the project process.

P7: All projects must have an approved plan with defined authorization points where the business case will be reviewed and approved. Decisions made at the authorization points must be clearly recorded. End-of-stage reviews can be used as authorization points.

P8: There are clearly defined key performance indicators for reporting project status and for escalating risks and issues to appropriate levels.

P9: The board and its delegated agents decide when independent audits of projects, programs and management systems are required and implement such audits as required. Audits may be undertaken because a project is known to be in difficulty. They may also be undertaken where a project must not fail, and the audit is undertaken to ensure it has been well established.

P10: Project stakeholders are engaged at a level that is appropriate for their importance and in a way that fosters trust and cooperation.

P11: The organization fosters a culture of continuous improvement and frank discussion and project reporting. The organization aims to be a learning organization.

Governance of the Project

The project is a temporary organization (Turner and Müller, 2003) and so it needs governance. With a little adaptation, Thomas Clarke's (2004) definition of corporate governance can be applied to a project:

> The governance of a project involves a set of relationships between the project's management, its sponsor (or executive board), its owner, and other stakeholders. It provides the structure through which the objectives of the project are set, and the means of attaining those objectives and monitoring performance are determined.

So there are three aims of project governance:

1   define the objectives of the project;
2   define the means achieving the objectives;
3   define the means of monitoring progress.

A project's objectives exist on three levels, Figure 4.3.

1   The output: this is the deliverable the project produces. It is some form of new asset, which the organization believes it needs to help it achieve its strategic objectives.
2   The outcome: these are new competencies which the output will help the organization achieve. The organization doesn't want the output for its own sake, it actually wants to achieve the outcome. The operation of the outcome will deliver benefits to the organization.
3   The goal: this is the longer-term strategic objective that the outcome will help the organization achieve.

I use two simple examples to illustrate the three levels. An organization wanted to increase its profits (goal) and to that end the new competencies it required (outcome) was to improve its marketing mix. To that end it developed a customer requirement management system (output). The Chinese government wanted to increase economic activity in Jiangsu province on the North side of the Jangtze river, near Shanghai. What was stopping economic development was poor traffic flows across the river, so the project outcome it needed, the new competencies, was faster traffic flow across the river. To that end it built a bridge (output).

Governance roles

Figure 4.4 illustrates the governance roles on projects. The inner loop shows the three steps of governance introduced above, and the second loop shows first the definition

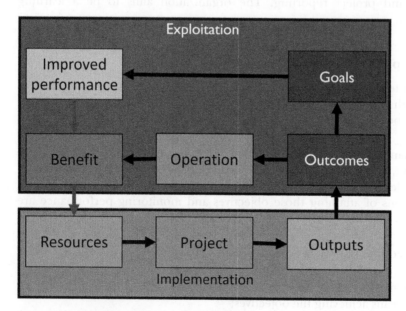

Figure 4.3 Three Levels of Project Objectives

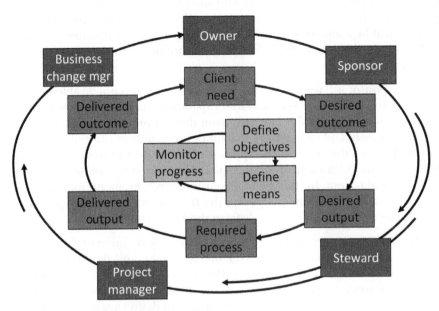

Figure 4.4 The Roles of Project Governance

and the delivery of the three levels of objectives. This illustrates that one level of objectives is the means of delivering the objectives at the level above. So the project outcome is the means of achieving the goal. That then becomes an objective, and the output is the means of achieving the outcome. That then becomes an objective, and the project process is the means of delivering that. You then need to control the project process to ensure the project is completed to time, cost and quality, and then as the project is completed you need to control the commissioning of the output, and the achievement of the outcome and the goal.

Figure 4.4 then illustrates that there are at least four project governance roles involved. (I don't count the client manager as a project governance role.)

Sponsor. The sponsor is somebody from the client or user department who identifies the strategic need, the possibility of achieving the goal and that there is a change (project output) that can be made that will deliver new competencies (project outcome) that will enable the organization to achieve the goal in a cost-effective way (the benefit will justify the cost). He or she identifies the possible new asset and capabilities (outputs and outcomes) that will solve the problem or exploit the opportunity. The sponsor approves the definition of the objectives (goals, outcomes and outputs) on behalf of the user or client organization and approves the statement of requirements. The sponsor also becomes the ambassador for the project, persuading the organization that the project is a good idea and trying to win resources in the form of money and people. He or she may be the holder of the budget that pays for the project or be a first report to that person. The ambassadorial role should continue throughout the project winning resources at the start and maintaining resources throughout the project. In the case of the customer requirements management system, the sponsor will be somebody from the marketing department, and in the case of the bridge, perhaps somebody from the economics department of central government.

Steward: The sponsor will not be a technical expert and so will not be able to finalize the definition of the new asset and new capabilities on his or her own. He or she will need to involve a senior manager from the technical department to help design the new asset and define the capabilities it can deliver through its operation. I call this role the *steward.* The sponsor and steward will work together to complete the project feasibility study and finalize the initial definition of the project outcome and output. In the case of the customer requirements management system the steward will be somebody from the Information Systems Department and in the case of the bridge somebody from the Ministry of Works.

Project Manager: The project manager is responsible for defining and managing the project process to design and deliver the new asset, and defining how the project will be monitored and controlled. He or she will then be responsible for monitoring progress during project execution to ensure the asset is delivered and is fit for purpose, that is, to ensure it is capable of delivering new capabilities that will solve the problem or exploit the opportunity. In the case of the customer requirements management system the project manager will probably form the Information Systems Department, and in the case of the bridge from the Ministry of Works.

Owner or Business Change Manager: I firmly believe that the project manager's responsibility ends with the delivery of the new capabilities. It is then the responsibility of somebody from the user department to ensure the new capabilities are used to work through the benefits map and ensure change is embedded and the problems are ultimately solved. You may use a benefits map as the means of monitoring progress for this last step of control (Turner, 2014), and so each step needs to be measurable. The owner of the new asset is ultimately responsible for this last step of control, but he or she may delegate it to a business change manager. In the case of the customer requirements management system, the owner and business change manager will come from the marketing department, and one in fact may be the same person as the sponsor. The marketing department are responsible for making the system work and obtaining the benefit, not the project manager. In the case of the bridge, the owner may come from the Ministry of Roads, and the business change manager from the provincial government.

The sponsor is essentially a pre-project role defining the objectives (goals, outcomes and outputs). This role also defines, through the benefits map (Turner, 2014), how the change will be embedded and performance monitored post-project. The sponsor is also the ambassador of the project, obtaining resources pre-project and maintaining their availability during the project. The owner and business change manager are post-project roles, responsible for embedding the change and achieving the performance improvement post-project. The sponsor and owner may be the same person, but do not need to be. PRINCE2 (The Cabinet Office, 2009) suggests you need two roles and calls the sponsor the project executive and the business change manager the senior user. Likewise the steward is a pre-project role defining the objectives (outputs and outcomes), and the project manager is an intra-project role defining the means of obtaining the objectives and monitoring progress (through the project plan). The project manager and steward may be the same person, but don't need to be. On large, stand-alone projects, they are more likely to be the same person, but the steward may just be a senior manager from the technical or projects department. On small projects the steward tends to be the program or portfolio manager. PRINCE2 calls the steward the senior user and the project manager just that.

The Principal–Agent Relationship

Ralf Müller and I (2004) demonstrated three necessary conditions for project success:

1   The project participants, especially the project manager and sponsor, should work together in partnership to achieve mutually consistent objectives.
2   The project manager should be empowered but not given total licence. The sponsor should set parameters within which the project manager should work, but the project manager must be given flexibility to enable him or her to respond to risk. If the sponsor imposes too much structure, the project manager has no flexibility to deal with the unknown; if the sponsor imposes too little, the manager has no guidance.
3   The sponsor should take an interest in progress.

We found in our sample that successful projects were clustered in the area of high cooperation and medium structure. However to operate there requires significant trust between the project manager and sponsor. We found the lowest success in the area of low cooperation and low structure. That was the worst position to operate the project. We found the lowest predictability in the area of low cooperation and high structure. In that quadrant, the project outcome was quite variable but never as successful as the area of high cooperation and medium structure. But it is in the area of low cooperation and high structure that many projects take place. The sponsor doesn't trust the project manager so adopts confrontational behaviours and imposes strict rules on the project manager's behaviour.

Most people, when they spend any time thinking about it, recognize that it is good practice to treat the project as a partnership, and to work to mutually consistent goals. They recognize that the best way of achieving a successful outcome is for all the project participants to gain from that outcome. If the project outcome is going to be detrimental to a given party, then you can expect that either they will be working for project failure, or they will be trying to change the project outcomes to be more beneficial for them and so may push the project in unintended directions. If you think about it, that is obvious, and so why is it that people adopt uncooperative behaviours on projects? The principal–agent relationship provides an answer.

Michael Jensen (2000) says that a principal–agent relationship exists if one party (the principal) depends on another (the agent) to undertake an action on their behalf. This is clearly the relationship between the sponsor (principal) and project manager (agent). Associated with this relationship are two problems, which lead to the lack of trust between the project manager and sponsor:

The Adverse Selection Problem: This problem occurs as the principal (sponsor) has to choose the agent (project manager) to act on his or her behalf and has to do that on inadequate information, and so can never be totally certain that the project manager is competent, nor that he or she was the best person available, nor that he or she will behave ethically. Having appointed the agent, the principal cannot know for certain why the agent is taking the decisions he or she does, and whether the agent is acting in their (the principal's) best interest. It is recognized that a fundamental transformation occurs at the moment the agent (project manager) is appointed that they now know more about the project than the principal (client or sponsor).

The Moral Hazard Problem: This problem arises because economic theory assumes that the rational human being will act rationally in any situation to maximize his or her beneficial outcome from the situation. That means the project manager will be taking decisions on the project to maximize his or her outcome and will only maximize the sponsor's outcomes en passant if their two sets of outcomes happen to be aligned. This is what I said above and is the need for the partnership. So if you are a sponsor on a project, don't expect the project manager to be working in your best interest if you have imposed a contract that will cause him or her to make a loss. He or she will cut corners or manufacture variations to turn his or her loss into a profit. Choose a form of contract that motivates the project manager to achieve your objectives. The board of directors of the contractor is in fact legally obliged to maximize returns for their shareholders and not the client's. So only expect the contractor to maximize returns for the client's shareholders if the project has been set up in such a way to align their objectives. Simples!

Bounded Rationality: Often the project manager would like to work in the sponsor's best interests, but can't because of human frailty. Economic theory labels this "bounded rationality" (Simon, 1955), and it is caused by three elements of human frailty:

- inability to gather all the information relevant to the decision;
- inability to fully process that information which is gathered;
- inability to foretell the future and so flawlessly predict all the risks.

The project manager ends up doing the best they can with the information he or she has, which is known as *satisficing*.

Agency or Transaction Costs: Against this background, the sponsor starts to impose structures on the project, which create additional costs that are over and above the cost of doing the work of the project. These are known as *agency costs* (Jensen, 2000), or *transaction costs* (Williamson, 1996). Michael Jensen identifies four agency costs:

1   the *cost of forming and managing the contract* and the contractual relationship between the principal and the agent;
2   the *cost of communication* between the principal and the agent, and of reporting progress and controlling the work;

3   *bonding costs* are things the agent does to win the principal's trust and support;
4   *residual losses* arise because the project's outcomes are not exactly what the principal needs.

An example of a bonding cost is the agent's membership of professional bodies. Such membership gives the principal trust in both their competence (Adverse Selection Problem), and ethical behaviour (Moral Hazard Problem). The agent had to prove their competence to get professional membership and needs to behave ethically to maintain it. This is why project managers want membership of organizations such as Project Management Institute (PMI). Other bonding costs are gifts and invitations to sporting events. Because the agent has to make a profit, the principal has to ultimately pay for all of these things through increased project costs. Residual loss occurs either because the project manager is acting in his or her own best interest and not the principal's or because of bounded rationality, or both. The new asset does not work exactly as the principal requires and they therefore fail to get the full benefit from the project.

Governance of the Context

There are two elements of the governance of the context:

1   The use of program and portfolio management to link project objectives to corporate strategy.
2   The development of organization capability to undertake the projects the organization is doing.

Program and Portfolio Management

Portfolios and programs are a key element in cascading corporate strategy down to project strategy and thereby linking project objectives to corporate objectives (Turner, 2014). They adopt the model developed by Rodney Turner (2009), shown in Figure 4.1. The concept of program and portfolio management is not new, but it is only recently that their key role in linking project strategy to corporate strategy has been identified.

I like to keep my definitions simple and focus just on the key point. So I define a program as follows:

A program is a group of projects that contribute to a common objective.

Often, to achieve the desired outcome from a change requires several project outputs. I define a portfolio as follows:

A portfolio is a group of projects sharing common resources.

The common resources can be money, materials, people, data, technology and so on. Portfolios can exist at several levels. Figure 4.5 shows a firm's investment portfolio, which is the sum total of all its investment activity. The investment portfolio can consist of large projects and programs, but also miscellaneous portfolios of small and

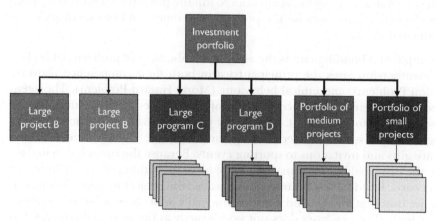

Figure 4.5 The Investment Portfolio

medium-sized projects. When you look at the sharing of money between projects in the investment portfolio, small and medium-sized projects cannot compete alongside the large projects and programs. We define medium-sized projects as being one-tenth the size of large ones and small projects one-tenth the size of medium. The estimating error in estimating projects is 5 per cent to 10 per cent and so medium-sized projects are the same size as the estimating error in large projects and so cannot be seen in the noise of the large projects. They have to be treated separately, and similarly small projects need to be treated separately again because they cannot be seen in the noise of the medium-sized projects.

Are programs a special case of portfolios? Some people say they are; a program is a portfolio that happens to have a common objective. However, they have very different key features: a program has common outputs; a portfolio has common inputs. Sometimes the projects in a program also have common inputs; for instance if you are developing a shopping centre. But sometimes they have quite different inputs.

Governing the Investment Portfolio

There are five essential steps in governing the investment portfolio:

Step 1: Maintain a list of all projects, programs and portfolios in a project database.

Step 2: Monitor progress on all projects, programs and portfolios.

Step 3: Prioritize all projects, programs and portfolios and assign resources appropriately.

Step 4: Plan the resource needs of all projects and programs in the portfolio and coordinate the assignment of resources between them.

Step 5: Evaluate business benefits post-implementation, to continuously improve selection and management procedures.

I call these "steps" which implies that one follows the other. But if you are doing port-folio management you do all five in parallel all of the time. However, if you are not doing portfolio management you tend to start at step 1 and work through in order.

Project Inventory and Progress

Steps 1 and 2 require the maintenance of an inventory of all projects, programs and portfolios, with progress shown on all projects. A traffic light report, Figure 4.6, is a useful tool for listing the projects in a portfolio and showing their progress against identified key performance indicators. (In the colour version of this the three types of circle are, left to right in the key, green, amber and red respectively.)

Prioritizing Projects

It is necessary to prioritize projects and only admit to the portfolio projects for which there are enough resources to do them. This will be the responsibility of a project portfolio committee. At the level of the investment portfolio they typically meet every three months. At their meeting they are presented with a list of proposed projects, in rank order of prioritization. They admit projects to the portfolio up to the limit of money and other resources available to do them. Once they have reached the initial limit, they may look at the next two or three projects and ask if they are higher prior-ity than projects already underway. If the answer is "yes" these current projects may be cancelled and the new projects admitted to the portfolio. Many of the projects

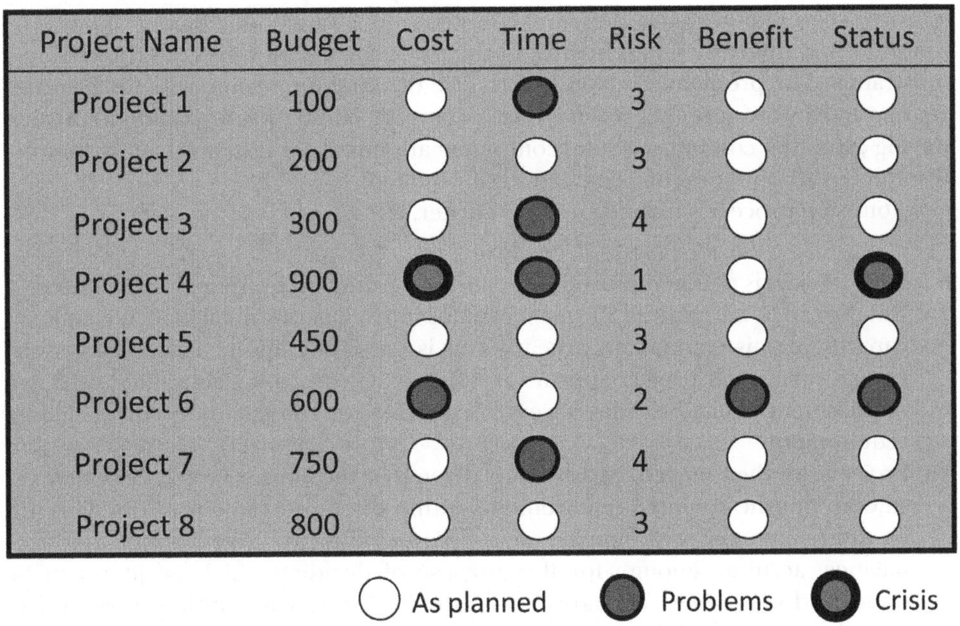

Project Name	Budget	Cost	Time	Risk	Benefit	Status
Project 1	100	○	●	3	○	○
Project 2	200	○	○	3	○	○
Project 3	300	○	●	4	○	○
Project 4	900	●	●	1	○	●
Project 5	450	○	○	3	○	○
Project 6	600	●	○	2	●	●
Project 7	750	○	●	4	○	○
Project 8	800	○	○	3	○	○

○ As planned   ● Problems   ● Crisis

Figure 4.6 Traffic Light Report

not admitted to the portfolio will be discarded. But for some it may be the decision this time around was borderline, or it may be there is reason to believe the priority will change in the future, and so some of the projects will be reconsidered at future meetings.

The two main criteria for prioritizing projects will be benefit and risk, but other criteria may include:

- stakeholder commitment;
- process effectiveness;
- learning opportunity;
- type of project.

You can use a weighted average (or balanced score card) to prioritize projects. Weighted average assigns a weight (often on a scale of 1 to 3) to each criterion. Each project is then scored against each criterion (again often on a scale of 1 to 3), and the overall score calculated. In a balanced score card, the weights are fractional numbers and sum to 100 per cent. If you use balanced score card, the balanced score card at the project level will be linked to that at the organizational level, with linked objectives.

Sharing Resources between Projects

The means of sharing resources between projects in a portfolio is now well understood.

Up to about ten years ago, the approach people adopted was to maintain a gigantic plan of all their projects in one database. Each project was planned in detail, with their resource requirements, and the plans merged into a single meta-project plan. The computer was then asked to schedule all the project activities subject to the resource constraints. The problem was, you had to give the computer some rule for prioritizing one activity over another when a clash occurred. These rules are called heuristics. Having given the computer a rule, computers are dumb things; it will apply the rule absolutely, without question. That led to silly outcomes.

A four-step process is now suggested (Turner, 2014):

1   Each project is planned individually, and its resource requirements calculated.
2   But instead of merging all the project plans into a gigantic meta-plan, a rough-cut capacity plan is maintained instead. This is called the Master Project Schedule. In that plan, each project appears as a single activity, with a simplified resource requirement. That provides a very rough view (a rough-cut) of the resource requirement.
3   Projects are then moved, extended or deleted in the Master Project Schedule, to smooth out the resource requirements within the resource constraints. This will be done manually, with management control. This produces a rough resource balance, accurate enough for the purpose of deciding which projects can be done, and when they can start and finish. That gives each project a window of when it can start and finish, and what its resource availability is.

4   Each project is then managed within its start and finish date and resource availability. As long as the project manager can keep to those constraints, there is no need to refer back to the Master Project Schedule. If some disturbance occurs, the project is delayed, or another project requires additional resources, the response can be planned in the Master Project Schedule.

This is not easy, but if you are doing it you have some semblance of control. If you are not doing it, you are out of control, and have no way of responding to disturbances.

There are three roles involved in this process, Figure 4.7. New projects and programs are given to the portfolio director. He or she asks the project managers to plan the projects and calculate resource requirements. The portfolio director receives predictions of resource availability for resource managers and balances the projects in the rough-cut capacity plan. They should balance because only the right number of resources should have been admitted to the portfolio. The project managers are then given projects to manage within the time and resource windows they are given, and make requests for resources to the resource managers.

Post-Project Evaluation

The last step in the portfolio management process is to evaluate projects post-implementation. The reason this is necessary is that without it people are encouraged to "lie" at Step 3, to overinflate the benefits of their projects and underinflate the costs and risks. A post-project evaluation must be held on all projects, and people held accountable if their projects have failed to deliver the benefits, within the envelope of risk. This is an essential step in the means of monitoring progress to ensure the organization's objectives are achieved.

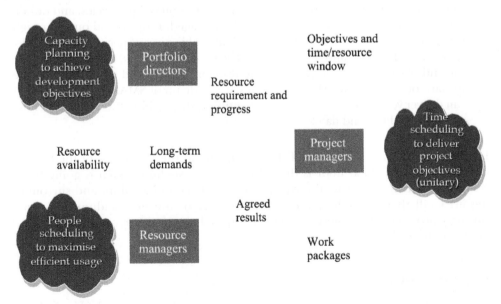

Figure 4.7 Project Portfolio Management Roles

Types of Program

There are three types of programs:

1   once through programs;
2   cyclic programs;
3   hybrid programs.

The once through programs are very similar to large projects. All the project out-puts need to be commissioned together because they are all needed to obtain the outcomes of the program. An example is Terminal 5 at Heathrow Airport. Outputs consisted of the main terminal building, the B pier, the baggage handling system, car parks and road access. And in the terminal building there were shopping and other facilities that were treated as separate projects to the terminal itself. Most of the projects needed to be finished for the terminal to be commissioned. Some of the terminal facilities could be left for later, and in fact the C pier was opened sometime later. There are also plans for D and E piers, but that is linked to the redevelopment of Terminals 1 and 2.

   With a cyclic program, the projects are done in several cycles. There are at least two advantages of the cyclic approach:

1   You get early benefits from the early cycles that can be used to pay for the later cycles, increasing the profitability of the program. In a project or once through program, you have to spend all the money before commissioning the output and getting any returns. But in the cyclic program, you only spend part of the money before getting returns, improving your cash flow.
2   At the end of each cycle, you can revisit the definition of later cycles, and decide whether to do more or less than originally envisaged. Projects and once through programs have what are said to be SMART objectives, Specific, Measurable, Achievable, Realistic and Timelined. Cyclic programs have sMARt objectives. At the end of each cycle you can decide to do more or less, and move the end date forward or back. Cyclic sMARt programs are made up of SMART projects, so you can deliver very specific outputs while continuously revisiting the objectives of the program, and the end date.

Hybrid programs are a mixture of the two. I work at the University of the Basque Country in Bilbao. Next door is the Bilbao football stadium which is going to be rebuilt on a new site across the road. The site of the old stadium and surround-ing area will then be redeveloped. The building of the new stadium is a once through program, the redevelopment of the old site and surrounding area is a cyclic program.

Program Life-Cycle

All types of program follow a similar program life-cycle, Figure 4.8 (The Cabinet Office, 2011), with four stages:

1   identify;
2   define;
3   govern;
4   dissolve.

However, during the govern stage, cyclic programs also follow a three stage embedded cycle:

1   plan;
2   deliver;
3   renew or dissolve.

Interestingly, the govern stage clearly shows the two governance roles:

- the project and program managers responsible for delivering the project outputs and new capabilities (project outcomes);
- the business change managers, working for the program owner, responsible for taking the outcomes and using them to achieve the desired benefit: this is significant in the cyclic programs because the benefits will be used to pay for the later stages.

Program Governance Roles

Figure 4.9 illustrates the program governance roles. These reflect the project governance roles in Figure 4.4. Figure 4.9 shows the roles in three columns. The middle column contains the program and project management roles, people responsible

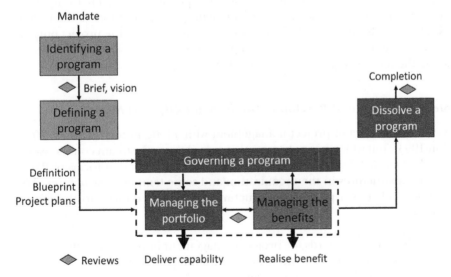

Figure 4.8 Program Management Life-Cycle

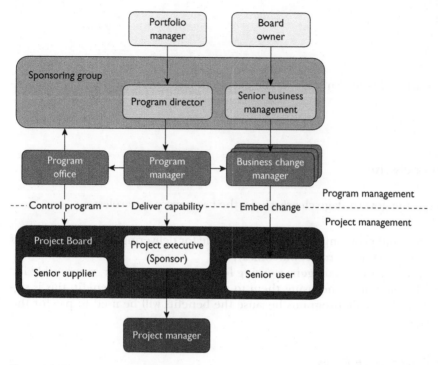

Figure 4.9 Program Governance Roles

for designing and delivering the project outputs to achieve the desired outcomes. The right-hand column shows the business roles, the people responsible for identifying the desired change and business goals, and acting as ambassadors to obtain the resources. They are also responsible for embedding the change as the project outputs are delivered. The left-hand column is the program office, responsible for establishing and enacting the monitoring and control mechanisms.

The Project, Program and Portfolio Management Office (PMO)

The PMO is another area of project management with a long history (Turner, 2014, first edition 1993), but which has only recently entered the mainstream consciousness (Aubry, 2014). Figure 4.9 shows that there are a number of different forms of PMO, some permanent structures in the organization and some temporary structures. The strategic project office is a permanent structure responding directly to the board, responsible for:

- setting policies and standards for project management in the organization;
- supporting project managers, and providing training and consultancy;
- aligning projects with corporate strategy;
- auditing projects and programs where necessary.

The portfolio office is also a permanent structure, perhaps in the projects department. It is responsible for:

- implementing the standards in a business unit;
- prioritizing projects and linking them to corporate strategy;
- prioritizing resources across projects within the portfolio;
- tracking progress of projects and programs in the portfolio.

The project and program office are temporary structures supporting a large project or program for as long as it exists. It is responsible for:

- supporting large complex projects or programs;
- implementing standards on the project or program;
- planning the project or program and managing progress;
- managing interfaces with clients and suppliers;
- managing materials;
- managing risk and issues.

Organizational Capability

The competence of the organization's staff is a key component of its capability, but organization capability is more than then competence of its staff. The whole is greater than the sum of the parts. Organizations need to know how to manage the projects they are undertaking. They need to have a defined methodology of managing projects and to be able to train project managers in the use of that methodology. (An organization may in fact have several methodologies, for different types of projects.) The organization's methodology needs to define several things:

1 The project process: The organization needs to have an understanding of the stages its projects go though from conception to completion. A standard process is concept, feasibility, design, execution and close-out (Turner, 2014), but the organization should develop a definition of the process appropriate to its types of projects. Organizations may also need to define a program process as above.
2 The management process: The organization needs to understand the management processes applied at each stage of the project life-cycle to deliver those stages. The management process suggested by the Project Management Institute (2013) is:

- initiation;
- planning;
- implementing;
- controlling;
- closing.

3 The project management functions: The organization needs to know how to manage the functions of project management. These may be the seven functions suggested by Rodney Turner (2014): scope, organization, stakeholders, quality, cost, time and risk. Or they may be the ten body of knowledge areas defined by the PMI (2013): scope, integration, quality, cost, time, risk, HR, communication, procurement and stakeholders.

Building and Maintaining Organizational Competence

So how do organizations build and maintain organizational capability? I suggest four themes:

Procedures: These are the explicit statements of how the organization manages projects; they are the codification of its knowledge and capability. Through its procedures an organization defines how it manages projects. An organization may in fact need several sets of procedures for different types of projects. Also, the procedures should be treated like flexible guidelines not rigid rules. Every project is different. So an organization should have its project management procedures, which are a statement of good practice. However, at the start of every project, the manager should develop the project-specific version to say how this project will be managed, and that will become part of the quality plan for the project. I worked with one engineering construction company that makes its apprentice project managers follow the procedures to the letter, but will not let someone manage a project on their own until they know how to adapt the procedures appropriately to meet the needs of individual projects.

Project reviews: It is through project reviews that an organization learns how it is doing on individual projects, but also learns how to improve its project management procedures and processes. There are several types of review:

- Audits: these are reviews conducted by people external to the project team.
- Health-checks: these are reviews conducted by the project team on themselves.
- Project control reviews: these are reviews conducted as part of the normal control cycle of the project, including end-of-stage reviews.

Benchmarking: It is important for the organization to know how it is performing compared to other people undertaking similar projects. The organization gathers data about its project performance and compares that to organizations doing similar projects. It is relatively easy to compare project data with other people in the same parent company. It is more difficult to compare data with other companies, especially competitors. Some professional organizations maintain benchmarking databases, where you can compare the performance of your projects to industry averages, but you can't compare your projects directly with the projects of your competitors.

Project management community: Through the project management community the organization develops its implicit or tacit knowledge. The project management community is an important part of the organization's learning processes, where apprentice project managers are trained and mentored. An effective community will also arrange events where project managers can meet and share experiences. Typically a meeting is arranged once every three months. There are perhaps one or two lectures lasting 90 minutes, followed by socializing. Project managers meet. Perhaps at some future time, if a project manager has a problem, he or she will remember discussing a similar problem with a colleague, and can contact the colleague to discuss it further.

Organizational Project Management Maturity

An organization's ability to deliver its projects successfully to achieve business benefit is often defined as its project management maturity. Many models of organizational project management maturity have been developed, and any models are based on the Capability Maturity Model developed by the Carnegie-Mellon Institute in the United States for information systems development (Paulk et al., 1995). That defines five levels of maturity:

Level 1 – Initial: The organization has no defined process for project management. It uses ad-hoc processes with no consistency.

Level 2 – Repeatable: The organization starts to develop individual processes for how it manages the project management functions. It may define how it manages scope, quality, cost, time or risk for instance. It begins to develop the project management community and give project managers guidance on how to apply the embryonic processes.

Level 3 – Defined: The individual processes become combined into a set of procedures for project management, defining holistically how the organization manages projects. The project management community is developed to provide project managers with group support.

Level 4 – Managed: Through the review process, lessons are learnt and metrics gathered. These are fed back into the procedures to continuously improve them. As further metrics are gathered project performance can be benchmarked against other organizations.

Level 5 – Optimized: The procedures are continuously improved and defects patched. Nirvana is achieved.

You will notice the four themes defined above are at play here, with procedures and the project management community dominating at levels 2 and 3, and reviews and benchmarking dominating at levels 4 and 5.

It costs money to achieve increasing organizational project management maturity. Is it worthwhile? Work done at the University of California in Berkley (Ibbs and Reginato, 2002) show that increasing project management maturity can lead to substantial improvement in cost and schedule performance. In more mature organizations, on average projects cost less, and deliver their expected benefits earlier, leading to performance improvement. Performance improvement of 30 per cent or more can be achieved from increasing maturity, but it comes at a cost. You can define a project management return on investment (PM ROI) where:

$$\text{PM ROI} = \frac{\text{Annual spend on projects * Efficiency gain from increasing maturity}}{\text{Cost of achieving that gain}}$$

A problem is that increasing maturity is a learning curve as shown. The efficiency gain of going from maturity level N to N+1 is half that of going from N-1 to N, while the cost of achieving the increased maturity is double. So the PM ROI of going from level N to N+1 is one-quarter that of going from N-1 to N. For many organizations with moderate annual spend on projects it is just not worthwhile going beyond maturity level 3. It is only large project-based organizations with substantial project spend for whom it is worthwhile achieving maturity levels 4 and 5.

Achieving Capability Improvement

We suggest a four-step process for achieving capability improvement:

Variation: New ideas are created, sometimes by deliberate problem solving and purposeful creativity, sometimes by random occurrences and fortuitous happenstance.

Selection: Through a review process, good, successful new ideas are chosen for reuse.

Retention: Those ideas chosen for reuse are stored in the organization's memory where they can be used by people in the organization.

Distribution: Ideas are distributed from the organization's memory to people working on projects, who may be working at some distance from the centre.

The first three steps in this process were originally suggested in the evolution literature to explain the evolution of species. New features (genes) in species occur by random variation. Successful features (genes) are selected by survival of the fittest, and are then stored in the memory (the gene pool). The three-step process was later adopted by the management learning literature to explain learning in organizations. New ideas arise in organizations, sometimes by chance, but sometimes purposefully with people deliberately trying new ideas. Good ideas are selected for retention, and those ideas selected for reuse are stored in the organization's memory.

In a functional organization it ends there. Knowledge is stored in the function for reuse by people working in the function. People's careers are limited to one function, climbing the ladder up the functional silo. As their career develops in the function, they are exposed to the retained knowledge in the function, where it is available for them to draw on locally. It is different in project-based organizations. New ideas occur on projects that come to an end; so they must be captured and transferred to the function to be stored. People also work on projects away from the functional centre, sometimes geographically quite distant. In order for the good new ideas to be used, they must be distributed somehow from the functional memory banks to people working on projects as new projects start. Thus distribution of the knowledge is an important fourth step in knowledge management process in a project-based organization, which is not necessary in a functional organization.

Top Management Support

We cannot stress enough the importance of top management support in improving maturity and enterprise-wide project management capability through innovation and learning. Without senior management support junior people will either fear making changes or not take the initiative. A manager in IBM told me that junior people may avoid making honest reports in project reviews for fear of upsetting middle managers. Particularly they fear that if they make an honest report it may put their boss in a poor light. Organizations must learn not to shoot the messenger, and the support of senior management will help junior people to make honest reports.

Some people may not make changes because they have done something a certain way for a long time, and they just don't want to try new things. They are locked into a competency trap. They may fear that if they try something new and it goes wrong they will lose their job. Senior management need to make it clear that it is the other way around, if they don't try something new they will lose their job. If they aren't occasionally making mistakes people will be asking why they aren't trying new things. Top management need to make it clear that they want to see new innovative ways of working.

Governance of the Relationship between the Client and Contractor

Above I described how an organization governs the projects it is undertaking though three levels, Figure 4.1. This applies equally well to the client organization and contracting organization, Figure 4.2, although there is a slight difference in emphasis. For instance with principles P2 and P3 from the APM guide:

- for the client, organizational strategy is to develop new business, and the project business case compares the cost of the project to the future revenue from the new business;
- for the contractor, organization strategy is to do projects, and the business case compares the cost of the project to the price the client will pay for it.

As I said above, the three interfaces in Figure 4.2 need governing. The interfaces between the client and the project and the contractor and the project are managed through the three levels described above. But the interface between the client and the contractor needs governing.

The main governance mechanism is of course the contract. This will:

- define the objectives the contractor is to deliver;
- provide some guidance of the means of achieving those objectives, although this will be more strictly defined on a remeasurement contract than a fixed price contract;
- describe the control reports the client wishes to receive.

However, Anne Keegan and I (2001) identified that the contracting organization may have several governance roles to support the relationship with the client.

The client may have all the governance roles illustrated in Figure 4.4. They should have a sponsor providing senior management support to the project, and a business change manager to embed the change and deliver the benefits on project completion.

They may also have a steward, or senior supplier, from the relevant technical department within the organization and a project manager overseeing the work of the contractor. However, it is not unusual for technically naïve clients to delegate the role of steward, or senior supplier, and project manager to the contractor.

Anne Keegan and I (2001) identified that the roles of sponsor, steward and project manager are usually mirrored within the contract organization, Figure 4.10. The broker mirrors the sponsor, and the steward and project manager fulfil those roles. The broker and steward had many different names in different organizations, but it was not uncommon for them to be called the account manager and solutions manager respectively.

> *Broker.* This role mirrors the sponsor within the contractor organization. He or she manages the client account. He or she helps the client define the business need, and identify the possible project outcome and output. He or she negotiates the contract with the client, and persuades the contract organization that this is business they want, and makes resources available for the contract.

> *Steward:* This role mirrors the steward in the client organization, and may even fulfil it for the client organization. He or she manages the frontend design of the project outputs and the initial definition of the project process, and so works with the broker in preparing the tender for the contract and preparing the contract. He or she will then identify a project manager and project team to deliver the project, and will in that role fulfil the program or portfolio management role within the contract organization.

> *Project manager.* The project manager manages the detail design and delivery of the project. He or she fulfils this role within the contract organization. The client may have a project manager overseeing the contractor's project manager, but in this case the client project manager mirrors the contractor project manager.

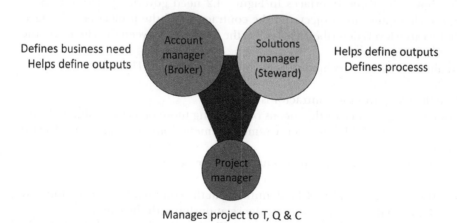

Figure 4.10 Contractor Governance Roles

Conclusion

Anne Keegan and I identified these roles both within contractors doing work for external clients, but also within back office departments doing work for front office departments. One company we interviewed was Ericsson in the Netherlands, who were building telephone networks for Dutch telephone operating companies. They described the three roles as Three Core. We also interviewed a back office department for British Telecom. They also called the roles account manager and solutions manager. Our interviewee told us that the back office departments combined had an account manager for each front office department and a solutions manager within each back office department. So when a front office department had a need, the relevant account manager would go to the solutions manager for the appropriate back office department and design the required solution. This was much more efficient than each back office department maintaining a direct relationship with each front office department; it reduced transaction costs. At the time of the interviews, BT was about to increase the number of front office departments from 15 to 18. All they had to do was create three new account managers, rather than each back office department having to create a relationship with each of the new front office departments.

References

Association for Project Management, 2004a, *Directing Change: A Guide to Governance of Project Management*, High Wycombe, UK: Association for Project Management.

Aubry, M., 2014, The project office, in J.R. Turner, (ed.), *The Gower Handbook of Project Management*. Farnham, UK: Gower.

Cabinet Office, The, 2009, *Managing Successful Projects with PRINCE2™*, 5th edition. London, UK: The Stationery Office.

Cabinet Office, The, 2011, *Managing Successful Programmes*, 4th ed. London, UK: The Stationery Office.

Clarke, T. (ed.), 2004, *Theories of Corporate Governance: The Philosophical Foundations of Corporate Governance*. London: Routledge.

Ibbs, C.W. and Reginato, J., 2002, *Quantifying the Value of Project Management*. Newton Square, PA: Project Management Institute.

Jensen, M.C., 2000, *A Theory of the Firm: Governance, Residual Claims, and Organizational Forms*. Boston, MA: Harvard University Press.

Müller, R., 2009, *Project Governance*. Aldershot, UK: Gower Publishing.

Müller, R., 2011, Project Governance, in P. Morris, J.K. Pinto, and J. Söderlund. (eds.), *Oxford Handbook of Project Management*. Oxford: Oxford University Press.

Müller, R., Andersen, E.S., Kvalnes, O., Shao, J., Sankaran, S., Turner, J.R., Biesenthal, C., Walker, D.W.T. and Gudergan, S., 2013, The interrelationship of governance, trust and ethics in temporary organizations. *Project Management Journal*, 44(4), 26–34, DOI: 10.1002/pmj.21350.

Paulk, M.C., Curtis, B. and Chrissis, M.B., 1991, *Capability Maturity Model for Software*. Pittsburg, KA: Carnegie Mellon University.

Project Management Institute, 2013, *A Guide to the Project Management Body of Knowledge*, 5th edition. Newtown Square, PA: Project Management Institute.

Simon, H.A., 1955, A behavioural model of rational choice. *Quarterly Journal of Economics*, 69, 99–118.

Stoker, G., 1998, Governance as theory: five propositions. *International Social Science Journal,* 50(155), 17–28.

Turner, J.R., 2014, *The Handbook of Project-based Management,* 4th edition. New York: McGraw-Hill.

Turner, J.R. and Keegan, A.E., 1999, The versatile project-based organisation: governance and operational control. *European Management Journal,* 17(3), 296–309.

Turner, J.R. and Keegan, A.E., 2001, Mechanisms of governance in the project-based organization: the role of the broker and steward. *European Management Journal,* 19(3), 254–267.

Turner, J.R. and Müller, R., 2003, On the nature of the project as a temporary organization. *International Journal of Project Management,* 21(1), 1–8.

Turner, J.R. and Müller, R., 2004, Communication and cooperation on projects between the project owner as principal and the project manager as agent. *The European Management Journal,* 22, 327–336.

Williamson, O.E., 1996, *The Mechanisms of Governance.* New York: Oxford University Press.

Winch, G.M., 2014, Three domains of project organizing. *International Journal of Project Management,* 32(5), 721–731.

Chapter 5

Corporate Governance of the Project-Oriented Company
Contributing to Its Sustainable Development

Roland Gareis and Laurence Lecoeuvre

Introduction

Different corporate governance structures are appropriate for different company types. Given the specifics of the project-oriented company, which manages unique business processes of medium to large scope by projects and by programs, specific governing structures are required. The elements governing the project-oriented company are:

- its specific objectives, strategies, and values;
- its specific processes, namely project initiation, project management, program management, and project portfolio coordination;
- its temporary organizations, namely projects and programs, and its specific permanent organizations, namely the Project Management Office (PMO) and the Project Portfolio Group; and
- its descriptions of the specific roles, namely project/program sponsors, project/program managers, and project/program teams.

By complying with guidelines and rules, companies can mitigate risk, can increase the quality of their processes, and can add value to their stakeholders. By appropriate governing structures the project-oriented company relates to these principles of sustainable development.

Model of the Project-Oriented Company

Companies perform business processes. A business process is a sequence of tasks with defined objectives and a defined start and end event. It is cross-organizational, i.e. it is fulfilled by different roles of one or more organizations. For the performance of different process types different organizations are appropriate. Repetitive routine processes with low strategic importance and of small scope are performed by the base organization of a company. A project is a temporary organization for the performance of a relatively unique business process of medium to large scope and short or medium duration. A program is a temporary organization for the performance of a relatively unique business process of large scope and medium duration.

Figure 5.1 shows the example of the process map for an Austrian Consulting Company as an example of the relationships between business processes and the organizations that perform them. This company with some 20 employees along with

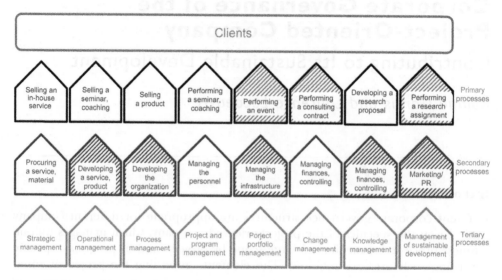

Figure 5.1 Process Map of an Austrian Consulting Company

a number of networking partners provides consulting and training services in Austria and in Eastern European countries. It also organizes international events and performs research activities. The shaded processes might require a project or a program for their performance. Therefore these project/program types are to be considered in the project portfolio of the company.

Projects/programs need to be initiated and managed. The objectives of the project initiation process are to decide the appropriate organization (base organization, working group, project, network of projects, or program) to implement an investment; to analyze the relationships of the new project to the projects of the existing project portfolio; to select a project sponsor; and to assign the project to the project manager and the project team.

The main objective of the project management process is to manage a project professionally by performing the sub-processes (project starting, project controlling, project coordinating, and project closing as well as possibly project transforming/new-positioning) efficiently. Further objectives are to manage the project complexity, the

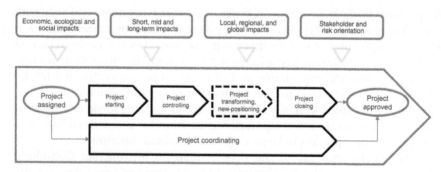

Figure 5.2 Project Management Process

project dynamics, and the relationships to project contexts efficiently, to optimize the economic, ecological, and social consequences of the investment implemented by the project, and to consider the local, regional, and global ecological as well as social consequences of the project. The process should also assure appropriate stakeholder participation in the project. A project management process organized with consideration of the principles of sustainable development is illustrated in Figure 5.2.

A project-oriented company can be defined as a company, which:

- applies "Management by Projects" as an organization strategy, i.e. it uses projects and programs for the performance of relatively unique processes of medium to large scope;
- considers projects and programs, the project portfolio, and networks of projects in addition to profit and cost centers as management objects;
- has a PMO, expert pools (e.g. of project managers), and a Project Portfolio Group as permanent, integrative organizations;
- has employees with competences in project and program, and project portfolio management;
- considers empowerment, team work, and sustainable development as important values; and
- provides governing structures for project, program, and project portfolio management.

The conceptional organization chart of the project-oriented company is illustrated in Figure 5.3 and shows projects and programs as temporary organizations as well as the specific permanent organizations PMO, expert pools, and Project Portfolio Group.

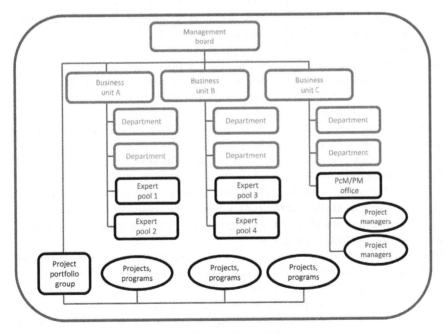

Figure 5.3 Organization Chart of the Project-Oriented Company

Companies have differing levels of projectization; that is, the extent to which their business is based on projects and the degree the project way of working pervades practice within the corporation. A framework is needed to enable corporations to choose their own appropriate governance structure for project management, according to their own level of projectization.

(Müller, 2009, p.29)

The project-oriented company requires specific governance structures.

Corporate Governance Concepts

Although corporate governance has only recently come to prominence in the business world, theories underlying its development and its elements can be found in a variety of disciplines including finance, economics, accounting, law, management, and organizational behavior (Mallin, 2010).

A generally accepted definition of corporate governance is provided by the OECD:

Corporate governance involves a set of relationships between a company's management, its board, its shareholders and other stakeholders. Corporate governance also provides the structure through which the objectives of the company are set, and the means of attaining those objectives and monitoring performance are determined.

(OECD, 2004, p.11)

In simple terms, "corporate governance is the system by which companies are directed and controlled" (Cadbury Committee, 1992, p.14). "New Corporate Governance" is defined as a system "by which companies are strategically directed, integratively managed and holistically controlled in an entrepreneurial and ethical way and in a manner appropriate to each particular context" (Hilb, 2012, p.7).

Elements of corporate governance are the organizational structure, size and ownership of a company, the authorities, roles and responsibilities as well as its strategic goals, objectives and key performance indicators. The organizational structure provides a "framework for planning, executing, controlling and monitoring activities for achieving overall objectives" (Moeller, 2007, p.12). Different individual and group roles and responsibilities are described in governance documents. "The assignment of authority is essentially the way responsibilities are defined in terms of job descriptions and structured in terms of organization charts" (Moeller, 2007, p.13). Different types of authority bodies are boards of directors, auditors, and various independent committees. According to Müller (2009, p.3), governance regulates the methods and processes of defining the objectives of an organization, providing means to achieve those objectives and controlling progress.

It is the objective of corporate governance to achieve transparent and repeatable company structures and processes. This is achieved by defining the objectives of the organization, the means of obtaining those objectives, the means of monitoring the performance and the relationships with and between stakeholders.

Corporate governance results are high level guidelines and rules, which are relating to all identity dimensions of a company, such as its strategies, objectives, and

Table 5.1 Examples for Corporate Governance Documents

- Corporate Governance documents relating to company strategies, objectives, values:

  - guidelines and rules about how objectives, strategies, and values are to be planned, communicated and controlled;
  - definition of overall objectives, strategies, and values.

- Corporate Governance documents relating to services, products:

  - rules regarding services to be provided for different markets;
  - guidelines and rules about the delivery of the services and products to different markets.

- Corporate Governance documents relating to the organization:

  - guidelines and rules about how role descriptions, organization charts are to be developed;
  - important role descriptions and organization charts;
  - rules about how processes are to be documented;
  - descriptions of important business processes.

values, its services and products, its technologies, its organization, its personnel, its infrastructure, its financials, and its stakeholder-relations. So the focus is not just on its financials. A list of possible corporate governance documents is shown in Table 5.1. As the examples show, governing is not managing but providing guidelines and rules for the daily management and operations.

Existence of corporate governance is insufficient if it is not communicated to and understood by the stakeholders. Communication of governing structures can be done through formal and informal channels, e.g. documents, staff meetings, announcements, intranet and internet, etc. This communication should be differentiated adequately for internal and external stakeholders (Cromme and Classen, 2009).

Even if corporate governance structures exist and are communicated appropriately, they have to be occasionally checked and adherence to them has to be controlled. Therefore, auditing and controlling should be regularly performed to track compliance with the governance structures.

Sustainable Development and Corporate Governance

Sustainable development can be perceived as a new management paradigm to cope with the complexity and dynamics of organizations. It is of relevance for permanent as well as for temporary organizations, i.e. for projects and programs.

The concept of sustainable development has acquired wide attention following the publication of the so-called Brundtland Report by the World Commission on Environment and Development (WCED) in 1987. The report defines sustainable development as a "development that meets the needs of the present without compromising the ability of future generations to meet their own needs" (WCED, 1987, p.41). Sustainable development is a normative concept and thus is representing values and ethical considerations. The basic values of sustainable development are inter- and intra-generational equity, transparency, fairness, trust, and innovation (Global Reporting Initiative, 2011). These values are defined at a societal level. They cannot be transferred to companies directly, interpretation is required.

"Sustainable development when incorporated by the company is called corporate sustainability and it contains all three pillars: economic, ecological and social" (Baumgartner and Ebner, 2010, p.77). Although many different definitions of sustainable development for companies can be found in the literature, some basic guiding principles can be identified. A generic, process-related definition of sustainable development considers the following principles: economic, ecologic, and social oriented, short-term, mid-term, and long-term oriented, local, regional, and global oriented as well as values-based (Gareis et al., 2013).

During the last years, companies committed themselves to implementing the concept of sustainable development as an active corporate engagement that goes beyond legal compliance. Critiques, such as Porter and Kramer (2011) argue that corporate sustainability initiatives performed by many companies can be understood as paying a lip service only. Often philanthropic activities are provided in order to do "good" for the society. Serious sustainable development means to integrate sustainable development principles into services, products, and processes of a company, means to "re-think the business."

Corporate governance is relating to the values of sustainable development, e.g. to transparency, accountability, responsibility, and fairness. Also the corporate governance objectives of stakeholder-orientation and risk-orientation are important values of sustainable development.

Case Studies: Examples of Corporate Governance

As examples, the corporate governance structures of Apple Inc. and of the Technical University Graz are described. Both organizations offer a hierarchy of governing documents. The consistency of the guidelines and rules is a success factor of corporate governance.

Apple Inc. is an American multinational corporation that designs, develops, and sells consumer electronics, computer software, and personal computers and is headquartered in Cupertino, California (http://en.wikipedia.org/wiki/Apple_Inc.—cite_note-Waymarkmark-2). Apple's web site dedicates the following paragraph to the corporate governance issues (Apple, 2012):

> Apple's Board of Directors oversees the Chief Executive Officer and other senior management in the competent and ethical operation of Apple on a day-to-day basis and assures that the long-term interests of shareholders are being served. To satisfy the Board's duties, directors are expected to take a proactive, focused approach to their positions, and set standards to ensure that Apple is committed to business success through the maintenance of high standards of responsibility and ethics.

Apple's Corporate Governance Guidelines (Apple, 2012, p.1) describe its governance to be "a working structure for principled actions, effective decision-making and appropriate monitoring of both compliance and performance." The guidelines list the following to be forming Apple's framework for governance: Corporate Governance Guidelines, corporation's articles of incorporation, bylaws, and the charters of the committees of the board. Apple's Corporate Governance Guidelines primarily focus on the duties, rights, competencies, and power of the board and its directors, emphasizing their independence and diversity in terms of experience and expertise and efficient performance of the oversight functions and specifying the level of director compensation, their competences and qualifications, as well as the term in the office. In addition to the board, various committees are formed to aid the governance process (e.g. Nominating and Corporate Governance Committee, an Audit and Finance Committee, and a Compensation Committee).

The Technical University Graz with over 12,000 students offers bachelor programs and research-oriented master and PhD programs. Corporate governance of the Technical University Graz is aligned to the Austrian Corporate Governance Codex. The corporate governance system consists of the following internal and external control mechanisms: Guidelines for auditors, board and senior management, regulations handbook, quality management handbook, regulations and principles of financial management, and general guidelines of governing bodies. An authority and guideline handbook of the Technical University Graz (TU Graz, 2007) includes the following: Authority and guideline for the dean, general guidelines for the heads of institutes, and guidelines for research projects.

The external control of the Technical University Graz is exercised through examinations by external auditors, the Austrian court of audit, the legal supervision of the government and audits of EU projects.

Corporate Governance of the Project-Oriented Company: Hypotheses, Models and Examples

The situational corporate governance model is based on the assumption that the optimal corporate governance depends on the situation of a company (Nötzli Breinlinger, 2006). Specific corporate governance is to be applied according to the structures and the business environment of a company. Therefore, guidelines and rules meeting the specific requirements of the project-oriented company are to be developed and implemented. In order to describe the specific governing requirements of the project-oriented company, hypotheses are formulated, models are presented, and examples are given from an Austrian consulting company.

The following hypotheses regarding the corporate governance of the project-oriented company can be formulated:

- The specific objectives of the corporate governance of the project-oriented company are to improve the management quality of its projects, programs, and project portfolios and to assure the consideration of the principles of sustainable development.
- Specific elements governing the project-oriented company are:
  - its specific objectives, strategies, and values;
  - its specific processes, namely project initiation, project management, program management, and project portfolio coordination;
  - its projects, programs, and project portfolios;
  - its specific permanent organizations, namely the PMO, expert pools, and the Project Portfolio Group; and
  - its descriptions of the specific roles, namely project/program sponsors, project/program managers, and project/program teams.

In a project-oriented company the management of projects, programs, and project portfolios is to be governed. Corporate governance structures of the project-oriented company include guidelines for project and program management, in order to standardize these processes and to assure quality (Gareis, 2005). In addition, guidelines for project portfolio management and project auditing can be provided. The guidelines for project and program management define what constitutes a project/program, which process steps to perform, which methods to apply, and which roles to perform in the project and program management process. The guidelines for project portfolio management define what constitutes the project portfolio, which project portfolio management processes to differentiate, which process steps to perform in each process, which methods to apply, and which roles to perform in the project portfolio management processes.

Examples of the lists of contents of a "Guideline for Project and Program Management" and a "Guideline for Project Portfolio Management" are shown in Tables 5.2 and 5.3. An extract of the list of project management methods to be applied and an extract of a role description of the project sponsor are shown as examples of the contents of the "Guideline for Project and Program Management" (see Tables 5.4 and 5.5). All these examples are taken from the Austrian consulting company mentioned above.

Table 5.2 Guideline for Project and Program Management: List of Contents (Extract from a Document from an Austrian Consulting Company)

1   Introduction
2   Definitions

    2.1   Definition: Small project, project, program
    2.2   Definition: Project discontinuities
    2.3   Definition: Project and program management
    2.4   Project and program types

3   Project management process

    3.1   Project management: Objectives, structure
    3.2   Project starting: Objectives, structure
    3.3   Project coordinating: Objectives, structure
    3.4   Project controlling: Objectives, structure
    3.5   Project transforming/new-positioning: Objectives, structure
    3.6   Project closing: Objectives, structure

4   Project organization

    4.1   Project organization chart
    4.2   Project roles and project communication structures
    4.3   Project values
    4.4   Project management methods and templates

5   Program management process

    5.1   Program management: Objectives, structure
    5.2   Program starting: Objectives, structure
    5.3   . . . .

Table 5.3 Guideline for Project Portfolio Management: List of Contents (Extract from a Document from an Austrian Consulting Company)

1	Introduction
2	Definitions

    2.1   Definition: Project portfolio, network of projects
    2.2   Definition: Investment/business case
    2.3   Definition: Project portfolio management

3 Project initiation process

    3.1   Objectives, structure of the process
    3.2   Project initiation roles
    3.3   Project initiation methods and templates

4 Project portfolio coordination process

    4.1   Objectives, structure of the process
    4.2   Project initiation roles
    4.3   Project initiation methods and templates

5 Networking of projects process

    5.1   Objectives, structure of the process
    5.2   Networking roles
    5.3   Networking methods and templates

6 Roles for project portfolio management

    6.1   Project Portfolio Group
    6.2   Project Management Office (PMO)

Table 5.4 List of Project Management Methods (Extract from a Document from an Austrian Consulting Company)

Methods for Project Starting	
Project scope planning	
Project objectives plan	Must
Project objects of consideration plan	Must
Work breakdown structure	Must
Work package specifications	Can
Project scheduling	
Project milestone plan	Must
Project bar chart	Must
Project critical path method (CPM) schedule	Can
Project resource planning and project budgeting	
Project resource plan	Can
Project budget	Must
Project finance plan	Can

(continued)

Table 5.4 (continued)

Methods for Project Starting	
Project context relationships	
Project stakeholder analysis	Must
Investment cost-benefit analysis	Must
Analysis: Relationships of the project to other programs and projects	Can
Analysis: Pre- and post-project phase	Must
Designing the project organization	
Project assignment	Must
Project organization chart	Must
Project role descriptions	Must
Project communication structures	Must
Methods for project controlling	

Table 5.5 Role Description: Project Sponsor (Extract from a Document from an Austrian Consulting Company)

Objectives of the Project Sponsor
Representing the interests of the company in a project
Coordinating the project interests and company interests
Assigning the project manager/the project team with the project
Leading the project manager
Supporting the project team
Organizational position of the project sponsor
Reporting to the project portfolio group
Being a member of the project organization
Receiving reports from he project manager
Tasks of the project sponsor
Tasks of the project sponsor in project starting
Selecting the project manager (and some project team members)
Agreeing about the project objectives with the project team
Contributing to the construction of the project contexts
Assuring the provision of the required resources
Initial project marketing
Performing a project sponsor meeting
Tasks of the project sponsor in project controlling
Performing project sponsor meetings
Making strategic project decisions
Continuous project marketing

Tasks of the project sponsor in project transforming and project radical new-positioning

Defining the project change
Contributing to the development of ad-hoc measures
Contributing to the development of a sense of urgency for the project change
Deciding about change strategies
Contributing to change measures and change controlling
Defining the end of the project change

Tasks of the project sponsor in project closing

Participating in the project closing workshop
Contributing to the project evaluation
Formal project approval

The following hypotheses regarding the implementation of corporate governance of the project-oriented company and the controlling of the compliance can be formulated:

- The board of directors decides about the specific corporate governance of the project-oriented company.
- The PMO contributes to implementing the specific corporate governance of the project-oriented company and to the controlling of its compliance.
- Stakeholders are involved in implementing and controlling the compliance with the corporate governance of the project-oriented company.
- Project and program audits/health checks performed by project/program external auditors ensure the compliance with the corporate governance of the project-oriented company.
- Project/program sponsors have content-related interests in projects/programs and therefore perform managerial roles in projects/programs. They don't have corporate governance related functions.

The functions of the PMO regarding the implementation of corporate governance of the project-oriented company and the controlling of its compliance can be described as follows:

- providing guidelines (including templates) for project and program management, for project and program consulting and auditing/health checking, and for project portfolio management;
- providing standard project plans, such as standard work breakdown structures for different project types;
- providing software for project and program management, for project portfolio management;
- communicating the specific corporate governance structures by brochures, newsletters, maintaining a PMO homepage, organizing events (e.g. project vernissages);
- controlling the compliance with the specific corporate governance by regular project/program audits and health checks.

Conclusion

Corporate governance provides mid-term to long-term-oriented structures for the overall company, including its permanent and temporary organizations. Corporate governance is to be differentiated from management; the corporate governance responsibility is different from the management responsibility. The project organization is responsible for managing a single project whereas the board of directors of a project-oriented company and the PMO are responsible for governing the management of projects generally. Specific corporate governance objectives of the project-oriented company are to define how projects, programs, and the project portfolio are to be managed. Within the governing framework the day-to-day management of projects, programs, and project portfolios is to be performed.

References

Apple (2012): Corporate Governance Guidelines. Retrieved January 23, 2013, from Apple: http://files.shareholder.com/downloads/AAPL/2336641731x0x443011/6a7d49f1-a3af-4e69-b279-021b81a93cdf/governance_guidelines.pdf.

Baumgartner, R. J., and Ebner, D. (2010): Corporate sustainability strategies: Sustainability profiles and maturity levels, *Sustainable Development*, 18(2), 76–89.

Cadbury Committee (1992): The Financial Aspects of Corporate Governance. Retrieved April 20, 2012, from http://www.ecgi.org/codes/documents/cadbury.pdf.

Cromme, G., and Claassen, J. (2009): Unternehmenskommunikation als Element der Corporate Governance. In: Hommelhoff, K.J. Hopt and A. von Werder (eds) Handbuch Corporate Governance, 2nd edition. Stuttgart: Schäffer-Poeschel.

Gareis, R. (2005): *Happy Projects!* Vienna: MA.

Gareis, R., Huemann, M., Martinuzzi, A., Weninger, C., and Sedlacko, M. (2013): *Project Management and Sustainable Development Principles*. Newtown Square, PA: Project Management Institute.

Global Reporting Initiative (2011): *Sustainability Reporting Guidelines Version 3.1*, Amsterdam, The Netherlands: Global Reporting Initiative.

Hilb, M. (2012): *New Corporate Governance. Successful Board Management Tools*, Fourth Edition, Berlin, Heidelberg: Springer-Verlag.

Mallin, C. (2010): *Corporate Governance*, Third Edition, Oxford: Oxford University Press.

Moeller, R. R. (2007): *COSO Enterprise Risk Management*, Hoboken, NJ: John Wiley & Sons, Inc.

Müller, R. (2009): *Project Governance*, Farnham: Gower Publishing Limited.

Nötzli Breinlinger, U. G. (2006): Situative Corporate Governance: Ein Modell für kleine und mittelgrosse Familienunternehmen in der Schweiz (Dissertation), St. Gallen: Universität St. Gallen.

Organisation for Economic and Co-operation and Development (OECD) (2004): OECD Principles of Corporate Governance. Retrieved March 02, 2012, from http://www.oecd.org/dataoecd/32/18/31557724.pdf.

Porter, M. E., and Kramer, M. R. (2011): The big idea: Creating shared value, *Harvard Business Review*, 89(1–2).

TU Graz (2007): Vollmachten und Richtlinien Handbuch der Technische Universität Graz. Retrieved February 20, 2013, from Graz University of Technology: http://portal.tugraz.at/portal/page/portal/Files/o97020/Richtlinien/Vollmachten_Richtlinien_Handbuch_Vers13_08102007_1.pdf.

World Commission on Environment and Development (1987): *Our Common Future*, Oxford: Oxford University Press.

Chapter 6

The Project Environment
The Key to Sustainable Project Performance in Project Intensive Organizations

Otto Husby and Halvard Kilde

Introduction

Project management involves planning, monitoring and controlling all aspects of a project and the motivation of all those involved, in order to achieve objectives on time and within cost, quality and performance parameters.

While the definition of project management is simple and sound, in practice, things become complex within the constraints of a project intensive matrix organization. The performance of projects and project management and the probability for project success will then very much depend on the organizational project management maturity and on how well the organization is designed and staffed for planning and execution of projects.

The main project-oriented company challenge is to create an *environment* in which there exists a continuous stream of successfully managed projects, where success is measured by having achieved a level of performance that is in the best interest of the whole company, as well as having completed a specific project (Kerzner, 2004).

A building or a system is designed to serve a purpose. Likewise, an organization must be designed for a purpose. Project intensive companies must be designed and built for the efficient and successful delivery of projects and project portfolios.

Project management used to be called the "accidental profession." People were assigned roles in project management teams without any project management experience or training. Project management was not viewed as a profession, but something that anyone with a little common sense could do. This of course led to accidents. Some projects succeeded and some failed. Projects succeeded because they had project management experience, a lot of common sense, hard work and a competent staff. Project failure was often a result of poor project management and lack of project governance. No time to plan and little risk management was a recipe for failure and it still is.

A Learning Organization–Maturity and Project Excellence

The situation is now changing. Competition, increased complexity and time and cost pressures have increased the need for and the impact of projects and mean that projects and project management are on the strategic agenda in most companies today. Thus, project management improvement initiatives are ongoing in over 70 percent of companies where projects are important (PwC, 2012). The main emphasis of such

Figure 6.1 Project Management Maturity Development

improvement initiatives is towards increased probability of success for all projects in the portfolio through increased project management maturity. This is illustrated in Figure 6.1.

The Y-axis reflects the number of projects in the organization that are either challenged (delays, cost overruns etc.) or successful. The X-axis reflects the time it takes to increase organizational maturity. As the project management improvement initiatives are implemented, the organization "matures" (it is not something that happens overnight). The number of successful projects increases as the organization improves their project management practices and streamlines their organization to fit both project and operational challenges. With persistence and focus, after a few years, a majority of projects in the organization will reach their objectives. The organization's ultimate objective is to reach the "project excellence" phase—where project success is repeatable—and stay there.

The Project Environment

A new expression has emerged to describe companies that rely on the success of their projects—the project intense company. These companies organize their people and disciplines according to several apparently conflicting needs, in terms of projects and operations/services. Resources and management are allocated to projects from a shared "resource pool" (functional organization), and top management have a number of agendas and strategies for both project performance and operational performance.

Managing projects in such an environment adds a level of complexity to project management in addition to that of scope or technology, namely organizational complexity. Many of these organizations are designed in a way that is neither optimal for running projects nor for operations—they are designed to serve both needs. The

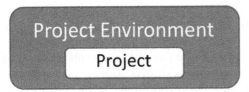

Figure 6.2 The Project Success Relies on the Project Environment

organizations must balance their focus between the two types of work, make choices and compromise.

"The NUMBER ONE reason for project failure is POOR EXECUTIVE ENGAGEMENT and an unhealthy project environment which is the responsibility of the EXECUTIVE TEAM" (Standish Group, 2012).

Thus, it is no longer enough to be an excellent project manager leading a highly competent team to succeed. A healthy project environment will promote project success, while an unhealthy project environment can cause the project to fail (see Figure 6.2).

Requirements for a Healthy Project Environment

The requirements for a healthy project environment creating a continuous stream of successful projects include, but are not limited to:

1   executive sponsorship;
2   an organizational structure designed for efficient project management;
3   common project model tailored to the needs of the organization;
4   application of "best practice" project management—knowledge and skills.

Executive sponsorship and support is essential for all kinds of changes and improvements in an organization. For any changes in an organization the initiatives must come top down with continuous support and backing. An organizational structure enabling efficient decision making through delegated authority and defined roles and responsibilities—from corporate management down to the project team—is another healthy project environment factor. The common project model includes the processes, guidelines and templates for efficient project governance and project management and a success criterion for a project-oriented company is an implemented project model. In addition, all organizations of course need skilled people to manage and perform the work, and the sign of a healthy project environment is that projects are managed according to the defined "best practice" in the organization and not according to what each individual project manager believes is the right approach.

Executive Sponsorship

Executive sponsorship is one of the key success factors for project success in project-oriented companies. Recent surveys by some renowned organizations show the following results:

1   Executive sponsorship. Ensuring top-level management support for the project (one of five project success factors in PMI's Pulse of the Profession, 2012).
2   Lack of executive sponsorship. The second most important factor (after poor estimates) contributing to poor project performance when implementing an organization's approach to project management (insight and trends by PwC, 2012).
3   The number one reason for project failure is poor executive engagement and an unhealthy project environment, which is the responsibility of the executive team (CHAOS report by the Standish Group, 2012).

Project management knowledge, insight and skills are just as important for executives in project-oriented organizations as they are for project managers. And processes combined with clear roles and responsibilities are of equal importance for the executives as they are for the project management team.

Project Governance Principles

Project governance is the project management shorthand for executive sponsorship and organizational design. Each organization should define a set of project governance principles as a framework for executive support in projects. Once key stakeholders agree on the principles it will be easier to define and implement a project governance process that works in practice. The following principles are examples:

- the project portfolio and the project's business and project objectives are aligned with the strategic objectives;
- the accountability for the success of each project is clearly defined;
- the roles and responsibilities for project governance and project management are clearly defined;
- project owners, project board members and other members of delegated authorization bodies have sufficient representation, competence, authority and resources to enable them to make appropriate decisions and to support the projects;
- disciplined governance arrangements, supported by appropriate methods and controls, are applied throughout the project life cycle;
- all projects follow the project model containing decision points at which the project performance is reviewed and approved;
- transparency and traceability in the planning and execution of all projects—including documentation, decisions and communication;
- all project stakeholders—from corporate management down to the project team members—operate within the project governance framework;
- all project managers have a mandate describing their responsibility and authority;
- there are clearly defined criteria for reporting project status and for the escalation of risks, deviations and changes to the level required by the organization.

The principles should be tailored to the organization and to the needs defined by the organization. Project governance is about doing the right projects the right way. This is the responsibility of the executive team.

Preconditions for Executive Sponsorship

Corporate management (the organization's leadership team: CEO, Director of Projects, Department Managers etc.) is responsible for project management maturity within the organization and for the project success rate. The most important issue is to make sure that projects are performed in a uniform way and according to best practice. The following are prerequisites for repeatable project success and executive sponsorship (project governance):

- corporate management message—project success is important and expected;
- corporate management support, involvement and backing;
- the project-oriented company—an organizational structure enabling executive sponsorship;
- project governance process—requirements, activities, defined roles, responsibilities and charters;
- project model and project management processes—phases, decision points and compulsory management products, to be tailored to the specific project;
- decision gate/stage gate reviews for support and control of progress (part of the project governance process);
- trained project management teams—corporate management, project owners, project board members, project managers and project team members;
- an organization with the ability and will to succeed—"we are all responsible for project success";
- open and honest communication within the organizational structure;
- benefit realization assessment should be performed to verify the success of completed projects and to optimize benefit realization;
- lessons learned and experience transfer—learn from past projects.

If the prerequisites are in place, make sure they are implemented and truly support the projects in an efficient way. The company will never achieve project excellence and long-term improvements without best practice project governance and project management implemented.

To check the status of project governance and project management in your organization, you can run a "Project Improvement Workshop" including key employees. The objective is to openly discuss improvement potential for projects and project management. This is a good starting point for an internal project management improvement initiative.

Organizing for Projects: The Project Intensive Company

Modern project management is very much about designing an organization suitable for both projects and operational activities. Most project-oriented companies choose to adopt a matrix organizational structure. The functional organization is designed and developed to meet the needs of projects and operational activities. The functional departments specialize in various disciplines and are staffed by engineers and technicians who work on developing products, supporting projects and supporting operations/services after project completion.

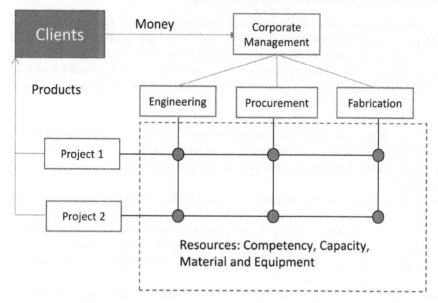

Figure 6.3 The Matrix Organization in a Project Intensive Company

Figure 6.3 illustrates how projects interface with the functional organization in a matrix pattern. The projects "borrow" resources from the functional organization to plan and execute projects. The main objective of the matrix organization is to ensure that limited resources are used in an optimal and cost-effective way in meeting operational and strategic objectives. Advantages of the matrix organization include:

- resource flexibility—resources can be shared among several projects and operational activities;
- resources can be moved around based on needs and priorities;
- key resources can share their important competencies with many projects;
- strong functional departments are developed to serve the projects and operational activities;
- lessons learned can be used on subsequent projects;
- lines of reporting and communication are clearly defined.

The matrix system is a complex organization with many communication interfaces and stakeholders balancing the needs of the temporary projects with the long-term development of the functional organization. Important challenges affecting most matrix organizations in project-oriented companies include:

1   Lack of management attention to project planning and execution. Focus is on operational activities. Management must support and control the projects (project governance).
2   Unclear roles and responsibilities. The responsibilities and authority of the project manager, project owner and project board must be clearly defined.

3   Inadequate resource planning, availability and capacity. Projects need resources to fuel them. Far too often, projects suffer from a lack of capacity and/or competencies. This is a corporate management responsibility.
4   Improperly implemented project management. Practices vary from project to project and success is achieved through both good management and good luck.
5   Executive management does not understand project management. They want the project to start without a proper project plan and/or risk assessment.
6   Ineffective communication. Updates on project progress, risks and challenges must reach decision-makers in time to minimize any negative consequences and optimize the positive consequences of risks, deviations and changes.
7   Lack of prioritization by corporate management. Too many projects can lead to low productivity and delays on all of them.

In a dynamic project-oriented company there is a need for processes, guidelines and rules to streamline cooperation between the functional organization and the project teams, as well as to avoid the potential pitfalls listed above. An implemented project model, including the project governance process, a suitable organizational structure, defined roles and responsibilities and a skilled workforce is the best guarantee for successful projects within a matrix organization.

Roles, Responsibility and Accountability

The corporate management level in a project-oriented company includes a dedicated project responsibility role, such as director of projects or CPO (chief project officer). This role reports to the CEO or other C-level manager. The director of projects is responsible for implementing the project model, ensuring that "best practice" project management is applied on all projects and making sure that the organization has the necessary knowledge and skills. In this way, the director of projects is *ultimately accountable* for the continuous stream of successful projects.

The roles shown in Figure 6.4 are involved in most projects.

The portfolio manager or the project owner may be a departmental manager, for example, assigned from the functional organization on a temporary basis. Alternatively, this post could be a fixed role in the functional organization. The director of projects delegates responsibility for project/portfolio success to the portfolio manager/project owner. He/she is responsible for assigning the project manager through a project charter and for the project business case, benefits realization (up to hand-over to the client/functional organization), and supporting and monitoring the project during the project phases. The project manager's responsibility, for which he/she is held accountable, is defined in the project charter. For a project manager in a supplier project, the responsibilities will include the following objectives: profit margin, scope/quality, time and cost (budget).

Most project-oriented companies also have a project management office (PMO) or a similar unit responsible for maintaining, communicating and supporting the project model, including project processes, tools and templates. A PMO with the necessary level of respect and authority can be a valuable tool for implementing and improving project management practices across the organization. On the other hand, a PMO with little authority to influence project practices is often ignored and serves little value.

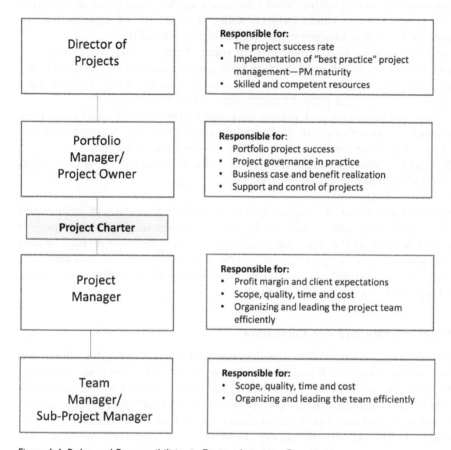

Figure 6.4 Roles and Responsibilities in Project Intensive Organizations

Responsibility and Authority

Projects are temporary organizations and each is unique, with their own distinct challenges and needs. This is why it is important to clearly define project roles for each specific project to ensure that all key team members understand their responsibilities and that authority is aligned to responsibility. Corporate management empowers the project owner who, in turn, is responsible for delegating responsibility and authority to the project manager (see Figure 6.5).

In this way, authority can be delegated from top management down to the level where decisions should be made. If a decision is needed outside a given level of authority, this decision is then referred to the right management level with the necessary authority.

The project manager is responsible for achieving the project objectives: scope, time and cost, and sometimes also benefits (profit margin). The project manager thus needs the necessary authority (control over resources—personnel, equipment, money) to realistically achieve the objectives and get the job done.

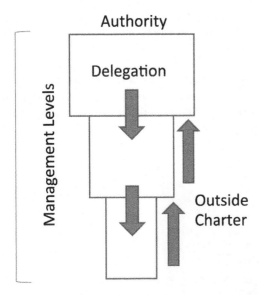

Figure 6.5 Delegation of Authority

Authority must be aligned with responsibility. A major challenge in project management is the *authority gap*—meaning that the project manager has a lot of responsibility for achieving ambitious objectives but lacks the necessary authority to get the job done.

For example, the project manager is responsible for meeting the scheduled completion date. However, if the project manager does not have access to the required resources, completion may be delayed. The project manager should refer the problem to the project owner. If the project owner has the necessary authority, the situation can be solved. If not, the problem bounces back to the project manager and delays will occur. However, it is still the project manager's responsibility to meet the completion date and avoid delay. So the entire difference between meeting and missing the planned completion date can come down to the power and influence of the project manager and the project owner. And if roles are unclear, it is usually the project manager who gets the blame. Authority must match responsibility. If not, you cannot be held accountable.

The Project Manager and Project Type

Selecting the right project manager is a very important decision for every project. Experience shows that the project manager is crucial for the project results. The wrong project manager can be disastrous for the project and most organizations have already experienced this.

In general, the ideal project manager should have skills and expertise within the following areas:

- Leadership—leading the project team.
- Meeting stakeholder expectations—business focused.
- The deliverables and their components—the products or output from the project.
- Project management—"best practices."

Projects vary in scale from small to large and can involve anything from a few individuals to many thousands of people. For this reason, the project manager's skills and capabilities will differ from project to project. Figure 6.6 below reflects the type of project manager needed in different project types:

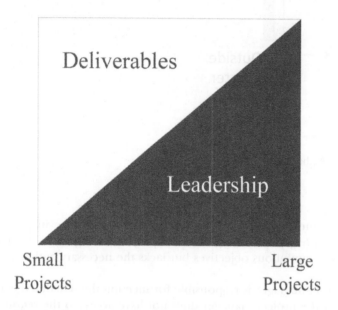

Figure 6.6 Project Size and Project Management Main Skills

In small projects, the project manager will be personally involved in producing the deliverables and his or her main role will be providing product or technical skills. Smaller projects are a lot more predictable than larger projects with less focus on leadership, project management and reporting.

In larger projects, the project teams and their members are responsible for performing the "job" while the project manager is busy leading the teams, optimizing benefits and managing stakeholder expectations. In this case, the project manager focuses mainly on leadership and project management. The required skill sets for project managers consequently vary from project to project.

The Project Model

A foundation for a healthy project environment is a high quality project model. The project model is the project's roadmap from A–Z. It guides projects through project phases, decision points (for management decisions) and mandatory requirements. It includes processes that describe how to plan, manage risk, monitor and control progress, manage business objectives and manage changes according to "best practice"

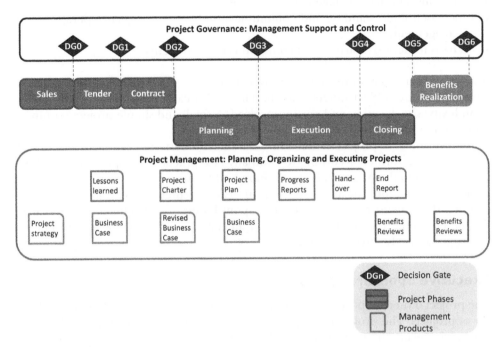

Figure 6.7 A Typical Project Model in a Project Intensive Organization

project management. It also includes tools such as document templates and checklists. The project model is the framework for a successful project and for a uniform way of planning and executing projects in an organization.

All project-oriented companies have a project model. The overall project model can look like Figure 6.7.

The project model, also called project method, project life cycle, project execution model, stage gate model or project methodology, includes the following elements:

- phases and decision points (also called stages and stage gates);
- project management processes planning, monitoring and controlling scope, quality, time, cost, risk and benefits;
- the project management requirements for each phase (defined in the processes);
- the decision process in each decision point/stage gate;
- checklists;
- templates and product examples; e.g. the project mandate or progress reports.

The project model should be used by all projects in the company. It is an important part of developing project management maturity and a healthy project environment within the company and it contributes to:

- a uniform way of managing projects—repeatable success;
- management buy-in, support and control—if the business justification no longer proves to be valid, the projects can be changed or stopped;

- a common project management terminology;
- increased understanding and communication between projects, operations and management;
- a basis for lessons learned and continuous improvements.

A company can have more than one project model as projects can differ greatly in nature. And the project model must be tailored to each project according to risk, complexity, size, location and parties involved. A small and simple project requires a more simple approach than complex and large projects.

An implemented project model is an assurance for corporate management that all projects are performed according to company best practice. The project model also links projects to the functional organization and to corporate management through decision points, reporting and communication arrangements and project owner/project board roles and responsibilities. If responsibilities for benefits, benefits realization and resource availability lie with corporate management, there will be real buy-in and support for the project manager.

Executive Sponsorship in Practice

The project owner supports, monitors and controls the project on behalf of the director of projects. The project manager is responsible within his/her project charter to plan and execute the project. The project owner's main responsibilities in a project are to establish the first business case, to assign the project manager, issue a project charter to the project manager, support the project manager during the project phases, update the business case and establish the benefit realization plan together with the project manager, make decisions if outside project manager's charter, review the project progress, make decisions in the defined decision points/stage gates and make sure the completed products are handed over to the client/operations for benefit realization.

The main executive sponsorship activities (the responsibilities of the project owner/portfolio manager/director of projects) are defined in the project governance process as illustrated in the project model figure above, and include the following:

- the project model is tailored to the project challenges;
- the project follows the project model;
- the business case is valid and updated—clear business objectives (i.e., the why);
- assigning the best project manager;
- a project charter is in place defining objectives, authority and roles/responsibilities;
- there is time and resources available to make a good plan;
- the project plan is based on clear and realistic assumptions; scope, quality, time, cost and risk;
- scope expectation gap is under control;
- risks are managed;
- the project manager and the project team have the required experience and competence;
- the project manager is focusing on managing and meeting client expectations;

- project progress is within tolerances;
- deviations and changes are managed according to procedures and the contracts in place;
- deviations and changes outside the mandate are escalated to the project owner.

In some organizations with professional project managers and an implemented project model and project governance process, the above items are not a challenge, while in other organizations with less experienced project managers and no implemented project model the project owner must follow up that the project manager is in control.

Application of "Best Practice" Project Management

People assigned to a project management role must perform their job according to the company's defined best practice in project management and other company processes such as the quality management system (QMS). This means that the company's project model should be tailored to project size and complexity, experiences from other projects should be used to reduce risk and exploit opportunity, and recognized methods and techniques in project management should be used to plan, organize, execute and close the project.

In addition, the managers at various levels in the project must arrange for good cooperation and teamwork, ensure open and sincere communication, and lead with a strong drive for success. Figure 6.8 illustrates the key elements in best practice project management.

It is important that each company defines what they mean by "best practice" in project management. And the requirements will differ from company to company as projects and project management challenges differ.

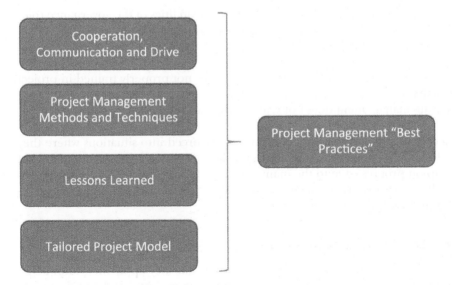

Figure 6.8 Best Practice Project Management

Project Environment and "Best Practice" Project Management

Some will say: "project management is easy and anyone can do it" or "project management is only common sense." Yes and no. The theory, processes, methods and tools are straightforward and easy to learn. But the practical application of project management in a complex project with a tough schedule performed within a complex organization and with a demanding client can be very hard.

A good project manager will adapt his/her knowledge of project management to the situation and will ensure that all the principles of project management are applied to the extent necessary; that there is a realistic plan, that the risks are assessed, that communication with the client is prioritized etc. The project manager can also deviate from the project model if this will benefit the project and has been agreed with the project owner. However, a common risk in project-oriented companies is that the project manager and the project team are forced to compromise on the application of "best practice" project management because of an unhealthy project environment:

- Corporate management is not making priorities. Everything is important. Resources are not allocated according to priorities.
- The project model exists mainly in PowerPoint. The project model is not important in practice.
- The project owner role is not taken seriously, and the project managers manage the projects according to their own private project models.
- The project managers do not get key resources at project start-up as they are busy on other assignments. Start-up gets delayed and the project loses valuable float.
- Start-up gets delayed and there is suddenly no time to plan. We enter the execution phase without a high quality plan and suddenly the domino effect hits the project and all focus is on fire fighting.
- There is no project charter. The roles and responsibilities of the governance roles such as project owner, portfolio manager and project director are unclear.
- Lack of important knowledge and skills in key knowledge areas such as risk management and change management.
- The project managers and the project teams are not properly trained in project management.
- Corporate management does not really understand the project challenges.

The project manager and the project team can be forced into situations where they feel they do not have time to plan, to manage risks, to agree scope with the client, and to follow up on progress due to the many fires they have to fight. The consequences are often delays, cost overruns, angry clients, failure to comply with quality requirements and negative profit margins.

Good or Bad Project Management

Project managers are also responsible for ensuring that they apply their knowledge and skills for the best of the projects. It is sometimes important that the project managers rise up and explains for corporate management/resource owners that the risk is too high or without a realistic plan we should not proceed. Project management teams should not expect that corporate management sees all the mechanisms of project management or that they understand the content of a healthy project environment.

To avoid a situation in which we deviate from best practice project management and common sense, we should think about the "good management" rule: there are two types of project management: *good* project management and *bad* project management. Good project management is the application of best practice project management in all phases of the project. Commercial hand-over, start-up, planning, execution, risk management, change management and managing client expectations according to the project model and "best practice." Bad project management is deviating from best practice because of time constraints, short cuts, inadequate competencies, etc. No time to plan, unclear scope, unclear roles and responsibilities, no risk management and poor change management leading to delays and cost overruns. "Good project management" and "bad project management" have nothing to do with the project management knowledge and skills. It is all about attitude, behavior and how the project management team fills their roles.

Challenging projects are also affected by many risks, some of which cannot be controlled. You therefore also need some luck. There are two types of luck: good luck and bad luck.

As Figure 6.9 illustrates, there are several possible combinations of project management and luck. The preferred one is good project management and good luck, which is a safe way to project success. You can also succeed with a combination of bad project management and good luck. But in complex projects you will need a lot of good luck to make up for bad project management. The combination of good project management and bad luck is also acceptable, as you may have done a great job as a project manager but the project failed for reasons outside your control and you are not to blame. The absolute guarantee for project failure results from the combination of bad project management and bad luck.

Ask yourself: Am I applying my skills and knowledge for the best of the project?

A Practical Example of a Typical Project Management Maturity Initiative—Advanced Project Supplier (APS)

Advanced Project Supplier (APS) designs, develops and installs advanced onshore and offshore facilities for the global energy industry. All facilities are tailor-made to client

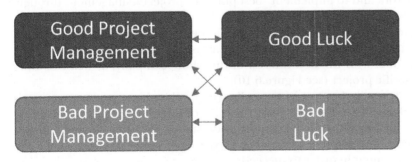

Figure 6.9 The Concept of Good Project Management

specifications and completed in accordance with frame agreements or Engineering, Procurement and Construction contracts (EPC contracts).

APS has offices in the US, Norway, Scotland, the UK, Singapore, Malaysia, Brazil and Argentina.

The APS business consists of projects and operations. The onshore and offshore facilities are planned and executed as projects using project management processes, methods and tools. Once the project has been completed and the products have been handed over to the client, operations will take over responsibility for maintenance, customer support, training and repairs.

APS performs most of its work through projects. Thus, APS is a project-oriented company and a "supplier" delivering to "clients." The success of the company depends on the success of individual projects and on the overall project portfolio.

Strategic Objectives

APS's strategic objectives for the next five years are:

*   position the company among the global top five suppliers in this industry;
*   increase revenue by 20 percent annually while maintaining an operating margin of 10 percent;
*   generate 30 percent of the revenue from emerging markets.

A strategic plan has been developed for achieving the strategic objectives, including activities and projects aimed at strengthening sales, project management and operations. The strategic plan has been approved by the board of directors, and corporate management is responsible for its implementation. APS shall become our clients' preferred supplier through outstanding performance and exceptional quality.

APS Project Excellence Project

Winning projects and succeeding with project planning and execution are the cornerstones of APS's business. APS sees the need for improving project management practices to improve project results and to avoid runaway projects. The main strategic project management goals are to develop and implement a professional project management framework and to implement "best practice" project management throughout the global organization. The project is called the APS Project Excellence Project. Its objective is to create an environment in which there exists a continuous stream of successfully managed projects, where success is measured by having achieved a level of performance that is in the best interest of the whole company, as well as having completed a specific project (see Figure 6.10).

APS wants to reach the "project excellence" level—where project success is repeatable—and stay there. The APS Project Excellence Project is the tool for maturing the organization. Corporate management understands that the change will not happen overnight. This improvement project requires investment, patience and the backing of management in order to succeed.

Figure 6.10 The Project Management Maturity Development

Business and Project Objectives for the Project Excellence Project

The business objectives are:

- meet or exceed customer expectations on 95 percent of all projects—at least 70 percent of customers shall also select APS for their next project;
- increase average project profit margins from 9 percent to 20 percent within the next two years;
- deliver 95 percent of projects on time and within cost within the next two years.

The project objectives are:

- Scope: Implement a professional project management framework and "best practice" project management.
- Time: Project duration: Two years.
- Investment: US$ 10 million.

Content

The APS Project Excellence Project includes the following key elements (see Figure 6.11):

- Project governance—A project governance process for management control and support.
- APS project model—A standard recipe for planning and executing projects, including processes, methods, tools and checklists.
- Project management high focus areas—Special focus on areas with high improvement potential; scope management, business focus, project risk management and stakeholder management.

- Project management training program—A training program including all necessary modules to train and develop project managers, project owners and project
team members.

It will be mandatory for all projects in APS to use the project model including the
project governance process once it has been implemented. This requirement will be
specified in project charters for project owners and project managers. The elements
of the project management framework will constantly be improved based on feedback
from the project teams.

Project Management Training Program

APS is introducing a tailor-made project management training program (see
Figure 6.12) to support the implementation of the project management framework
and "best practice" project management. All course modules have been adapted to
APS's project management framework and project challenges. The training program
is designed for global delivery and busy work schedules. It is based on the blended
learning approach combining professional e-learning modules and interactive
workshops facilitated by world-class instructors.

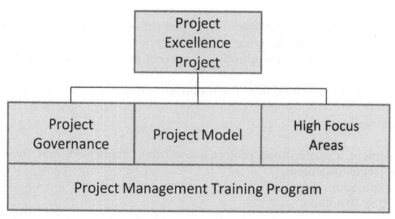

Figure 6.11 The Content of the APS Project Excellence Project

Figure 6.12 The APS Project Management Training Programme

Employees who complete all of the modules will earn the APS Advanced Certificate in Project Management. Employees who complete the modules on the first level will earn the APS Diploma in Project Management.

The target is for all project managers and key project team members to have earned the Advanced Certificate within two years. The Advanced Certificate will then become a requirement for project managers. All project team members will be nominated to start the program. Regular project team members shall complete the Diploma in Project Management within two years.

Project owners, line managers and corporate management should all complete the Project Governance module as soon as possible.

References

Garland, R. (2009). *Project Governance: A Practical Guide to Effective Project Decision Making.* London: Kogan Page.

Husby, O. and Kilde, H. (2013). *Professional Project Execution.* Oslo, Norway: Metier.

Kerzner, H. (2004). *Advanced Project Management: Best Practices on Implementation.* Chichester: John Wiley & Sons.

Muller, R. (2009). *Project Governance.* Aldershot: Gower.

PMI (Project Management Institute). (2012). *Pulse of the Profession: Driving Success in Challenging Times.* Pennsylvania, PA: PMI.

PwC (PriceWaterhouseCoopers). (2012). Insights and Trends: Current Portfolio, Programme, and Project Management Practices. The third global survey on the current state of project management.

Standish Group. (2012). CHAOS Report.

Part III

Project Teams and Sustainable Performance

Dans les autres classes, on leur apprenait sans doute beaucoup de choses, mais un peu comme on gave les oies. On leur présentait une nourriture toute faite . . . . Dans la classe de M. Germain, pour la première fois ils sentaient qu'ils existaient et qu'ils étaient l'objet de la plus haute considération: on les jugeait dignes de découvrir le monde.

In other classes, you probably taught them many things, but a bit like force-feeding geese. They were presented with a ready-made food . . . . In the class of Mr. Germain, for the first time they felt they existed and were the subject of the highest consideration: they were deemed worthy to discover the world.

Le premier homme,
Albert Camus, 1994

Project Teams and Sustainable Performance

Chapter 7

Intra-Organizational Networks and Communities of Practices as a Platform for Project Innovation and Sustainability?

Stefano Borsillo, Danièle Chauvel and Geneviève Poulingue

Introduction

Nowadays, project management is widely spread over many organizations, and it participates in structuring creation of knowledge within enterprises. Approaches to project management are various and differ according to specified contexts. But in the complex and dynamic ecosystem in which enterprises are (always) evolving faster and faster, there is a need to invent new ways of coordinating activities to produce goods and services that are suited to the information flows and the requirement of continuous innovation as a main source of competitive advantage.

The purpose of this chapter is to study the role of communities of practices (CoPs) in the project management environment. First, after an overview of the evolution of project management, the co-existence of project management and some forms of networking are addressed. Then we examine to what extent networking and CoPs are useful to boost innovation and bring some stability and a perspective of continuity.

The world is changing at an increasingly rapid rate, as are dynamics in the business environment and in managerial practices. In this complex, fast-growing and uncertain landscape, companies need to face rapidly changing challenges, to seize immediate opportunities, and to innovate continuously if they are to sustain their position in the marketplace. Nothing is to be taken for granted and everything needs to be configured within a context of ephemeral situations. Companies need to manage the complexity of today's challenges through the tools of project and innovation management. Joel de Rosnay (2012) qualifies this society as "fluid," meaning that it tries to invent new ways of coordinating activities to produce goods and services that are suited to the information flows within our economic environment and thus within companies. It turns out that a favored option is to organize networks in which project driven knowledge and processes are shared.

Indeed project managers focus more and more on words like "agility," "innovation" and "sustainability." This means that mastering a project through its different steps until delivery is far from being enough. Besides being flexible, the general demand is to be innovative, perhaps creating added value in addition to the project outputs and contributing to the quest for sustainability. Sustainability means that it necessarily includes long-term equilibrium. Allying the words "sustainability" with "innovation," we understand "the long-term maintenance of responsibility" in terms of the human, social and management implications of innovation (Chauvel, 2013).

Potential answers to these challenges can be found by seeking new ways to coordinate, insisting on the horizontal dimension of organization and transposing hierarchically structured organizations onto networked.

Based on a review of literature on CoPs, project management and innovation, our research objective is to investigate the relevance of developing networking within organizations to enhance innovation and sustainability. One of our key guiding principles is to consider that CoPs are islands of knowledge and skills endowed with certain stability due to their human/social roots; as such they represent invaluable resources for project teams whose lifetime is rather temporary. Communities are places from whence new project teams emerge; in other words they are the "seedbeds" of innovations. They equally constitute a springboard for ideas and the capitalization and regeneration of knowledge.

Questions that arise are (1) how should we create and develop networking in a project oriented organization? (2) How far is project management affected by the coexistence of networks? and (3) To what extent will these networks/communities contribute to the objective of innovation and sustainability?

The chapter is organized as follows: the first part focuses on the evolution of the concept of project management so that it addresses agile organization as well as organizational improvisation. The second part presents inter- and intra-organizational networks as a means to make sense of knowledge flow, integration and creation in project management. The third part builds on these managerial foundations to discuss possible ways to enhance innovation and sustainability in projects. The leitmotif of these successive approaches remains the dynamics of human interaction and the strength of knowledgeable teams for leveraging innovativeness and creating sustainable value in the project environment.

This debate is at the crossroads where strategy management and sustainable performance meet. In the world of management, recurrent strategic changes correspond to the need to maintain competitive advantage by renewing demand for products and services. Hence management of innovation is implemented to meet market "demand." These changes require structural adaptations and new combinations of company resources, which themselves generate other changes (Chandler, 1962). We can put it this way: structure follows strategy. And yet strategic intention is rooted in structure.

Project Organization Matches Corporate Strategy within Uncertain Environments

Evolution of Project Management

Historically speaking, project management has been developed within pyramidal structures in order to respond to special requests under time and cost constraints: according to the Project Management Institute (PMI[1]), it is defined as a temporary organization with the purpose of creating a product, a service or unique result

---

1   PMI : www.pmi.org.

(Declerck et al., 1983). Project management is at once a management tool, a form of organizational structure, and a strategy as a key objective for the whole company. Today, project management still plays this role in order to develop products or services efficiently. But it is evolving towards agile approaches where a specific purpose is coupled with flexibility so as to grasp additional value added opportunities during its course.

Besides defined guidelines related to the management of a project, any project in its development phases depends on organizational context. In some organizations with knowledge oriented and collaboration based cultures, conducting a project or a portfolio of projects adopts a transversal approach that can be adjusted in line with changes and opportunities. In such organizations, porosity between departments or functions has become more natural. A collaborative spirit spreads throughout all layers of the project and is enhanced by the project manager. Indeed, the project manager plays the role of a great enabler who empowers his/her team, encouraging collaboration and the development of collective intelligence. The tools used for planning and scheduling remain necessary for formatting and assessment at the macro level, but they act as guidelines and are no longer strict predictors of the whole process. If the project process is "over planned" there is a risk that actors will remain attached to a initial projection that has required considerable effort on their part, but which is no longer strictly relevant because the context has changed since the original planning. Options for change always need to be built into initial objectives or into decision-making approaches in order to allow resilience in unexpected situations and these options must be taken into consideration by those in charge. Agile project management has emerged from this type of uncertainty management (Rota, 2010). This evolution has grown in importance over the last few years by focusing on collaborative systems that should also include clients to ensure that the true sense of the project is never forgotten.

The Link between Project and "Agility"

This evolution from traditional project management to agile projects is synthesized in Table 7.1 below. This table results from combining a 1991 analysis presented in a workshop at the Club Montreal with a more recent study of a more flexible approach to project management. Club Montreal is an informal community of practice comprising of French-speaking project directors, among them project directors from Renault SA, Cap Sesa, Fougerolle, Aérospatiale (Dutrait-Poulingue, 2009). Christian Navarre (1993) presented the contrast in approach between the current dominant paradigm emphasizing control and that of practitioners seeking more effective methods. These practitioners refute the dominant paradigm, particularly project management based on detailed à priori planning and posteriori controls. The evolution shown in Table 7.1 confirms the need for a change of paradigm and the relevance of the concept of agile firms (Preiss and Warnecke, 1997; Badot, 1997). Companies sell highly differentiated global solutions while maintaining a competitive market price (Nagel and Dove, 1991). Production is ensured by transversal teams operating largely autonomously and directly linked to top management. The organization supplies resources and consolidates knowledge capitalization fuelled by all actors. Innovative responses to clients are encouraged.

Table 7.1 From Risk Management to Flexibility Management: A New Way of Learning to Create More Value

Systems	Dominant Paradigm (1960) Sequential Model and Compression (Griffin, 1997)	Trends towards Highly Efficient Forms of Project Management (1990) Model towards More Autonomy and Flexibility	Agile Project Management (Rota, 2010) Model Valuing Flexibility
Definitions	Tasks are performed one at a time by individuals and scheduling conflicts are eliminated by prioritizing activities and/or priorities. The parallelism of activities (standardization, synchronization) is the result of organizational effort organization, including scheduling. The interfaces are static. Culture is monochronous.	Tasks are performed by people simultaneously. Conflicts are processed in parallel by direct negotiation and dynamic management interfaces. Organizational parallelism means that individuals are "parallel inside the organization" (they format the project from different angles). Culture is polychronous.	Project evolves through iterations in an incremental approach. Iterations occur within a space-time (time boxing) where intermediate versions are developed and tested. This limits the risks of development without testing and involves stakeholders such as customers. The highly customer oriented culture is also collaborative to encourage both macro and microscopic interpretations.
Rules Segment the Project	Segment tasks and activities. The planning is conceived in relation to the object (work breakdown structure or WBS).	Segmented into "deliverables." Planning is conceived in terms of territories and sub-projects.	Segmented into "deliverables" by iteration within fixed dates, and cost/benefit before proceeding with the project.
Governance	The project manager coordinates, arbitrates and administers the project.	The project manager is an entrepreneur and a pilot.	The project manager facilitates and encourages rather than commands and controls. He/she promotes information sharing and knowledge creation to deal with complex situations.
Basis of the Management	The overall conduct of the project is carried out through a Program Evaluation and Review Technique (PERT). Design by stages. (Metaphor of relay race.)	The conduct of the whole project is operated through a communication system. Concurrent engineering design. (Metaphor of rugby team.)	Leadership from the project manager encourages collaboration within the team, and is a source of motivation. Shared or distributed leadership. (Metaphor of the conductor.)

Basis of the Operation	Detailed rules and procedures. Detailed and comprehensive definition of the objectives, tasks and activities associated with, coordination plans, procedures for discipline. Project management.	Comprehensive guidelines detailed in waves and levels, meta-rules, invariant processes "instantiated" loosely. Freedoms, creation, energy, challenge result. Portfolio management projects and portfolios methods.	Making a list of macroscopic resources, macro planning and setting milestones. Each iteration corresponds to a part of the testing process in consultation with the project stakeholders. Project management with an integration process.
Vision	Participants are isolated in their sphere and their specialization. Their horizon is limited to the following activities assigned. They have no overview (metaphor of the transceiver).	Participants have all the information all of the time (metaphor of the hologram). They have an overall vision. Exhaustive definition of territories and autonomy for all inside the project, intelligent interfaces negotiation.	Participants have the information available and have an overall vision through which many elements are subject to revision in the iterative and incremental development system. The customer is associated at different stages.
Planning Style	Planning once at the beginning of the project (one shot).	Planning by successive waves of increasing accuracy (horizontal and vertical over time within the organization).	Two levels: macro planning for the overall project planning and micro testing in each iteration.
Spread Management	The deviations from the reference plane (baseline) are attributed to deficiencies related to poor definition of objectives, poor planning or from the inability to control size. Behaviors are reactive.	The project is adjusted at all times by bottom-up interactions in its objectives and scope. This involves very sophisticated systems and fast "redesign." Behaviors are proactive.	The differences are identified early and corrected downstream at the iteration. At worst, the iteration may be cancelled if tests fail. The project continues incrementally and can produce a high quality product.
Controlling the Conduct of the Project	Control relative to the plane of reference (baseline). Efficiency is more important than effectiveness.	Project by objective by freeing itself from schedule. Effectiveness is more important than efficiency.	Control by the value created and risks involved. The client is involved in the project and the project team adapts to the changing needs and remaining work to do. The project can be stopped in case of lack of budget.
Teams	Temporary or permanent matrix teams of specialists.	Multidisciplinary teams, dedicated and multifunctional integrated project. The teams are in a position to challenge.	The team has expanded to involve the different project users.

Agile project management is highly quality-oriented, but dependent on customer involvement and responsiveness to change.

Capabilities of Project Members to Define Possible Options in a Flexible Model

Unlike the predictive approach, agile project management is organized around a system of options determined throughout the project's development by simplifying processes; its main constraints reside in respecting a "set" budget and assessing "added" value for the client. This agile approach implies a management style that empowers actors to be able to define possible options throughout the project's evolution. It also requires competitive intelligence activities to be integrated into the project management team in order to achieve the most effective developments (Perbal et al., 2009). It is crucial that the corporate culture encourages innovative flexible projects consistent with strategic orientations.

The margin of autonomy allocated to project actors is defined through collective decision-making. The risk here is that the project will be modified and adjusted to the context, while its previous objectives may be forgotten. Another risk lies in generating or being attracted by a great number of new ideas, which are sometimes far from the initial value creation objectives and which may lead to project failure (Chedotel, 2005, p.136). An experimental approach that offers the possibility of ongoing testing and analysis is one way to limit risk. This type of management can cope with failures regarding innovation and capitalization of experiences (Weick, 1999).

Barrand (2010) discusses "Analysis through actual options" (Myer, 1977) as an assessment method suited to uncertain environments. Such environments entail multiple challenges: they imply developing capacities analyzing produced value, envisaging different possible scenarios and, after disseminating these within the organization, generating solutions from various viewpoints. Blum (2010) uses the table of projects (e.g. see Figure 7.1) devised by Copeland, Koller and Murrin (2000) and offers an

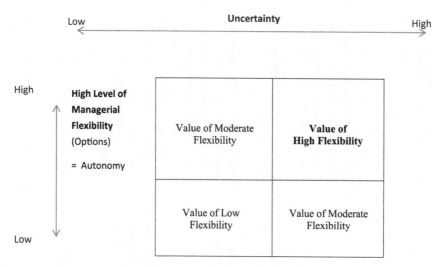

Figure 7.1 When Flexibility becomes "Valuable" (according to Barrand, 2010)

assessment of projects as regards flexibility (possible options). He thus goes beyond the negative notion of flexibility (seen as a risk), transforming it instead into potential risks and opportunities.

The higher the uncertainty of the context, the higher the value of managerial flexibility. When the future is not predictable, actors look for managerial action that can be adopted step by step while keeping a sharp eye on the final objectives. This stance is the embodiment of change in the managerial paradigm.

A Big European Transport Company: A Pyramidal Structure on the Move

This company periodically redefines its strategic orientation by focusing on the evolution of the organization and the renewal of tools used in conducting projects. The challenge for this type of organization is to be able to capitalize on employees' internal experience and knowledge while helping them to learn from external context. The company, a pyramidal structure, under study corresponds to this change and must fight silos. In its discourse, top management announces strategic plans emphasizing the priority of creating communities of shared experience. The reality studied often refers to local blockages by middle management. There is a need for explaining that collaborative participation announces new managerial perspectives where the hierarchical system will be rethought. Agility has to be developing according a change in the company culture, which has to promote new forms of leadership and collaborative processes in order to manage projects in complexity.

Building options by the project team members relies on a spirit of information sharing, which enables contributors to develop open-minded capabilities to analyze information. Project members are both actors of competitive intelligence within the scope of the project but also outside it. Gathering and evaluating information collaboratively has become an integral part of project management in the global knowledge economy.

Communities of Practice to Stimulate the Exchange of Knowledge and Experience among Project Actors

The nature of "agile project" management is part of the logical framework of a *structured project organization*. Under this organizational paradigm, a corporation is similar to a large network in which project actors constantly create collaborative relationships across functional silos and hierarchical levels of the organization. Such a collaborative and dynamic mix of skills is fertile ground for the continuous emergence of new project teams. In the *buffer spaces* separating various project teams, actors share their knowledge and experiences related to the expertise developed in their respective projects, generating over time a repository of common knowledge. A particular form of these buffer spaces are called "communities of practice" (CoP). A CoP is a group of individuals who share a common interest in a specific theme, and share knowledge, expertise, and experiences across organizational boundaries (Wenger et al., 2002), with the common motivation of cultivating trust, learning together (McDermott, 1999), and improving decision-making in the conduct of current or future projects (McDermott and Archibald, 2010). What actually binds members of a CoP is a shared dedication to and identification with one area of expertise, or a particular topic. These communities develop as a learning space within many organizations, often in the background of various project teams (Josserand, 2004; McDermott and Archibald, 2010). A CoP is a "reservoir of intellectual capital" that offers individuals the opportunity to draw from it information and knowledge, enabling them to supplement their missing knowledge and improve their decision-making process (Wenger and Snyder, 2000). Finally, such CoPs often emerge spontaneously, or they may be initiated by company management (Wenger et al., 2002).

The theme (or "practice") around which a CoP evolves is often related to an area of expertise that is relevant to carrying out various projects within the organization. For example, the practice can be *scientific* in nature (e.g., calculations, measurements, molecular structures, chemical dosing), *methodological* (e.g., project management, time management, launching new products), *procedural* (e.g., manufacturing process, security protocol, logistics, process optimization) or *creative* (e.g., virtual animations, augmented reality, audiovisual and 3D). Whatever the nature of a CoP's theme, it often brings together project actors in order to solve a problem common to several projects carried out within the organization (McDermott and Archibald 2010; Wenger and Snyder, 2000). Figure 7.2 illustrates the relationship between a CoP and project teams.

As such, CoPs play a unifying role, one of support and coordination, as well as serving as a body of knowledge for project teams. What then, specifically, is the difference between a CoP and a project team? Wenger et al. (2002) draw a very clear distinction between CoPs and project teams. Indeed, members of a CoP have no direct responsibility for the achievement of a final result, or for the continuous deployment of an operation or process. No specifications or any other type of contracting formality exists to spell out the role of each participant in the fulfillment of an expected result.

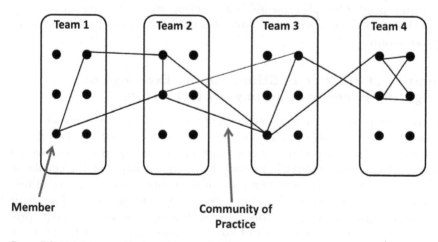

Figure 7.2 Link between Project Teams and COPs

Another aspect that sets the two apart is that a CoP's membership delineation is *vague*, whereas that of a project team is well defined. Finally, unlike a project team, a CoP does not dissolve as soon as the end result is delivered, but instead persists as long as the topic is relevant to members and to the organization and as long as there is value to, and interest in, members learning together.

As is the case for a project team, a CoP must maintain a certain degree of momentum and dynamism so that its members are stimulated to share knowledge, stories and experiences common to their respective projects (Lank et al., 2008). To maintain a vibrant CoP in knowledge sharing, McDermott and Archibald (2010) advocate active and ongoing network management. CoP guidance is mainly achieved through the ubiquity of one (or more) leader(s)—also known as facilitator, coordinator or moderator—whose role it is to stimulate the exchange of knowledge among network members. Typically, leaders devote 20 to 50 percent of their working time to supervising CoP activities, so as to ensure that the CoP remains active in sharing ideas and knowledge (Wenger et al., 2002). An effective coordinator can encourage member participation in the exchange of knowledge and experiences—and in more ways than one. First, he or she can build links among certain members, based on their complementary knowledge (McDermott, 2001). Second, he or she can regularly respond to requests from members, thereby accelerating the process of mutual learning relevant to a common practice (Lesser and Everest, 2001; Wenger and Snyder, 2000). Third, the leader can arrange regular meetings among members on a particular issue. This allows members to build relationships, thereby enabling them to exchange knowledge related to the CoP's practice and create discussion spaces (Wenger et al., 2002). Indeed, the exchange of experiences and knowledge among project actors of the same CoP requires the organization of regular interfaces, so that they can exchange on an ongoing basis. This is what Wenger et al. (2002) and McDermott (2001) called "routinization of activities." This is defined as the organization of regular plenary sessions, workshops, conference calls, videoconferences, or informal group gatherings "around the cooler" to keep the CoP active in the sharing of knowledge and experience. Finally, the moderator can nudge members to document their ideas, stories, experiences, knowledge and best practices (tools, methods, processes) using appropriate media (e.g., databases, electronic platforms, wikis, written documents, guides, etc.). This makes exchanges more fluid within the CoP (Wenger et al., 2002).

A good pilot is crucial in coordinating a CoP. Obviously, such guidance does not derive from the traditional and statutory duties of the head of a formal organization, whose powers are well defined. It is more of a "way of doing and being" intended to foster emulation and stimulation about exchanging innovative ideas and experiences among project actors. Wenger (1998) adds that to foster the emulation of ideas and new knowledge, the leader may occasionally invite renowned experts to share their ideas, vision, knowledge and best practices with members of the CoP, who in turn can disseminate them in their respective projects. The type of active management that we have presented thus depends largely on the individual initiative of CoP leaders committed to creating collaborative relationships among CoP actors. However, in addition to CoP leadership, another factor exists that is intrinsic to the informal nature of any CoP: the environment must be "psychologically safe" for members to feel confident and spontaneously share innovative ideas, experiences and knowledge. This is what we show in the following vignette.

Illustrative Case: The "Futuristic Public Transportation" CoP within Company XYZ, a Large European Public Transportation Company

XYZ is a European company (60,000 employees) that manages a public transportation network (subways, tramways and buses) in a large European city. The "futuristic public transportation" CoP comprises approximately 50 project stakeholders working at XYZ who all participate in innovating projects aimed at improving various areas of public transportation. For instance, projects evolve around areas such as (1) the design of modern subway stations with improved mapping systems, electronic ticketing and passenger assistance, (2) the conception of eco-friendly and energy-efficient subway trains, tramways and buses, (3) enhanced security systems in subway and bus stations, and (4) adapting the size of the public transportation infrastructure (size of trains and stations) to a fast-growing urbanism. The "futuristic public transportation" CoP has a leader, who is assisted by three external facilitators hired by company XYZ to help the leader facilitate CoP activities, coordinate interactions, dialogues and knowledge sharing between the members of the community. In addition to leadership, there is an element of "psychological safety" that project stakeholders feel by participating in this community, which has a positive impact on their sharing of ideas, knowledge and technical expertise. Psychological safety prevails for three reasons that are detailed below.

The CoP Is Perceived by Project Stakeholders as a "Buffer Zone"

Project stakeholders perceive this CoP as a place where, after a discussion, their project-related problems, frustrations and stress are absorbed by the group, hence the term "buffer zone." Being part of the community is considered as a great opportunity for sanction-free discussion; this in turn encourages members to return to the buffer zone, because they don't feel they will be judged or called "incompetent" by their peers. This free expression and sanction-free zone is a fertile ground for stimulating project stakeholders to share the successful and less successful technical expertise they have developed and applied in their respective projects.

During group discussion, the sharing of problems and frustrations encountered during projects is highly encouraged by the CoP leader, or by the three external facilitators. Such an atmosphere has a psychological impact on the members who then feel that they are allowed to make errors during these regular group meetings. During these discussions, or one-to-one interactions, criticism of their ideas is perceived differently to the criticism that their superiors or colleagues in their project teams offer. Members do not feel looked down upon by superiors and/or teammates, and are not made to feel diminished by making mistakes, or by admitting that they have encountered problems during their project. As a consequence, the atmosphere is more relaxed and members are able to come up with numerous ideas and suggestions for improving aspects of the different projects being discussed, simply by talking and exchanging insights with other participants in the group. As freedom of speech is encouraged, the existence of joint expertise that exploitable in different projects could even be discovered during discussions with other group members.

No Hierarchy-Related Pressure

Within the CoP's boundaries, project stakeholders are no longer under their direct superiors' orders since it is a hierarchy-free zone. Consequently, they are not subjected to the usual daily pressure from their project team superiors. Taking part in the CoP enables them to switch from a working atmosphere, in which people are held together by formal rules, to an atmosphere of informal collaboration, where liberty of expression is highly encouraged. The "futuristic public transportation" CoP has an atmosphere of trust and friendship. The CoP is thus a "safety zone" for these project stakeholders. This lack of hierarchy-related pressure enables them to be inspired and motivated to develop together and share their project-related expertise, knowledge, and innovative ideas.

In this CoP, members have no fear of being judged and/or sanctioned by their direct superiors if they ask naïve questions, make mistakes or show that they have gaps in their knowledge. The consequences of the lack of hierarchy-related pressure are that the members do not fear to lose their reputation and position in their project, if they admit to being ignorant about certain topics; they also develop a sense of freedom to criticize ideas put forward by other project stakeholders or developed by themselves.

A "Think Outside the Box" Approach

During CoP group discussions, the CoP leader, or the three external facilitators, encourages the members to think outside the norms of their respective projects with a view to finding ideas and solutions to apply in a variety of innovative projects related to futuristic public transportation. The CoP leader or the three independent facilitators thus encourage members to break the barriers of the normal mental processes they use for the routine formalized tasks in their project. The central idea is for them to be more creative in the process of developing new ideas together, as a community. This approach applies to experimentation with ideas for knowledge development.

This "think outside the box" approach is fully legitimized within the CoP, and takes on a concrete form at meetings (and smaller workshops) through trial and error sessions. These sessions include brainstorming for ideas that could serve the purposes of innovative projects related to areas such as: the conception of eco-friendly and energy-efficient subway trains, tramways and buses, the design of modern subway stations with improved mapping systems, electronic ticketing and passenger assistance, enhanced security systems in subway and bus stations, and the rethinking of the size of public transportation infrastructure (size of trains and stations) in a context of fast-growing urbanism.

When the CoP leader or the three external facilitators start trial and error sessions, they stimulate members to be as experimental as possible in their ways of perceiving and defining how they could develop and improve the ideas and expertise they use in the various innovative projects. At the beginning of sessions, the CoP leader external facilitators spread the word that making errors during group discussions is not only permitted, but also necessary to find good ideas.

(continued)

(continued)

The brainstorming that occurs at these sessions stimulates members' spontaneous participation. It forms a fruitful environment for the emergence of spontaneous ideas and creativity that goes beyond normal operational patterns of thought. The strong flow of ideas related to ideas' enhancement offers increased opportunity for selecting solutions from members' various propositions. Consequently, the project stakeholders discuss the multiplicity of paths and perspectives that they could explore to enhance the ideas under discussion. Through a process of iteration to detect the best ideas for improvement, the group eventually reaches consensus on the best ideas or solutions. The members then export this selection of best ideas and solutions to their respective projects, and have them on standby for concrete application.

Developing Sustainable Innovative Projects

With an Agile approach to performance improvement, people are seen as the source of value that propagates through the system, rather than the problem that needs fixing, and tools and processes are designed to free teams to perform the irreducible activities that only people working together can accomplish.

(Rudd, 2009, p.2)

The nature of "agile methods" in project management implies a focus on collaboration based on flexibility and a quest for establishing close connections between individuals. This can, for example, be implemented through inter/intra-organization networks and CoPs. The collaborative dynamic leads to develop what Weick and Roberts (1993) call "collective mind" in which members of an organizational system strive to develop relations and connect their actions with those of others to achieve best outcomes. This concept is close to the notion of "collective intelligence" a phenomenon defined by George Por (1995) as the capacity of human communities to evolve towards higher order complexity and harmony through such innovation mechanisms as differentiation and integration, competition and collaboration.

Talking of "agile projects" or/and networks and "CoPs" reveals a human-centered approach because it is about people and relationships and about the knowledge they possess and develop through these relationships. An agile environment, indeed, encourages actors to establish links and constitute effective teams, appropriate to the task in hand, by selecting required expertise as well as knowledge, know-how and *savoir être*, recognized from the execution of former projects. Informal vs. formal networks of individuals and teams or communities, which underlie the agile project-led organization, are elements of a collective system of knowledge creation and use.

In this collective system, project or community members develop, through their interactions and to accomplish the allotted tasks, a set of activities through knowledge acquisition, knowledge flow, knowledge integration and knowledge application; this results in knowledge creation and comprises many feedback loops between the different stages. Knowledge sharing is then the central activity; it is enhanced by knowledge empathy, which bolsters the comprehension of the context where the knowledge originates and makes sense to all. It is encouraged through the structuring of knowledge flows and leads obviously to knowledge creation. Knowledge is created through learning processes at the individual, group and organizational levels. Communities are learning systems; in fact they are structures with an inner emergent culture that facilitates members' learning; this culture is in a continuous state of transformation (Pedler et al., 1988). This aptitude for continuous learning and progress focuses on people's capacity to take effective action. This also contributes to deploying shared mental models between members who are able to behave cooperatively and innovatively (Johannessen and Olsen, 2011). The "silver thread" here is to explain that in such an environment, teams or networks possess the ingredients to develop innovation.

A constant trend in the literature of knowledge-based theory of the firm is to consider that the process of knowledge exchange and recombination that leads to knowledge creation is strongly tied to innovation (Galunic and Rodan, 1998; George et al., 2008; Nonaka and Takeuchi, 1995). Most business experts and academics have focused their attention on the question of how to apply resources in order to generate, organize and utilize knowledge to trigger innovation (Johannessen and Olsen, 2011). These intra-organizational networks and communities act daily to acquire, generate, internalize and use knowledge; in doing so, they shape projects, which are/could/should be innovative and contribute to the organizational value chain.

Indeed, aligned with Por's definition above, our line of reasoning follows Johannessen and Olsen's assumption (2011, p.1396) that is, "social mechanisms among individuals and organizations [that] initiate and sustain processes related to innovation." An analysis of this internal network structuring, in line with the literature, can evidence five important social mechanisms that stimulate deployment of knowledge conducive to innovation: connectivity, knowledge diversity, collaboration, collective creativity and creative leadership.

By definition, these networks imply connectivity, the most important prerequisite for innovation; it is mainly about establishing relationships with unexpected things or contexts; it is the capacity to forge interactions within the company to unleash expertise, creativity and knowledge combinations. Learning derived from these connections and consequently combinations of various subjects, domains, people and organizations, underpins innovative activity (Mitra, 2000).

Connectivity calls for knowledge diversity through the broad scope of common and singular knowledge and expertise held by network members. A multiplicity of knowledge feeds a mixture of intuitive associations among different contexts and insights and creates groundwork for higher levels of creativity that are used to stimulate innovation (Corriera de Sousa, 2006; Quinn, 1993). Connectivity stresses complementarities that can foster development in other fields, enhancing the absorptive capacity to exploit external knowledge innovatively (Dosi, 1988; Quintana-Garcia and Benavides-Velasco, 2008). Employee diversity should generally have a positive effect on innovation since diversity affects the way knowledge is generated and applied in the innovation process (Ostegaard et al., 2011).

Collaboration consists of operationalizing knowledge diversity in such a way as to create value. It facilitates the link between various types of knowledge, encourages dynamic synergies and co-creation, liberates energy in teams, and helps knowledge and ideas reach implementation.

If knowledge diversity has a positive influence on innovative capacity, this capacity is scaled up if the knowledge is used and deployed creatively (Basadur and Gelade, 2006). Organizational or collective creativity is defined by Woodman et al. (1993, p.23) as "the generation of a valuable new idea, process, thought, knowledge but also action and progress, by individuals working together in a social context." According to the system model, proposed by Csikszentmihalyi (1997, p.6), creativity results from "the dynamic operation of a system composed of three elements: a culture that contains symbolic rules, a person who brings novelty into the domain and a field of experts [the community] who recognize and validate the innovation." This highlights the crucial role of contextual culture in inhibiting or, on the contrary in unlocking, creativity at the different levels of social aggregation. Research also shows that group creativity is much more than the "simple sum" of individual creative skills, and depends on organizational and social processes like communication processes, positive affective behavior and activities scheduling (Bissola and Imperatori, 2011), as well as collaborative leadership, all of which are features of constructive communities.

It can be said referring to Por's definition (1995) that these social features—connectivity, knowledge diversity, collaboration and creativity—are intrinsic "working components" of communities and networks. But they need to be leveraged by a strong creative support leadership to lead to innovation. According to a recent study by IBM Institute (2010), the ability "to embody creative leadership" is one of the most critical attributes enabling companies to ensure rapid agility and to take advantage of their environment complexity. "Creative leaders invite disruptive innovation, encourage others to drop outdated approaches and take balanced risk. They're open-minded and inventive in expanding their management and communication styles, particularly to engage with a new generation of employees, partners and customers" (p. 3). Indeed, in the age of knowledge—when knowledge is disseminated in the sense that everybody has some knowledge that can be of interest for others, leadership is envisioned on a horizontal dimension. In other words, Wheatley and Frieze (2011) talk about the age of complexity, in which leaders have to abandon their "heroes habits" to take the role of "hosts," empowering their colleagues by inviting them to develop their own skills to solve problems and contribute to the organizational value chain. Leaders are expected to possess the capacities to lead teams in taking on uncertainty, progress and risk-taking, encouraging them to think beyond accepted wisdom and giving them a vision conducive to creativity and innovation (Amabile, 1998; Andriopoulos, 2001). Support leadership is indeed a significant enabler that appears to have a positive and seminal influence on the innovative process.

All these social mechanisms result from and at the same time boost human interactions within agile project teams and inter/intra-organizational networks; they enable innovativeness and liberate teams to perform innovative projects. This perspective leads to considering innovation as a social phenomenon, if it is agreed that "social" according to the definition by Putman (2000, p.19), means the result of dynamic connections: "social capital refers to connections among individuals—social networks and the norms of reciprocity and trustworthiness that arise from them."

In prior research (Chauvel, 2013), it has been argued that innovation capability highly depends on the quality of these interactions (Nonaka et al., 2000; Wang and

Han, 2011). The capacity to organize collective human efforts aimed at establishing a social context specific to knowledge flows is here stressed to enhance relations and collaboration able to generate valuable innovation. Since only people have, can develop, use and maintain knowledge through interactions with others, they are the central actors of this innovation dynamic.

In our perspective, it is this social dimension that confers sustainability on innovation. This sustainability resides in the fact that humans play the leading role in the innovation act through their capabilities to generate knowledge and use it appropriately; such sustainability also depends on their capacity to preserve innovation for both present and future application, and remain aware of the necessary adjustment of the whole system in which they operate. Indeed, in the concept of sustainability, we have adopted Jorna's approach (2006), insisting on the "long-term maintenance of responsibility": making innovation sustainable with a focus on human, social and management implications. This means emphasizing the sustainability of the innovation act and its outcomes, its potential long-term durability, sense making and coherence with the world today as well as for the future.

Conclusion

The soul of this chapter has focused on the strength and capacity of human interactions to steer change and sustainable value creation in an organizational project based environment. Agile, innovative and sustainable project management cannot be reduced to a few main principles of coordination, communication and *in fine* decision-making, even if the managerial approach prevails. The latter should encourage organizational actors to be actively responsible for the knowledge and information necessary to their own analysis and action and must empower them on a general basis. It is up to senior management to organize this "orchestration," giving the pitch and bolstering managerial maturity seen in taking over autonomous and responsible attitudes that are rewarded. Organizations moving from a pyramidal model to a networked system must rewrite their "orchestral score" as well as be open to new interpretations proposed by actors who are dealing with the real challenges.

Even if collaborative systems have become popular and have been widely disseminated for several decades, they have not really affected the foundations of the traditional organization based on power relations. CoPs should remain spaces of positive/constructive confrontation.

Tensions in the enterprise are a source of innovativeness; they may be part of a constructive duality of disorder and order for action, capacity of unlearning without "uncapitalizing" fundamentals and of learning how to think out of the box, in other words, letting go while keeping to the right course. Such a creative organization, strongly rooted in human interactions dynamics with mature behaviors, managerial methods and sharing routines, may deploy proficiently while staying on course to serve the global strategy. In this period of organizational change, intra-organizational networks and CoPs may represent privileged spaces where it is possible to create new relational dimensions which facilitate knowledge exchange and creation, enhance responsibility and autonomy while boosting the creativity conducive to innovative and sustainable projects.

References

Amabile, T.M. (1983) *The Social Psychology of Creativity*. New York: Springer-Verlag.

Amabile, T.M. (1998) "How to Kill Creativity," *Harvard Business Review*, Vol.76, No.5, pp.76–87.

Andriopoulos, C. (2001) "Determinants of Organizational Creativity," *Management Decision*, Vol.39, No.10, pp.834–840.

Badot, O. (1997) *Théorie de l'entreprise agile*. Paris: l'Harmattan.

Barrand, J. (2010) *L'entreprise agile*. Paris: Dunod.

Blum, V. (2010) "Logique financière court terme vs logique financière long terme" in Barrand, J., *L'entreprise agile*. Paris: Dunod.

Basadur, M. and Gelade A.G. (2006) "The Role of Knowledge Management in the Innovation Process," *Creativity and Innovation Management*, Vol.15, No.1, pp.45–62.

Bissola, R. and Imperatori, B. (2011) "Organizing Individual and Collective Creativity: Flying in the Face of Creativity Clichés," *Creativity & Innovation Management*, Vol.20 No.2, pp.77–89.

Chandler, J. (1962) *Strategy and Structure: Chapters in the History of the Industrial Enterprise*. Cambridge, MA: MIT Press.

Chauvel, D. (2013) "Toward a sustainable approach for innovation in the knowledge society" in JFBS ed., *Sustainable Development and Innovation*. Tokyo: Chikura Publishing.

Chedotel, F. (2005) "L'improvisation organisationnelle concilier formalisation et flexibilité d'un projet," *Revue française de gestion*, Vol.1, pp.154.

Copeland, T., Koller, T. and Murrin, J. (2000) "Valuation—measuring and managing the value of companies" in Copeland, T. and Antikarov, V., *Real Options—A Practioner's Guide*. New York: Texere Publishing.

Corriera de Sousa, M. (2006) "The Sustainable Innovation Engine," *The Journal of Information and Knowledge Management Systems*, Vol. 34, No.6, pp.398–405.

Csikszentmihalyi, M. (1997) *Finding Flow, the Psychology of Engagement With Everyday Life*. New York: Basic Books.

Declerck, R.P., Debourse, J.P. and Navarre, C. (1983) *Méthodes de direction générale, management stratégique*. Paris: Dunod.

de Rosnay, J. (2012) *Surfer la vie—comment sur-vivre dans la société fluide*. Paris: Les liens qui libèrent.

Dosi, G. (1988) "The nature of the innovative process" in Dosi, G., Freeman, C.H., Nelson, R., Silverberg, G. and Soete, L., *Technical Change and Economic Theory*. London: Pinter, pp.221–238.

Dutrait-Poulingue, G. (2009) Historiographie d'une communauté d'experts en management de projet: le Club de Montréal, Thesis presented at the University of Caen Basse—Normandie for obtaining the PhD in Management, IAE de Caen, July.

Galunic, C. and Rodan, S. (1998) "Resource Recombination in the Firm: Knowledge, Structures and the Potential for Schumpeterian Innovation," *Strategic Management Journal*, Vol.19, pp.1193–1201.

Garel, G. (2003) "Pour une histoire de la gestion de projet," *Gérer et comprendre*, Vol.74, pp.77–89.

George, G., Kotha, R. and Zheng, Y. (2008) "Entry into Insular Domains: A Longitudinal Study of Knowledge Structuration and Innovation in Biotechnology Firms," *Journal of Management Studies*, Vol.45, No.8, pp.1448–1474.

Griffin, A. (1997) "PDMA Research on New Product Development Practices: Updating Trends and Benchmarking Best Practices," *Journal of Product Innovation Management*, Vol.14, No.6, pp.419–458.

IBM Institute for Business Value (2010) Capitalizing on Complexity: Insights from the Global Chief Executive Officer Study, www.ibm.com/capitalizingoncomplexity, accessed January 2016.

Johannessen, J.A. and Olsen, B. (2011) "What Creates Innovation in a Globalized Knowledge Economy? A Cybernetic Point of View," *Vine Emerald*, Vol. 40, No.9/10, pp.1395–1421.

Jorna, R. (2006) *Sustainable Innovation: The Organizational, Human and Knowledge Dimension.* Sheffield, UK: Greenleaf Publishing.

Josserand, E. (2004) "Cooperation within Bureaucracies: Are Communities of Practice an Answer?" *M@n@gement*, Vol.7, No.3, pp.307–339.

Lank, E., Randell-Kahn, J., Rosenbaum, S. and Tate, O. (2008) "Herding Cats: Choosing a Governance Structure for Your Communities of Practice," *Journal of Change Management*, Vol.8, No.2, pp.101–109.

Lesser, E. and Everest, K. (2001) "Using Communities of Practice to Manage Intellectual Capital," *Ivey Business Journal*, Vol.65, No.4, pp.37–41.

McDermott, R. (1999) "Learning across Teams: How to Build Communities of Practice in Team Organizations," *Knowledge Management Review*, Vol. 8 (May/June), pp.32–36.

McDermott, R. (2001) "How to Design Live Community Events," *Knowledge Management Review*, Vol.4, No.4, pp.5–6.

McDermott, R. and Archibald, D. (2010) "Harnessing Your Staff's Informal Networks," *Harvard Business Review*, March, pp.1–7.

Mitra, J. (2000) "Making Connections: Innovation and Collective Learning in Small Businesses," *Education + Training*, Vol. 42, No.4/5, pp.228–237.

Myer, S. (1977) "Determinants of Corportate Borrowing," *Journal of Financial Economics*, Vol.5, No.2, pp.147–175.

Nagel, R. and Dove, D. (1991) *21st Century Manufacturing Enterprise Strategy.* Bethlehem, PA: Iaccoca Institute, Lehigh University.

Navarre, C. (1993) "Pilotage stratégique de la firme et gestion de projets: de Ford et Taylor à Agile et IMS," in V. Giard, C. Midler, *Pilotages de projet et entreprises. Diversité et convergences*, coll. Gestion, Ecosip. Paris: Economica, pp.181–215.

Nonaka, I. and Takeuchi, H. (1995) *The Knowledge Creating Company: How Japanese Companies Create the Dynamics of Innovation.* New York: Oxford University Press.

Nonaka, I., Toyama, R. and Konno, N. (2000) "SECI, Ba and Leadership: A Unified Model of Dynamic Knowledge Creation," *Long Range Planning*, Vol.33, No.1, pp.5–34.

Ostegaard, C., Timmermansa, B. and Kristinssonb, K. (2011) "Does a Different View Create Something New? The Effect of Employee Diversity on Innovation," *Research Policy*, No.40, pp.500–509.

Pedler, M., Boydell, T. and Burgoyne, J. (1988) "Towards the Learning Company," *Management Learning*, Vol.29, No.3, pp.337–364.

Perbal, S. Vergno, L. and Quazotti, S. (2009) "Le processus de veille intégré au processus de management de projet," *Les Cahiers du numérique*, Vol.5, No.4, pp.79–92.

Por, G. (1995) "The quest for collective intelligence" in K. Gozdz, *Community Building: Renewing Spirit and Learning in Business.* San Francisco, CA: New Leaders Press.

Preiss, K. and Warnecke, H.-J. (1997) *Agile Enterprise*, A new publication for organizations competing in the 21st century, ai@absu.amef.lehig.edu, accessed January 2016.

Putnam, R.D. (2000) *Bowling Alone: The Collapse and Revival of American Community.* New York: Simon & Schuster.

Quinn, J.B. (1993) *Intelligent Enterprise.* New York: Free Press.

Quintana-Garca, C. and Benavides-Velasco, C.A. (2008) "Innovative Competence, Exploration and Exploitation: The Influence of Technological Diversification," *Research Policy*, No.37, pp.492–507.

Rota, V. (2010) *La gestion de projet agile.* Paris: Eyrolles.

Rudd, C. (2009) Raising the Bar with Agile, http://www.projectsatwork.com/article.cfm?ID= 247127, accessed January 2016.

Wang, C. and Han, Y. (2011) "Linking Properties of Knowledge with Innovation Performance: The Moderate Role of Absorptive Capacity," *Journal of Knowledge Management*, Vol.15, No.5, pp.802–819.

Weick, K.E. (1999) "The aesthetic of imperfection in orchestras and organisations" in M.P. Cunha and C.A. Marques, *Readings in Organisation Science*, Lisbon: ISPA, pp.541–563.

Weick, K.E. and Roberts, K.H. (1993) "Collective Mind in Organizations: Heedful Interrelating on Flight Decks," *Administrative Science Quarterly*, Vol. 38, pp.357–381.

Wenger, E. (1998) *Communities of Practice: Learning, Meaning, and Identity*. Cambridge: Cambridge University Press.

Wenger, E., McDermott, R. and Snyder, W. (2002) *Cultivating Communities of Practice: A Guide to Managing Knowledge*. Boston, MA: Harvard Business School Press.

Wenger, E. and Snyder, W. (2000) "Communities of Practice: The Organizational Frontier," *Harvard Business Review*, Vol.78, No.1, pp.139–145.

Wheatley, M. and Frieze, D. (2011) *Walk Out Walk On: A Learning Journey into Communities Daring to Live the Future Now*. San Francisco, CA: Berrett-Koehler Publishers.

Woodman, R., Sawyer, J. and Griffin, R. (1993) "Toward a Theory of Organizational Creativity," *The Academy of Management Review*, Vol.18, No.2, pp.293–321.

Chapter 8

Project Team Life Cycle
The First Steps of a Methodology for Management Reflection

Carole Daniel and Sandra Walker

Introduction

The way a project team is set up and functions is fundamentally different from a team working in operations. The project team's assignment consists of turning the initial intangibility of a project into reality. Considering the project team as a temporary group helps us to visualize why the right development of the group is one of the key factors in the project's success. The concept of life cycle for a temporary group was developed in the work of R.D. Laing who provides an analysis of group dynamics and helps us to understand the inner mechanisms of project teams, which are subconscious and highly emotional. Concepts, such as a part or transitional object, are helpful to create a methodology for a temporary project group's management and merit in-depth exploration.

In the same way that project activities differ from operational activities, project teams differ from other types of teams. Operations are known to be statistically stable; team members can identify and understand causes of problems. Projects are statistically unstable; causes of change are difficult to assign. The project path starts in a virtual phase, when ideas and intentions prevail. The role of the project team is to transform these aspirations into a real project. An individual worker assigned to operational activities can be easily interchanged with another. By contrast, an individual on a project stands apart from other team workers as they play a highly distinct role (DeClerk et al., 1997). The reason for this lies in the simple fact that professionals working on operational "routines" follow well-known procedures, which are put in place through quality assurance in order to guarantee the efficiency of the company. The unique nature of projects implies that it is impossible to follow existing procedures. Each project team member's individual personality, experience and managerial skills contribute to the project team performance, which in turn is a success factor on a project. The fundamentally different nature and dynamics of projects make it difficult then for project managers to lead a project team effectively. Furthermore, a project is not a "closed system"; it is a creative endeavor in a company's ecosystem, that it will necessarily and temporarily destabilize. Also, the project dynamics in the implementation phases impact the project team's dynamics, affecting its capacity to cope with all the situations that can arise later. Understanding the dual dynamics is thus critical to lead project teams successfully. Within team dynamics, there are three different levels, namely individual, interpersonal communication and the group dynamics level, which will be at the core of this chapter.

Several authors have described[1] various steps in team development and the literature indicates some agreement that project team development follows its own logical steps before reaching the phase of an effective, united project team. R.D. Laing (Laing and Cooper, 1971), in his comment on J.P. Sartre's (1960) *Critique de la Raison Dialectique*, develops what he calls the group "life cycle." A project team is a group of people and, more precisely, a temporary group. Therefore the group "life cycle" could apply to project teams' development. Indeed, this model can provide fundamental understanding of project teams' dynamics.

In addition to the presentation of this project team life cycle pattern, we will suggest the first steps of a methodology for management reflection. We will also provide business examples drawn from our consulting activities.

Project Teams as Temporary Groups

When the idea of a project emerges in a company, rarely is thought given to the question of the mix of human resources available to work on it. Too often, project team members are selected because they have the time rather than the right intellectual capital. This can be a key factor in the failure rate of projects. In a more reflective world, a project team member would be selected firstly on a strong motivation that they should be part of the project team. Indeed, one of the main characteristics of a project team is the incredible energy it needs to produce to survive against external threats, or to overcome internal tensions, since humans have a natural tendency toward inertia (practico-inert social field, see Laing and Cooper, 1971).

The Notion of a Group

R.D. Laing insisted that, a priori, several individuals together do not necessarily create a group. The most common mistake consists of considering a group as a super-organism, bigger than the sum of its individual parts. An outsider's initial observation of the group may produce this illusion. However, a group is fundamentally different to what Sartre calls a grouping, a mere mathematical sum of the individuals present (see Table 8.1). A grouping is passive and deeply anchored in inertia. On the contrary, a group is action-oriented, stimulated by opportunities for change.

"A group is a dynamic whole, in movement, in action, with inner conflicting associations between the parties" (Sartre).

In the first tome of *Critique de la Raison Dialectique* (1960), Jean-Paul Sartre examines the problem of man in the face of both a group and collective history. According to him, human relations are built on the struggle against scarcity. He makes a fundamental difference between a grouping of people and a group. In a grouping, individuals constitute a passive crowd bowing to their destiny.

---

1 See bibliography.

Common interests are felt as being imposed from outside. To become a group, the common interest must become sufficiently strong so as to resonate with people. Then there is a sense of purpose, eventually becoming a common interest. The members of the group must discover the necessity of interdependence in order to serve this interest well. Interpersonal knowledge increases and communication takes place. Concern for the common interest overrides the group preoccupation with sub-groups that have hidden agendas. It also overcomes the passive resistance of a few individuals who refuse to commit themselves to a common venture. The group must also move from indirect communication to direct communication or from one-way communication to bilateral communication with feedback. Finally, groups with opposing interests emerge and are quietly drawn into a struggle against one other.

Table X.1: Sartre on groups and groupings.

The creation of a group, according to psychosociologists, comes from "a movement of tension between a common danger and objective." Sartre goes further in his affirmation that relations between members are qualitatively transformed. It is important to understand that the birth of a group arises from *common action*, freely undertaken. This "praxis unites the members in a new way, drawing them away from group passivity, the impossibility to act and superficial relations. Then, through praxis, they rediscover the concrete use of freedom, enabling new solutions and transforming reality instead of succumbing to it" (Anzieu and Martin, 1997). In order for a project team to characterize this definition of a group, then there must be some knowledge and analysis of group dynamics.

The Temporal Nature of a Group

The "temporal nature" of a project team is of fundamental importance. The works of J.P. Sartre are interesting because he started to analyze temporary groups. He considered the phenomenon of group dispersal that he felt had its own logic and significance. The discontinuity in the different project phases impacts the project team. The behavior of team members is affected as a result of multiple stops or waiting time that is typical on projects due to late deliveries, inevitable delays linked to administrative procedures and so on. A cohesive project team achieving high results can be paralyzed by a lack of strategic decision from its management, which can with time break the project team's energy and lead it back to inertia, frustrated by the idea that "nothing is never decided." This pathway is in some ways "non-linear," with "breaks" and "irreversible movement." For instance, a managerial decision coming from the top to support the project team by using a team of consultants can have dramatic consequences. The group self-confidence can be jeopardized to a point that the group loses its creativity and no longer dares to implement the necessary managerial actions. The group dynamics can be changed, sometimes at a superficial level, where productivity slows down for a moment, but sometimes at a deeper level with regression phases.

The second impact of the temporal nature of a project team concerns the arrival and exit of various participants in the Project/Context Ecosystem.[2] Citing the above example, following management's inability to take decisions, the project manager—or any team member—can decide to leave the team creating a split in the group. This is irreversible in the sense that the group's positive energy was linked to the quality of the team's interactions based on a precarious balance of the team members. If one team member disappears, the equilibrium is forever destroyed. There is also frequent separation anxiety before departure, either at the end of a stage or of a project, which is often overlooked under pressure to deliver. Project managers should be able to understand these issues and to adjust their behavior accordingly.

The Notion of Life Cycle

Project teams display, or should, the characteristics of temporary groups, following a designated path with clearly defined phases. This is what R.D. Laing calls the "life cycle." This path begins with the appearance and creation of the team and finishes with the dispersal, the "symbolic death" of the group.

Other authors outline, in an essentially descriptive manner, the development stages of a team. Some identify different natures of the various groups that can adapt to situations as they evolve to the next phase or, on the contrary, stop at a certain stage in their development. This is the case for J.R. Katzenbach and D.K. Smith (1984) in their "team performance curve." These authors seek to position different types of groups on two scales: performance impact and team effectiveness. The groups can be identified as follows: "working group," "pseudo-team," "potential team," "real team" and "high-performance team." According to the authors, you should choose which type of team corresponds best to a specific project situation. Even if this seems logical in terms of group development, no means of evolving from one type of group to another is suggested. There is no analysis of the specific way in which each team functions. Neither is there, apart from an outline of simple processes, any suggestion of how to identify or control the team types to influence them.

Other approaches that we think are more realistic but still remain descriptive, propose a framework for the composition of a project team. H.-Pierre Maders(2000) equates the development of the "high-performing team" to a five-storey house featuring stairs that you go up from the lowest to the highest storey. The author suggests the following "steps"; observation, cohesion, differentiation, organization and production. Another author, Olivier Devillard (2000), suggests four team development stages: latency, belonging, team and performance.

The life cycle proposed by R.D. Laing provides a much richer analysis of temporary group dynamics, going beyond descriptions. Although he does not specifically examine teams working on projects, Laing's model is based on the works of Sartre,

---

2   The concept of a Project/Context Ecosystem is well-developed in the different works of Roger P. Declerck (see the bibliography). Briefly, it concerns all the players who have a stake in the project (stakeholders) or who have an interest in it (shareholders) and the project team should make efforts to manage the Ecosystem.

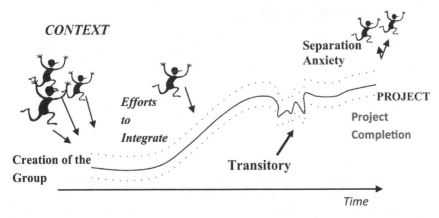

Figure 8.1 Examples of Sensitive Phase during the Life Cycle of a Project

who had founded his reflections on two elements that justify this transposition. Sartre had started with the analysis of temporary groups. Secondly, he structured his argument around logic of action, a human thought process in the struggle between Society and Nature, which corresponds exactly to the logic of action for a project team as defined earlier.

Figure 8.1 represents a few specific issues associated with temporary groups. On the well-known life curve of the project appear problematic issues linked to the creation of the group, namely the exit of participants during the project that can cause anxiety separation, the arrival of players who should "make efforts to fit in" with the existing group members and reactions of teams during transitory periods on the project.

In the book, *Le management stratégique, Contrôle de l'irréversibilité*, J.P. Debourse, R.P. Declerck and J.C. Declerck (1997) highlight the model developed by R.D. Laing showing how temporary groups develop.

In accordance with R.D. Laing, we can characterize the life cycle of temporary groups as follows:

* a group coming together around an object;
* a group in fusion;
* a pledged group;
* a developed group;
* a group in partial dispersion.

This dynamic is of interest as our many observations on group life provide clear evidence of this chronological sequence. We saw that the absence of movement from one stage to another leads almost systematically to a regression phase in the temporary group.

It seems important to determine the rationale of collective action, the genesis of a group, and the structure of its praxis (Laing and Cooper, 1971).

Description and Illustration of the Different Phases in the Life Cycle of Temporary Groups

To better understand the different stages in the life cycle of temporary groups, as defined by R.D. Laing, we have observed a certain number of groups on projects. We chose to use the "participant observation" research method to avoid being totally outside of the group under observation. Being inside made it possible for us to capture emotions in the group, which was essential to achieve a minimal understanding of group phenomena.

We digress a little following this remark. We note that the scientific study of groups has long been delayed for the simple reason that researchers thought that they could not analyze group phenomena. M. Sherif was the first to prove in 1936 that it was indeed possible to study the behavior of groups in a controlled situation. All groups contain a strong dimension that could be described as enigmatic. A group under observation can react in unexpected ways, sometimes even dangerously. We can cite several examples from crowd phenomena, often expressed as "unruliness." We should not under estimate the strong emotional substructure in a group. It is a substructure that, in project situations, could appear as embers that a light breeze of uncertainty and instability could easily set alight.

In most of the illustrative examples that follow, we were "participant observers." In all cases we were either a participant on a project team or in a training role during real projects or indeed accompanying project managers and workers. We also cite examples that have been provided to us by various people. In each case, we will detail the framework for the observation as well as the role that we had, without going into contextual details that are irrelevant to the purposes of this study.

We have drawn up Table 8.1 to summarize the level of the invariables (on the top line) that seem to be the most characteristic of the different stages in the life cycle (listed in the first column).

We then give details of each of the stages.

First Stage: Coming Together around an Object

"Grouping"[3] does not come about via a complex web of interpersonal relations, but through a mediating object.

Initial observations from R.P. Declerck, J.P. Debourse and J.C. Declerck (1997) indicate that groups form through the "focus of attention" of different members of the team "at an intellectual level" toward the "vision," the perception of the project

---

3 This word comes from Anglo-Saxon literature with an emphasis on the action process and not on the specific noun that corresponds to the final result; the word "group" has a more static meaning.

Table 8.1 A New Framework of Team Dynamics

Stages \ *Characteristics*	*Resistance to Threats*	*Importance of the Task*	*Importance of the Relation*	*Productivity*	*Psychosociological Level*
1 Coming together around an object	Weak	Weak	Very strong	Very weak	Individual
2 Group in fusion	Medium	Medium	Strong	Weak	Interpersonal
3 Pledged group	Strong	Strong	Medium	Strong	Groupal
4 Developed group	Very strong	Very strong	Weak	Very strong	Groupal
5 Group in partial dispersion	Very strong	Weak	Strong	Medium	Individual
6 Symbolic death of group*	–	–	Strong	–	Individual

* This stage is the real disbandment of the team. That is why columns 1, 2 and 4 are no longer relevant, as the project has finished.

goal. Also, they form "at a sensory level" through the activation of one of the senses (touch, sight and perhaps smell) around a model, samples, cards and so on. This focus of attention of all the members on a common "object" is perceived as a stage in the process known as the "creation" of the group, without which no group will truly form and no entity will arise. We are thus only dealing with a given number of individuals: a grouping.

During other complementary observations, we appreciated how important it is for a group to have a shared meaning of the purpose of the project, an initial idea of what it could be.[4] We observed that when there is no common vision, the group is condemned to simply being an assembly of individuals communicating in a designated interpersonal mode. The group could not at all be considered as a team with its characteristics, strengths and dynamics. In this stage, the pseudo "group" has no strength enabling it to face potential threats in the project/context ecosystem.

There is no feeling of solidarity or any other notion of trust. There is just a series of works carried out by individuals without any real coherence, so the group is exposed to multiple conflicts.

> At this stage, we highlight the fact that we have witnessed failures evidently linked to the importance of the will of individuals to participate in a project. It is essential, before assimilating an individual into a project team, to ensure that the person is both motivated and shows "will." On a project, considerable energy is expended just for the survival of the group. If the motivation of each project member is not strong enough, then the wolf is let into the sheep's pen . . .

4 We are still in the totally virtual stage of the project and to progress, the group needs a "part-object" (see Segal, 1997).

During this stage, the production level of the team is not yet an issue. Moreover, it would be illusory and incoherent to begin production at this stage: to produce what and to go where? Every group member arrives with their own background, culture, way of seeing the world and notably their own perception of what one expects of a team. The psychosociological level is still individual.

We do not intend to discuss "team building" techniques. We believe that to function effectively a group should come together around an object, a phenomenon that we position at two levels:

- *at an intellectual level*: the group must achieve shared understanding, and to that end, develop "a common language" just as any other group of human beings might do. In general, the group does so, but often in an ad hoc manner, partially or ineffectively. The group could use a flipchart, scribbled diagrams, schedule, or work breakdown, for example, as well as lengthy discussions (we are only referring here to groups that manage to pass through this stage).
- *at a sensory level*: very often, we have recognized the relative poverty of words as a uniting force that could reach everybody in the same way. How many times though has some form of graphic re-launched the productivity and creativity of a group!

We let a group reflect for half an hour on the position of a given plot of land for agricultural use. The discussion became heated with various arguments given by everyone, but then fell into a silence that, as the minutes passed, became increasingly difficult to break. We suggested to the group to draw a map of the land in question, as well as the area represented by the agricultural zone to try and position it according to different suggestions. The person standing next to the flipchart started to draw an outline of the map and, as if by magic, some others began to calculate the surface area, while others looked for a rectangle of paper that could represent the agricultural zone . . .

This phase of analysis is essentially virtual, but by referring to tangible objects rather than abstract words, the project group members can keep coming back to concrete elements. These materials constitute what we shall later describe as a transitional object (Winnicott, 1975), an ersatz of the project. This allows the group to practice on what could become the real project and already to loosely identify any problematic aspects.

Second Stage: A Group in Fusion

Once the group has come together, it enters the fusion stage, to restate it in the terms of R.D. Laing. Quite simply, the group becomes aware of its difference, its identity and of the clear frontier between it and others. The individuals feel more inclined to defend group interests and they no longer defend, or express less, their own interests.

Emotions are still very present, but the group starts to direct its energy toward the project itself. During this phase, the group is faced with real threats, as all project groups are. The threats are concrete and measurable, such as being in competition with other groups, changed deadlines, administrative difficulties, problems with financial resources and so on. These threats weigh on the group and contribute to welding it into constructive action that is proactive or defensive. This reaction is quite healthy and arises from fear, which is natural and useful for the strong fusion of a group.

The emotional atmosphere has sufficiently calmed down to enable direct interpersonal communication. The team members get to know one another better. At this stage, geographic co-location is still necessary for group members to exchange their still differing points of view about the project and, in the face of threats, for initial decisions to be taken together. Working methods should also be set up.

The ability to withstand threats is still weak. An accumulation of them, in intensity or frequency, could transform the feeling of fear, which is healthy and constructive, into a state of separation anxiety.[5] This leads to regression, which we will discuss later or, worse still, to the dissolution of the group.

The members of a group in fusion, according to J.P. Sartre, live through three different experiences: solidarity, belonging to a new collective reality and considering the other as a third party regulator. An individual's action is part of the common action to escape from and ultimately triumph over the impossibility to transform life (acting on reality). The action of the group affirms "the impossibility of the impossibility." Sartre cites a French republican motto that he sees as an example of the experience of a group in fusion. "Freedom" is a collective *praxis* which can break through the impossibility of action. "Equality" is how each person is seen as being the equivalent of another: one's "similar contemporary." "Fraternity" is holding interdependence as a necessary means for the group to exist.

Third Stage: A Pledged Group

A priori, the term "pledged group" is not easy to understand. R.D. Laing explains it as a collective reaction toward threats that are too strong. It ensures group survival. There is a "solemn pledge of loyalty," symbolic or real, from each member toward the group.

The group is never safe from reverting to the state of the initial grouping. Every group must set up mechanisms to survive and guard against collective inertia. The group defines rules, working procedures and decision-making methods. It creates or recognizes certain collective norms. This does not occur without a fear of betrayal; every person is considered as a potential traitor in a position of power. To fight

---

5   A concept of Max Pagès. To be developed further in the fifth stage.

disloyalty, each member of the group must pledge allegiance to commit and maintain group belonging.

During our observations, we saw that each stage is necessary so that the group can achieve optimal productivity. The pledged group stage is the moment where the group members, however they may have promised allegiance, start to fulfill the group's purpose. Furthermore, there is mutual trust between group members and confidence in the realization of the project. From this moment onwards, doubts concerning the effective realization of the project disappear. It is possible that the project will not meet at all, or only partially meet, its objectives in terms of budget or timing, but something will have been accomplished. From this moment, the "energy" expended by the group to come together to face threats from the inside and outside, can be used solely for the production of the project.

Physically, the group no longer feels obliged to be in the same geographic location. Also the information flows can be "purged" of the "noises" that constitute emotional messages (these are expressions of assurance of the goodwill of the team members, of the motivation of each person, of positive feelings toward each other . . .).

During a training exercise, a team of five people had to hurry as one of them had to go and negotiate a contract with a client. Previous to that, a discussion about the position to adopt had taken place. After a long while, the person in question came back into the group. None of the conditions on which the group had agreed had been respected. The negotiator had accepted, against considerable financial advantages, a number of changes of which some, admittedly, were imposed by the client without any possible discussion. In this situation, one of the team members started to express some doubts about the technical feasibility of the project in view of the new information. This was quickly followed by a member announcing that, in any case, the negotiation was finished and they should now organize follow-up actions.

Fourth Stage: A Developed Group

A developed group is one whose members are sufficiently united to give all their energy to the project. The members can confidently allocate tasks with no worries about the quality of work produced by the other members.

At this stage, the group is truly resistant to threats. We have a notable example of a team, that we put under pressure during a pedagogical exercise: keeping one of the members off the project for an hour, changing technical parameters, changing financial limits, introducing a major constraint in the context of doing the project and so on. Instead of succumbing to divisiveness, the group alternated moments of work in sub-groups of experts with necessary team regrouping. They kept the project coherent, shared information and held short decision-making meetings.

A developed group has rapid reactions and is united in its decisions. Commitments taken by one of its members are adopted by the whole team without any discussion (at least in public). It is clear that at this stage any betrayal is "severely punished."

We affirm that from this moment onwards, geographic distances are manageable, however great they may be. They no longer present an obstacle to group production. It is still of course necessary to set up a system of effective communication, especially including "rich" media, allowing for a regular transmission of more relationship-oriented messages. This can be the telephone, possibly video-conference and, of course, face-to-face meetings. However, most information can be transmitted very concisely via emails, intranet, mail or fax.

The project manager should manage this system of information flow. It is up to him to ensure a high quality of communication. The opposite would be bad communication as defined by J. Ruesh (1972): "Too much, too little, too early, too late, at the wrong place."

Fifth Stage: A Group in Partial Dispersal

When the project draws to a close, the group views this finality with apprehension. We are faced with what Max Pagès (1997) calls "separation anxiety." It is a primary, deeply felt phenomenon, coming from the process of separation. It can be physical, affective, imaginative or even symbolic. It happens when one person leaves another in whom a great deal of positive energy was invested. It is a physical state as a strong emotion is experienced.

Separation anxiety is potentially present as soon as a relationship starts. It thus appears due to the very nature of projects. For a simple understanding of what we are referring to, just remember the feeling that you have when accompanying a loved one to the railway station, when you must separate for a long and undefined period. If, and only if, the group has correctly followed the different stages described above, each member of the group will have made a considerable emotional investment.

This period is often neglected on project teams, in the same way as the transition from project to operation. This phase is known as project closure (Debourse, 1991).

Three main reactions can be observed. The first and the most reasonable is the reaction toward "acceptation of the closure." The members have accepted the emotional commitment involved in group life for a project length that can sometimes run into years. They know that once the project is complete, the members will separate to perhaps never meet again (Figure 8.1).

The second as well as the third reactions are less "healthy," but unfortunately human and often observable. These reactions are sadistic and masochistic. In both cases, one of the team members prefers to harm the relationship rather than to consent to live through the delicate moment of a separation, where one sometimes feels torn apart. In a sadistic case, one of the members becomes a little aggressive toward other team members. It is less a question of hurting the other person, than avoiding being hurt oneself. In a masochistic case, one of the members leaves the group before the end of the project, in general with the best excuses possible. We can all admit to examples of this sort of behavior that we have ourselves displayed; we have cut short a meeting to catch a train that we could have taken later, we were unable to agree on the layout of a report and got annoyed even though most of the work had been done.

On project teams, these phenomena can be managed using personnel management techniques, such as career plans, reallocation of team workers, or simply by a stage clearly defined as the termination stage followed by a post-evaluation meeting.

Dysfunctions Linked to the Dynamic of Temporary Groups

After having described the general dynamic of the life cycle of temporary groups as we envisage them, we now suggest an original approach toward certain aspects of this dynamic. We draw ideas from the field of psychiatry, coming from studies of young children. These approaches are essentially based on the Klein approach. The contributions of Mélanie Klein focused on the discovery of early stages in the development of very young children, before the famous Oedipus complex from Freud, where she identified phases of fundamental depression in the construction of Oneself.

We will now discuss specific points, previously brought up by Roger P. Declerck, which we deem to be rich and useful in management terms.

Regressions in Temporary Groups

We will provide some illustrations of this phenomenon that we observed in groups with whom we worked. By regressions, we mean moments when a group ceases to produce, to do concrete and effective work on the project. During these periods, it seems that the group is no longer grappling with anything "real." Its members seem to share one of the emotional states that we shall describe below.

These regressions can emerge in any phase in the dynamics of the life cycle of the temporary group. We have noted however that they appear more often in the first stages: coming together around an object and group fusion. This is in accordance with the degree of resistance to threats, both internal and external.

W. Bion (1987), following his work in the army at Northfield hospital during the Second World War, identified three types of regression: dependence, fight/flight and pairing.

The Regression of Dependency

The group behaves as if they are waiting for the arrival of the ideal leader. This type of group makes a low level of sound with unfinished, broken sentences and interrupted conversations with questions left unanswered. There is low mobility of members and a generally passive attitude that could be described as slack, dull and inattentive. We suggest that this regression clearly occurs when the potential leader of a group, for whatever reason, does not fully play their role and another person attempts to replace him. The group stalls until each person has found their place. Another situation that provokes this type of regression could also be a misunderstanding of the project objectives.

In company X, a group of four people were working on a strategic analysis using initial partial data. Mr T stood up and started writing some questions on the flipchart. After a short while, Mr T turned around to ask the opinion of his fellow team workers. Mr V stated that he was not comfortable with the step of listing some questions, suggested to the team by Mr T. The latter then asked the group to suggest another method. Half an hour went by and Mr T continued to draw up a list on his own. The others insisted on silently reading and re-reading the information available on the project. After an hour, Mr V., who incidentally had simultaneously started to look for complementary information on the internet, declared: "I am sorry but I really don't see the point of what we are doing, nor where we are going." On the following day, Mr V. adopted a more active entrepreneurial attitude and the group seemed to come to life around him with each of the members bringing their contribution to the project.

Fight/Flight Regression

The group displays aggressive behavior toward its environment. This behavior can express itself as a flight, which is the refusal to face the necessity of productive work to advance the project. There are, for example, endless discussions and a refusal to write anything down. Alternatively, the group takes a combative stance with confrontational attitudes or words toward superiors, other groups, consultants and so on. It clearly takes place when the group feels strongly threatened against its survival.[6] This trouble can even appear from within the group. Sometimes the group goes as far as to invent an enemy. It prepares itself to unite against the Other that is positioned as a threat, be it imaginary or real.

We have witnessed several examples of this type of regression. It especially appears when there are two projects that are geographically close and linked either in a competitive or complementary way. Sentences starting with "yes, but we . . ." or "yes, but they . . ." frequently border on the inevitable and, in the case of team regression, no-one is short of clever excuses for the lack of productivity.

Three people that we had to coach on their project declared themselves to be totally blocked in their progress, because they were waiting for others' decisions so that they could move onto the next phases. After listening to them giving a lengthy explanation about how impossible it was to be productive, I asked them how these decisions stopped them from drawing up their report for the project, as an entire chapter was dedicated to an analysis of their sector of activity. They admitted that they couldn't work and that, although they were well-aware of the approaching deadline, they were only dealing with details of the layout. They were not getting stuck into heavier tasks or, quite honestly, the necessary constructive tasks to move forwards.

Pairing Regression

A "couple" is created between two group members who start to have a conversation together or do an unproductive exercise in a "private working session." Symbolically,

---

6 Beyond the constructive fear that we mentioned earlier.

the other members of the group seem to wait for this pair to produce something or for someone (like a leader) to appear. This type of regression is rarer than the two others but interesting to observe. From the outside, it would seem that the two people are deep in concentration, dealing with an important issue. The other members hang around them, without really listening or watching what is going on, but without moving away. The general impression is of a scene where there are two parents in discussion, surrounded by their children awaiting a decision to move to action, even if they have no idea what is going on.

> We had a discussion with a group in which we had observed this phenomenon. Listening to us bringing up the regression phenomenon and before we could cite any specific example, they looked at each other and burst out laughing. They recognized having experienced this phenomenon the day before. They described the particular atmosphere in which they found themselves. The "couple" explained that they were not really trying to go forwards, but were both engaged in a calculated move to avoid appearing inactive. As for the other members, they admitted that they had waited calmly for this operation to end, in the certainty that they could advance on the project whatever happened.

Managerial Contribution

- The first managerial contribution of this chapter is to offer clear indications on how to "decipher" group regression situations, and to enable a project manager to identify these stages. Identifying a problem is the first step toward a solution.
- The second contribution is to provide some "axes for reflection" on the way to manage these situations. We would underline W. Bion's assertion that it is impossible for a group in regression to admit its state. We suggest that to move a group in regression into a phase of production, there are two types of energy to leverage: extraction and incitation energy. We will not examine this any further at this point though, as it will be the focus of later studies.

> We are always surprised by the considerable efforts that we have to make to encourage members of a team to write anything down. They can hold a long discussion and be in agreement, without ever producing any evidence of the fruit of these discussions. Time after time, we find ourselves repeating: "Why are you not writing down what you are saying?"

We also wish to highlight that we are convinced of the power of the "mediating object." It is not by giving a speech to team members, however charismatic, that a temporary group can be pulled out of a regression. It is preferable for the group to tune into a concrete reality that it has lost sight of, which is the need to produce.

Conclusion

The life cycle of temporary groups, developed on the basis of the works of R.D. Laing, enables an in-depth analysis of the dynamics on project teams, whose similarity to groups is clear. As such, project teams have a strong emotional dimension and especially in the stages of creation. These underlying emotions make their behavior often incomprehensible to the uninitiated. Especially in periods that are known as transitory and sometimes even without any discernible cause, the group can generate some feedback, increase the instability experienced and resort to operational modes that are characteristic of regressions. The production of the project group stops and the various actions of the team members can seem childish, moody and illogical. It is at this moment that the project manager can benefit from understanding the internal workings of the project team to discover a reality he was hitherto unaware of. This knowledge of reality is inaccessible to the different team members but can guide the manager toward appropriate actions.

The application of the life cycle to the development of a project team opens the way toward effective managerial actions. If the part object enables a common model to be set up and facilitates the movement from a regrouping to a true group, then the project team can build reality, "becoming it." In the same way that a part object helps the group to form, then the transitional object provides a concrete way into the project when it still resides in the virtual world.

References

Anzieu, D. and Martin, J.-Y. (1997), *La dynamique des groupes restreints*, 11th edition, Puf, Paris.

Bion, W.R. (1987), *Recherches sur les petits groupes*, 5th edition, Puf, Paris.

Debourse, J.-P. (1991), "La terminaison des projets," *La Cible*, no. 38.

Declerck, R.P., Debourse, J.-P. and Declerck, J.C. (1997), *Le management stratégique, Contrôle de l'irréversibilité*, Les éditions ESC Lille, Euralille.

Devillard, O. (2000), *La dynamique des équipes*, Editions d'Organisation, Paris.

Katzenbach, J.R. and Smith, D.K. (1984), *The Wisdom of Teams*, HarperBusiness, New York.

Katzenbach, J.R. (1998), *The Work of Teams*, 8th edition, Harvard Business Review Book.

Laing, R.D. and Cooper, D.G. (1971), *Reason and Violence: A Decade of Sartre's Philosophy 1950–1960*, Pantheon Books, New York.

Maders, H.-P. (2000), *Conduire une équipe projet*, Editions d'Organisation, Paris.

Pages, M. (1997), *La Vie affective des Groupes*, Dunod Editeur, Paris.

Petit, M. (1999), *Management d'équipe*, Concepts et pratiques, Dunod, Paris.

Ruesch, J. (1972), *Distributed Communication. The Clinical Assesment of Normal and Pathological Communicative behavior*, W.W. Norton and Co, Inv., New York.

Segal, H. (1997), *Introduction à l'œuvre de Mélanie Klein*, 8th edition, Puf, Paris.

Winnicott, D.W. (1975), *Jeu et réalité—L'espace potentiel*, Editions Gaillimard, Paris.

Chapter 9

A Sustainable Approach for Project Management Performance

Jean-Charles Hainglaise and Laurence Lecoeuvre

Introduction

In the context of a changing world and a competitive market, business performance is a moving feast. Performance in managing projects implies not only improving project practices but also training and educating project teams.

This chapter, based on a case study, analyses the organization of a company whose aim is to sustain knowledge and know-how for project implementers. More generally it points out the conditions for providing sustainable practices to the people working on projects.

There are three factors that enable performance optimization within project management practices, which seem to be pre-requisite:

1   a baseline of internal project management practices;
2   efficient improvement process of those practices;
3   an organization that sustains a high level of skills among its project teams.

These three key issues need to be integrated effectively in order to provide the company with a high level of competencies and sustainable performance in project management.

If any one of the components of this triad-system fails, project performance will be undermined.

This chapter proposes a view of the interaction of these key issues, and suggests a way to optimize a systemic golden triangle.

Recent research by Eric Verzuh (2003) based on the study of 26 companies of varying sizes determines that implementing specific project management practices allows actual project performance improvement; particularly in terms of completing projects on budget and on time.

In this perspective the chapter investigates the relation between project management practices and the project team and its effect on project performance.

For Parking et al. (2005), "Sustainable project management consists also in developing sustainable skills in the company." In other terms project performance implies not only having the best processes, but also the knowledge and the systems to use and adapt them.

Thus this chapter also investigates the ability to set a baseline of practices that continuously improve within time and company environment changes. In particular it will analyse interactions between different roles involved in project performance.

The chapter opens with a literature review, notably around the notions of baseline, of process improvement and of training within the field of project management. There follows an analysis of the case study itself, describing the causes and the effects of an organizational change; and finally the authors propose a systemic approach to improve and sustain project management competencies.

Project Management: Baseline, Process Improvement and Training

Project Management Baseline

A project management baseline is a methodological point of reference that enables people to work together on the same processes, templates and glossary (Vanhoucke, 2012). It notably lists the practices that project teams have to apply on their project (Schwalbe, 2010).

Sustainability in project management practices is easier if a common baseline exist. Indeed if project teams use different glossaries, processes or templates, the aim of keeping a permanent level of performance in running project will be difficult to reach (op. cit., 2010).

Figure 9.1 provides an example of how a company can structure a methodological baseline of practices. The focus is done on risk management but the logic will remain the same for other project management practices such as cost management or procurement management.

A proper risk baseline enables project teams not only to share a common vision on the risk management objectives and processes but also it will provide them the means to implement them.

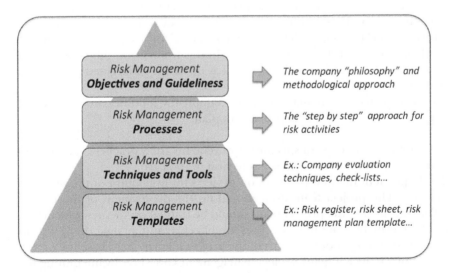

Figure 9.1 An Example of a Risk Management Baseline

It is the "maturation" of individuals' experiences, good or bad, which a baseline of practices attempts to summarize. For example, imagine a rugby team where the players are required to reinvent the rules at the beginning of each match: their performance can never be anything but immature.

Moreover a project management baseline needs be adapted on a continual basis to the company environment that moves with the market, with the customer's habits, with new laws or changes in recognized standards. Thus the practices on projects should be adapted to match the new environment. Of course, some core elements of the baseline remain the same over time, but the operational processes that describe the detailed steps to achieve an activity will need to be adjusted.

A new project environment might be defined by new mandatory legislation (environmental duty of diligence, for example) or by the decision of the company itself to seek certification and apply a set of norms (ISO for example). Either factor will involve changes in the way you implement projects. The market also can influence the scope of requisite practice for example in the application of new type of contracts; many companies are moving from "selling simple products" to "selling product and service bundles." A typical example is Public–Private Partnerships (PPPs) which operate against a contractual environment that focuses on services.

Consequently, it's not sufficient to provide teams with a project management baseline. You also need to put in place an effective improvement process alongside (see also Kerzner, 2002).

Project Management Process Improvement

An improvement process is basically a set of structured activities that enable the improvement of practices in a domain. Different approaches for improving processes exist, many of which involve a reflective loop (see for instance, Adesola and Baines, 2005).

The typical example is the Deming's Plan Do Check Act (PDCA); an iterative four-step management method used in business for the control and continuous improvement of processes and products. This method consists of four steps, each leading to another, and aims to establish a virtuous circle. In this framework, the frequency of the "improvement loops" is to be defined as well as the scope of targeted practices to be improvement.

The PDCA can be declined in many ways. As example the following steps represent the possible activities for a specific improvement plan:

- Plan (P): Identify the scope of specific improvements (new practices) and organize their implementation on a chosen selection of projects.
- Do (D): Implement the new practices on projects for evaluation of the practices effectiveness. The project team itself should do the deployment of those practices. That means that the project team should be trained on the new practices.
- Check (C): Verify that the new practices are effective and analyse the results in order to decide if they should be part of the project management baseline or not.
- Act (A): Improve the company project management know-how by integrating the new practices that have been validated in the previous phase into the project management baseline.

The ability of the organization to manage an improvement process efficiently is a key issue if it is to meet the market expectations. It is a long-term process that many stakeholders of the company must take into consideration. This is the same idea that one trainer developed in StudyCo (see our case study described later): "The business needs of the organization must drive the improvement work. If you are not able to correlate the work of improvement with the benefit to the specific organization, the senior management will not support the improvement work for the long run."

PDCA provides a global approach for setting an improvement process methodology. The project management baseline must not only exist and continuously improve, but also the project teams have to be trained and skilled in order to implement the processes efficiently. This last point implies adapted training.

Project Management Training

According to the Project Management Institute (PMI):[1] "organizations that offer training in project management are more efficient and better equipped for the challenges of the constantly evolving business environment . . . . People manage your projects. Even if your organization's established processes have been refined over the years, it's up to your employees to follow and further improve them."

Training in project management consists of providing project members and stakeholders with all the skills needed to run projects. Those skills include not only "hard skills" (techniques, methodologies etc.) but also "soft skills" such as the ability to work in team, or to communicate.

As described in the International Competencies Baseline (ICB) edited by the International Project Management Association (IPMA), the scope of skills is wide; and for that reason, special attention should be paid to identifying the training scope.

An observation over a period of ten years carried out by one of the authors (working as consultant and trainer at this period) reveals that the efficiency of a training programme is strongly linked to the ability to precisely identify the training scope. Since this process depends on different factors such as the operational need, the project management baseline evolutions and the trainee's skills, it can be a complicated and time-consuming activity.

Indeed, project management training scope can be surprisingly broad. As one speaker said to introduce a training into an international company:

> Gone are the days when a project manager was simply required to plan, do reporting, monitor his progress through appropriate measures, manage the requirements of the customers and manage sub-contractors; today the role of a programme manager is expected to face challenges that require more than simple management techniques as quoted above. He faces decisional management based on very precise knowledge of market issues, to be able forecast risks and opportunities and manage them permanently. He is expected to be able to communicate internationally to handle not only integrated programme teams but also go a step further to handle programme management quantitatively.

---

1 See http://www.pmi.org/Business-Solutions/Talent-Management-Project-Management-Training.aspx, accessed January 2016.

As the scope of project management training becomes more complex so the need for it to be strongly linked with the reality of project grows.

The following case study will analyse how project management baseline and training interact and play a role in providing the company with effective practices and project teams.

Research Methodology

This chapter is based on a case study that takes place within an industrial and international large company recognized for its know-how in managing complex contracts. The company will be called "StudyCo."

StudyCo is organized into different business units that manage contracts and projects in their specific fields. The headquarters of StudyCo manages the overall strategy of the company.

The qualitative approach used for this research corresponds to a longitudinal study of 12 years, based on participant observation and interviews. More than 100 stakeholders were interviewed (top managers, project managers, project team, quality managers). Fifty projects of different natures (technical projects, training engineering projects and process improvement projects) were observed, analysed and evaluated.

The aim of the study was to identify the key elements that can provide performing project management practices; and how those elements interact together.

To do so one question was particularly analysed: did the organizational changes in StudyCo influence the performance in in the implementation of project management practices?

The study analysed the causes and consequences of organizational changes on project teams and proposed a consequent organization based on a systemic approach.

The method of long-term observation fits the aim of the study as it enables first, to have a "helicopter view" (overall view) and second, to get a detailed analysis of the causes and consequences of organizational changes over the project management baseline control.

Results and Discussion

The research showed a decrease in project management performances within StudyCo over a period of 12 years. Based on the causes analysis of this declining situation, the authors suggested practical recommendations; they also proposed an organization to prevent such a problem with an efficient implementation in the framework of a "systematic approach."

The authors focused on analysing the interactions between the organizational changes and evolutions regarding project management baseline and training.

Case Study Analysis

Over a period of 12 years, the performance of StudyCo in project management has decreased significantly. This has been notable in the difficulty shown by the project team to implement the project management baseline properly in 2012, whereas in 2000 the project management baseline was well applied on project.

The following part will first provide a "status" of the respondent's perception over three periods: from 2000 to 2004, from 2004 to 2008 and then from 2008 to 2012. Second it will analyse the changes, notably in the responsibilities regarding project management baseline, project management improvements and project management training.

Evolution Regarding Project Management Baseline

The project management baseline is composed of a set of practices that project teams implement on projects. In this context, the perception of the project team seems relevant in order to evaluate the effectiveness of a new practice.

Table 9.1 shows the evolution of the project management baseline and the "ability" for the project teams to implement the practices coming from the project management baseline. In the table, the term "ability" means the perceived level of effort and/or difficulty of the respondents to implement practices.

Table 9.1 shows that changes made on the project management baseline had an effect on the ease and ability for the project teams to implement the practices.

Table 9.1 Project Management Baseline Evolutions over Time

	Description of the Project Management Baseline Evolutions over Time	Ability to Implement the Practices
2000–2004	Project management baselines are based on core practices at the company level and detailed at the business unit level. Those core practices are more "engineering oriented" than "process oriented."[2]	Good "Engineering oriented practices well understood and considered as an operational guideline."
2004–2008	The previous baseline has been replaced by a new baseline, more process oriented. Project management processes defined at the group level are to be adapted by each business unit depending their projects specificities.	Quite good "Process oriented practices quite well understood but considered too generic and not easy to adapt."
2008–2012	Another new and much larger process oriented baseline has replaced the previous baseline. The company baseline includes detailed processes that each business units must apply depending on the project's typologies. Some adjustments remain possible by business units but they are more limited than in the previous baseline.	Poor "Process oriented practices not well understood and considered as a constraint to be applied."

2 In this context "engineering oriented" means that the project life cycle is strongly linked to the engineering process and that the project management practices focus on delivering engineering milestones. "Process oriented" practices means that project management activities are defined by a process to be applied.

The perception of the project teams in 2012 is that the project management baseline becomes too hard to implement efficiently, notably for the following reasons:

- baseline's scope is too wide: project teams cannot find the good document;
- difficulties in identifying what is mandatory and what is not;
- complexity of processes: lack of time in critical phases of projects;
- complexity in adapting the processes to the project context.

The project management baseline identifies practices that are to be implemented on a project and its successive evolutions have to be adopted by the project team.

Within the studied period, the project management baseline moved from "engineering oriented" core practices to a full set of "process oriented" practices.

Figure 9.2 helps to understand the project management baseline evolutions between 2000 and 2012. It shows the estimated volume of documentation linked to each project management baseline components.

In 2000 the project management baseline was composed of core guidelines and recommendations to be completed (and eventually adapted), whereas in 2008 the project management baseline was composed of detailed processes to be adapted (and eventually completed).

The size of the project management baseline itself has increased, growing from approximately 50 core documents in 2000 to more than 120 documents in 2008. This major change is mainly due to project management processes, the number of which has significantly increased between 2004 and 2008.

This strategic change, decided by the StudyCo headquarters, is a key issue for understanding the impact on project teams' work.

Interviews with project teams reveal that an appropriate project management baseline should include sustainable processes that should be:

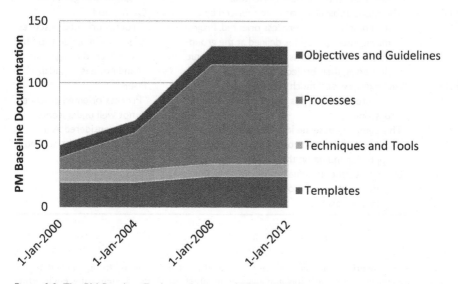

Figure 9.2 The PM Baseline Evolution between 2000 and 2012

Note: PM—Project management.

- adapted to the company organization;
- adapted to the project's typologies;
- adapted to the skills of the project teams who are in charge of their implementation;
- always improving, taking into consideration the points below.

Processes aim to secure project delivery. Nevertheless inappropriate processes may lead to the following question: "Should the project team deliver performance or processes?" In other words, a possible reaction towards processes is to reduce the project team "Respons-Ability," notably because they feel they have less autonomy. Those questions are not analysed in the present study but should be one of the key issues in project management performance.

The changes on the project management baseline have impacted the training contents. Indeed the skills needed to implement guidelines (project management baseline, version 2000) are slightly different to the skills needed to adjust a large set of processes (project management baseline, version 2012).

Evolution Regarding Project Management Trainings

Over the studied period, the project management training also evolved, having an effect on the projects teams and practices. The project teams' perception of project management training have been analysed thanks to feedback and interviews.

Table 9.2 shows the evolution of project management training within the group and the respondents' perception.

Table 9.2 Project Management Training Evolutions over Time

	Description of Project Management Training Evolutions over Time	Suitability for Project Teams' Needs
2000–2004	Training content oriented on "product management": Pedagogical approach based on the "product life cycle" including engineering processes and project management techniques and tools.*	Very well adapted. Project management techniques and tools are in accordance with operational needs and the engineering process.
2004–2008	Training content oriented on "project management": Pedagogical approach based on the "project life cycle" including project processes and project management techniques and tools.	Well adapted. Project management processes are presented in order to fit with the engineering practices on projects.
2008–2012	Training content oriented on "processes management": Pedagogical approach based on the processes baseline including project management techniques and tools.	Poorly adapted. Project management processes are seen as a "must do" with little leeway affecting the ability to apply project management techniques and tools properly.

* PM techniques and tools are the activities implemented to deliver the PM core elements such as PERT, WBS, PBS, Risk analysis etc.

Table 9.2 shows that evolutions over time have made the project management training less adapted to the project teams' needs.

The perception of the project teams in 2012 is that the project management training has become less adapted for the following reasons:

- training contents are too much focused on the processes and not enough on project management techniques;
- they are not business related enough;
- processes are seen as a "must do" with little room for manoeuvre;
- too much time is spent on learning about "processes" instead of learning about core project management techniques and tools.

The next part of the chapter will address the organizational changes in StudyCo and notably which entities were responsible for the project management baseline and for the project management training.

Organizational Changes Analysis

During the observation period, there have been changes within the StudyCo organization regarding who is in charge of project management issues. Those changes impacted not only the "responsibilities ownership" but also the "scope of responsibilities."

The "scope of responsibilities" that has been studied is the following:

- Project management baseline: Who is responsible for providing an efficient project management baseline to the project teams? This includes baseline update and configuration management.
- Process improvement in project management: Who is responsible for managing the improvement approach towards project management processes?
- Project management training: Who is responsible for providing the project management training for the project team? This includes training engineering and implementation.

The main actors ("responsibilities ownership") involved in the project management issues are the following:

- Headquarters: Its role is to manage the overall strategy of "StudyCo."
- Programme directors: Located in the business units, they supervise projects.
- Quality managers: Located in the business units they manage all quality aspects.
- Project management baseline owner: Located in a dedicated transverse unit in charge of capitalization and methodology shared between the business units.
- Project management training manager: Located in "StudyCo" corporate university. They have a transverse role on project management training.

Table 9.3 shows the evolution of the responsibly sharing over a period of 12 years within StudyCo.

Table 9.3 Evolution of Responsibility Sharing

R: Responsible A: Accountable C: Consulted I: Informed	Headquarters	Programme Directors	Quality Managers	Project Management Baseline Owner	Project Management Training Manager
2000–2004 Project management baseline	C	C	A	R	C
Process improvement in project management	C	C	R	A	C
Project management training	C	C	I	A	R
2004–2008 Project management baseline	R	C	A	C	C
Process improvement in project management	A	C	R	C	I
Project management training	A	C	I	C	R
2008–2012 Project management baseline	R	C	A	C	I
Process improvement in project management	R	I	A	C	I
Project management training	R	C	I	I	A

Table 9.3 reveals that decision-making over project management issues has moved from the business units to the headquarters; but the most important element pointed out by respondents is that all key decisions have been centralized and not shared among different instances.

The study shows a decrease in effectiveness of decision-making processes that has affected:

- the quality of the project management baseline that, in 2012, is considered too far from the operational needs;
- the effectiveness of the training in project management that are consider too "process oriented";
- and finally the skills of the project team themselves that are lost in too wide a baseline which is more process oriented than project oriented.

Observations and interviews reveal that failures in the decision-making process are not a question of competencies of the people themselves but more about having a centralized organization. As a manager said, "Decision-making dealing with project management issues is centralized into one hand and PM stakeholders are not always involved." Consequently centralized decision-making can lead to poor decisions if it is not linked to people's needs.

As underlined by the study, the decrease in organizational efficiency is mostly due to a centralized decision-making system. Consequently, the following part of the chapter proposes an organization and decision-making approach that aims to provide a high level of performance in the implementation of project management practices.

Proposition of a "Triad-Systemic Model"

The term "systemic" refers to the idea of global, integrated correlative elements; for example, when a company puts in place a system of knowledge management, a purely technical vision of the project, without taking into account human and economic aspects, will certainly lead to failure.

Based on the previous analysis, the next part of the chapter will present an organization which aims to clearly split the responsibilities over three key areas: project management baseline, process improvement and project management training. This organization can be seen as a triangle where each angle of the triangle represents the key core activities that are linked together. This "triangular vision" proposes a way to implement a strategy that enables organizations to reach high-level performance in the implementation of project management practices.

Each angle of the triangle represents the activities that must be carried out in order to contribute to sustainable and efficient project management practices. The "objective tree" in Table 9.4 resumes the triangle strategic vision.

Each "intermediate objective" not only contributes to the achievement of the "overall objective" but also interacts with the others and facilitates improvement. For example project management processes must continuously improve in order to maintain an effective project management baseline.

To implement this vision several stakeholders need to be involved. The next part of the chapter presents the key roles of such an organization.

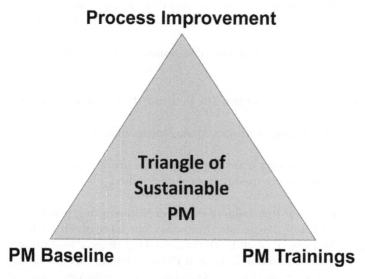

Figure 9.3 Triangle of Sustainable PM

Note: PM—Project management.

Table 9.4 Objective Tree of Sustainable Project Management

Overall Objective

To Provide the Organization with Sustainable Performance in Project Management

Intermediate Objectives

Process improvement	Project management baseline	Project management training
To continuously improve project management processes.	To maintain an effective project management baseline.	To provide the organization with the highest level of skills on projects.

Roles in the System

Various players need to be involved and the analysis of StudyCo showed that lots of interactions, either formal or informal, exist between those stakeholders. The study revealed that the three core responsibilities that must be part of the decision-making process regarding project management issues are:

- A representative of the process improvement: To continuously improve the project management processes.
- A representative of the project management baseline: To maintain an effective project management baseline.
- A representative of the project management training: To provide the organization with the highest level of skills on projects.

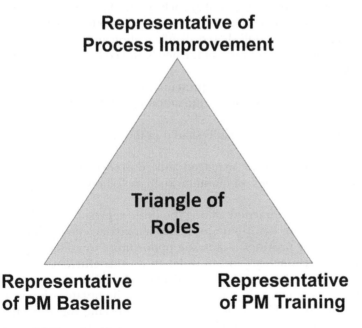

Representative of Process Improvement

Triangle of Roles

Representative of PM Baseline

Representative of PM Training

Figure 9.4 Triangle of Roles

Note: PM—Project management.

Table 9.5 Strength of the Interactions between Stakeholders in StudyCo

Strength of Interactions: 1 = low 5 = high	Project Teams	Quality Managers	Training Managers	HR Managers	Process Owners
Representative of project management baseline	2	4	2	1	3
Representative of process improvement in project management	5	5	1	1	5
Representative of project management training	4	2	5	4	1

Those three key roles need not only to interact with each other but also with StudyCo's many other stakeholders.

Table 9.5 shows the strengths of interactions among a selection of key stakeholders. In our case study the strength of interactions is the estimated frequency of contacts between two stakeholders.

Table 9.5 shows that the strength of interactions is the highest between the three representatives and the project teams. This result is actually expected, as project teams indeed learn and implement the project management practices.

Quality managers and training managers also play a role in the system, as they are involved in process improvement and training respectively. Of course some interactions occur with the process owners because of the transversal action of project management.

Moreover the main result of this analysis is that each of the three representatives of the triangle had a part of the information. This information is complementary and must be shared. If each representative duly shared all information and interacted with each other they would be able to identify most of the needs and constraints of project management stakeholders.

It means that, working together, the three representatives can analyse and elaborate the best solutions for the company, taking into account a global systemic vision of the needs.

Table 9.6 lists some of the information that is shared in the case study among the three representatives.

These flows of information should be managed and controlled by someone in authority who is able to make decisions on questions such as "Where do we want to go and how?"

An example is an interesting interaction among the three representatives below on how the training feedback can contribute to the project management baseline improvement. Indeed training provides a fantastic opportunity to collect operational feedback about project practices and in order to do this efficiently strong interactions between the three representatives are needed. Those three actors interact together to achieve the main aim, that is, to provide the organization with sustainable project performance. If they don't succeed in working together, the overall aim may not be reached.

Table 9.6 Information Case Study

	Inputs	Outputs
Representative of Process Improvement	Operational needs Problems faced during project implementation (process or tools implementation...) Results of projects audits Project team member needs, training feedbacks, company orientation and audit results...	Proposed new practices Identified best practices on projects Lessons learned documentation...
Representative of Project Management Baseline	Operational needs Proposed new practices New methodological standards of the market Change in company quality baseline Specific requests from customers Top management request for changes...	Benchmark on project management practices: International standards Other company practices Baseline engineering: Status of the baseline Main evolutions New release of the project management baseline...
Representative of Project Management Training	Operational needs New release of the project management baseline Identified best practices on projects Lessons learned documentation Typology of population to be trained...	Forecast training needs Training feedbacks: Problems faced during project implementation (process or tools implementation...) Difficulties in implementing certain project management processes Proposition of good practices implemented on project...

Interaction and Governance between Key Players

The three representatives of the triangle shown in Figure 9.5 need to interact, make common decisions and share information.

Each arrow between the three roles represents a flow of information or decision to be made. An example of those interactions, the following "logical approach" aims to keep high-level skills people in the company:

- If we want sustainable project management, we need project teams to be well skilled.
- If we want project teams to be well skilled, we need to provide them with good training.
- If we want good training, we need an adapted project management baseline.
- If we want an adapted project management baseline, we need to continuously improve it.

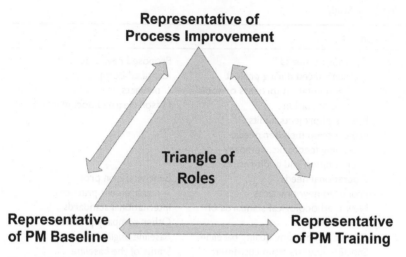

**Representative of
Process Improvement**

**Triangle of
Roles**

**Representative
of PM Baseline**   **Representative
of PM Training**

Figure 9.5 Triangle of Roles—Interactions

Note: PM—Project management.

The study shows that proper governance is crucial to enable efficient decision-making. According to respondents, the governance is specific to each organization and the following recommendations could help to define governance rules:

Recommendation 1: Not Cumulating the Roles

The study reveals that cumulating the three above-mentioned roles would significantly decrease the efficiency of the system for different reasons:

- Be judge and party: human nature will lead to make non-effective "shortcuts" (for example because lack of team objectives etc.).
- Lack for challenging options: the three roles should challenge themselves and cumulating those roles may reduce the opportunities for constructive debate. Self-challenging our own ideas is a challenge itself.
- Mind-oriented: preference for one role of the triangle and neglecting the two others roles will have a consequence on the overall objective.
- Lack of competencies: each component of the triangle represents a specific field of expertise; and one actor could have difficulties in achieving all three intermediate triangle objectives.

Recommendation 2: A Dedicated Committee

In order to control the decision-making, the case study reveals that a dedicated committee accountable for the "overall objective" should coordinate the systemic approach. That guarantees the effectiveness of the "triangle approach."

This committee shall be composed of at least the three representatives of the triangle but other stakeholders may contribute directly or indirectly in order to "feed" the committee, such as:

- The project teams: they represent the operational needs and their feedbacks are to be taken into consideration.
- Process owners: their work concerns mainly processes that have an interaction with the project management processes (procurement, human resources, information system etc.).
- Human resources managers: they present the forecast in terms of project manpower needs at the company level.
- Training managers: training in interaction with the project management processes (procurement, system engineering etc.).

Finally, the "triad-vision" needs to be monitored at the company level and challenged by the project management stakeholders.

Recommendation 3: A Strategic Vision

In order to develop project management sustainability those recommendations should also be supported by a strategic analysis at the company level:

- Where do we want to go? Question to be addressed to top management taking into account the company objectives towards projects typology and complexity.
- Where can we go? Question to be addressed to economic environment taking into account opportunities and threats.
- Where should we go? Question to be addressed to the market environment taking into account the internal and external stakeholders.
- Where are we able to go? Question to be addressed to the company itself taking into account its resources and competences.

Those four questions help to develop a strategic vision as a framework for the committee.

Managing performance in projects becomes more and more strategic for companies as they are increasingly involved in complex and numerous projects. For that reason sustainability in project management is strongly linked with sustainability of the company itself.

Conclusion and Perspectives

The components of the system presented in the case study that enable sustainable project management practices are the following:

- a project management baseline that is the reference for project management practices;
- an improvement process that enables continuous improvement of the project management practices;
- a training organization that enables people to apply those practices efficiently.

The case study shows us that each of the three components of the triangle is important and can't be neglected without having a negative impact on project management sustainability.

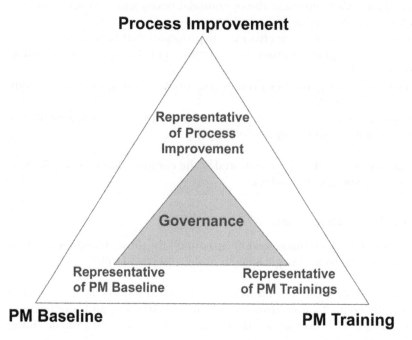

Process Improvement

PM Baseline

PM Training

Figure 9.6 Triangle of the Triad-Systemic Model

Note: PM—Project management.

These components interact together and have to be coordinated if we want to be efficient. The recommendations made within this study must be adapted, taking into account the company environment. Indeed, even if the logic remains the same, each context has to be analysed before implementing any methodological approach.

The environmental factors that can have an impact on the tailoring of the activities are, for example:

- Company typology: size, type of activities, international/regional context, culture etc.
- Project typology: size, internal/external projects, project scope, contractual constraints in terms of project management practices etc.
- Project management practices maturity: existing methodological baseline, level of skills of project teams and so on.
- Training approach: internal/external solutions, mandatory training or chosen training, ways to access to training etc.

A key issue is to have an efficient decision-making system that enables effective interactions between the three components of the triangle.

The authors recognize that the recommendations would be difficult to apply in small-sized companies where limited resources may mean that the three roles need to be cumulated.

Finally, future perspectives for the research would be: (1) to validate the robustness of the triad-system with a significant number of case studies and in different environments of projects; and (2) to analyse how the triad-system could contribute to projects' governance.

References

Adesola, S. and Baines, T. (2005) "Developing and evaluating a methodology for business process improvement," *Business Process Management Journal*, Vol. 11, No. 1, pp. 37–46.

Kerzner, H. (2002) *Strategic Planning for Project Management Using a Project Management Maturity Model.* Chichester: John Wiley & Sons.

Parking, S., Johnston, A., Buckland, H., Brookes, F. and White, E. (2005) "Learning and Skills for Sustainable Development," Forum HEPS Learning and Skills for Sustainable Development.

Schwalbe, K. (2010) *Information Technology Project Management*, 6th edition. Course Technologie, Cengage Learning.

Vanhoucke, M. (2012) *Project Management with Dynamic Scheduling—Baseline Scheduling, Risk Analysis and Project Control.* Berlin: Springer.

Verzuh, E. (2003) *The Portable MBA in Project Management.* Chichester: John Wiley & Sons.

Part IV

Project Standards and Sustainable Performance

Pour l'instant vivez les questions. Peut-être, un jour lointain, entrerez-vous ainsi, peu à peu, sans l'avoir remarqué, à l'intérieur de la réponse.

For now, live issues. Perhaps, in some distant day, you will gradually, without noticing it, enter within the answer.

Rainer Maria Rilke, 1929 (Lettres à un jeune poète)

Project Standards and Sustainable Performance

Chapter 10

Sustainable Capability Building in the Public Sector—Focus Gateway™ Reviews

Sarah Ross[1,2]

Introduction

Independent Quality Assurance (IQA) has been adopted as common, if not best practice, in public sector Projects for many years. One form of IQA is Gateway™, a best practice approach, licensed from the UK Cabinet Office that has wholesale Central Government-led uptake in the United Kingdom (UK), Australia and New Zealand (NZ). My interest in Gateway™ as a structure, process and outcome is in its intent, design and delivery for better public spending results in NZ, having based an earlier work on Gateway's™ role in sustainable capability building in the public sector.

From a NZ perspective, Gateway™ Reviews have successfully contributed to Project and Programme outcomes using an independent assurance approach. They are, however, an additional Project or Programme (initiative) cost that has been mandated since 2008 by NZ Cabinet for certain high risk initiatives and initiatives whose Whole of Life (Project and post Project) costs exceed a threshold value in importance, complexity and risk profile. Reviews are designed to periodically assess at key decision points along the trajectory that the continuing investment decision remains justified as linked to forecast Benefits Realisation and attainment of strategic objectives. For risk-sensitive organisations, such as those in the public sector, uncertainty reduction in the form of objective assurance offered by independent experts can be considered a safety net for "brand" government. Assurance reviews are apolitical and confidential to the government organisation concerned. They aim to have free and frank discussions with stakeholders (thus, statements are designed to be non-attributable to permit this) on a periodic basis (key milestones where performance can be assessed).

The review itself is wide reaching and entails significant planning to appropriate levels of depth and breadth to give confidence that these government-sponsored initiatives add value. This is achieved through independent and integrated assurance

1 Thanks to the New Zealand Gateway Unit for its assistance: Celia van Vliet, Programme Manager, Gateway New Zealand Treasury and Mel Wallwork, Senior Advisor, IMAP (Investment Management and Asset Performance), New Zealand Treasury.
2 Disclaimer: the views expressed in this chapter do not purport to represent the views of the UK Office of Government Commerce (for Gateway™) nor any part of the New Zealand Government Sector. Data for this chapter was originally gathered as part of an earlier doctoral thesis using New Zealand as a case study where Gateway™ Reviews are accepted as Best Practice.

from a review team of experts who report recommendations in the form of confidence ratings to the go/no go decision makers on whether an initiative is likely to achieve its objectives pre and post implementation. Like *Janus*, the Roman God, the review team looks backwards and forwards to literally "project" and "predict" and "recommend" whether intended results can be achieved and remain desirable, achievable, viable and that the investment remains sound.

If the above can be seen as the upside value there can also be considered a down-side of occasional distraction for the host organisation. Reviews are a "Project" in themselves—expensive, time consuming, require resourcing and must work within matrix management constraints where expert judgement, interviews, meetings, evidence-based work performance information and the like are all required to com-pile review findings for the host Project/Programme organisation and monitoring units. These findings and confidence ratings have sway but do not have authority in themselves; and when coupled with occasional confusion as to whether reviews are conducted as advisory (that can be ignored/accepted) or as assurance where a poor rating does not mean stop, nor does a favourable rating mean go; may be misunder-stood and their importance underestimated.

Role of Gateway™ Review and Responsibility of Government—a Marriage Made in Heaven

A purpose of a monitoring unit requiring Gateway™ Reviews on initiatives is to seek organisational consistency, frequency, reliability, precision and predictability of prac-tice towards goal achievement. Some of the recommended underpinning capabilities (practices)—building sustainability processes—can be classified under Compliance and Performance, Assurance and Guidance, and Strategic Alignment, Risk reduction and Benefits Realisation (State Services Commission (SSC), 2011b). Gateway™ is the bridge between capability development and sustainable outcomes through ensuring the initial candidate Project/Programme remains "right" for the customer (business, users, influencers, governance roles, and beneficiaries). While the Gateway™ Reviews themselves are confidential, longitudinal analysis of recommendations has pointed to a number of shortcomings in capability (across a number of areas) and pointed to a number of recommendations for improvement.

At Project level, Gateway™ Reviews are as follows and may be periodically repeated as needed i.e. Gates 3 and 5:

- Review 0: Strategic Assessment.
- Review 1: Business Justification and Options—Indicative Business Case.
- Review 2: Delivery Strategy—Detailed Business Case.
- Review 3: Investment Decision.
- Review 4: Readiness for Service.
- Review 5: Operational Review and Benefits Realisation.

At Programme level:

A series of Gate 0 review is repeated at intervals throughout the Programme life. A Programme will generally undergo three or more Gate 0 Reviews: an early review, one or more reviews at key decision points during the Programme (e.g. inter-tranche boundaries), and a final review near the conclusion of the Programme.

(SSC, 2013, p.2)

Gateway's introduction to NZ was via a successful pilot in 2008, its subsequent control was assigned to one of Government's "assurance arms," the SSC,[3] through their monitoring unit functions. In 2011 SSC published a benchmark summary review of findings from all Government sector Gateway™ Reviews, 2008–2011[4] (SSC, 2011a) (a second summary from 2011–2013 has since been published and will be referred to later). Whilst Gateway™ Reviews are confidential and the details confined to those principal stakeholders, these two studies permitted an insight into contextual lessons for the public sector and pointed to a number of good practices and shortcomings in capability (across a number of areas). In so doing, it informed with a number of recommendations for improvement as a basis of sectorial (inter-sectorial and cross-sectorial) better practices. In the first study of 2008–2011 608 summary/non-attributable recommendations linked to the 12 domains below were made; these were:

1 Business Case.
2 Project and Programmes.
3 Risk and Issue Management.
4 Stakeholder Management.
5 Resourcing.
6 Governance.
7 Programme and Project Planning.
8 Management of Change.
9 Sourcing Strategy.
10 Dependencies Management.
11 Financial Management.
12 Methodology.[5]

Positive, neutral and negative performance issues (capability) were highlighted against these primary domains;[6] they in turn related to wider relevant areas of structure, process and/or outcome. By way of example, findings concerned delivery mechanisms such as Project tools used, techniques applied, methods chosen and structures concerning governance arrangements for controls such as decision making, role delineation and accountabilities, documentation requirements and reporting. Whilst outcomes are a product of the structures and processes, the very quality of

---

3 Responsible for the policy making, review, roll out and coordination—Gateway™ Unit (a department within the SSC).
4 53 reviews undertaken across 33 Projects involving 25 Agencies entitled "Gateway™ Reviews Lessons Learned Report—2008–2011" (SSC, 2012).
5 SSC (2013)—second report—included additional categories of Transition into Service, Benefits Realisation and Capturing Previous Lessons.
6 The systemic approach of Projects means one issue could involve other issues. Example of risks affecting Business Case.

the initiative (Project selection and continuity) is as key as the outcome measurement perspectives. Expected capabilities were both evidenced and absent and whilst patterns emerged of accepted practice, common practice, good practice, better practice and best practice these were never consistently in one area, one sector, one location, one type of initiative when considering trended and single circumstance issues. Nonetheless, a sectorial performance picture emerged.

Assuring Sustainability and Defining Capability

The NZ SSC (2008, pp.6–7) states: "In a State Services context, capability is what an organization needs to deliver its outcomes now and in the future in a high-quality, efficient and timely way. Building and sustaining capability across all parts of an organisation and across the wider State Services is central to delivering results for New Zealanders." Organisational health, another term associated with capability, is a snapshot of capability—it describes an organisation's capability at a particular point in time. High levels of organisational health can be directly linked to high levels of overall performance. If sustainability were mathematically represented it might look something like the equation below.

$$\text{Innovation (Context + Capability + Transition)} = \text{Embedded Change (Outcomes Factored by Benefits − Disbenefits)}$$

Where:

- innovation is the idea/initiative;
- context is the organisational environment from which the Project is commissioned;
- capability is the things/outputs produced by the Project—ready to use;
- transition is changeover/hand over of outputs from Project into business as usual;
- outcomes are the changes and impacts occurring as a result of using Project outputs—the using;
- embedded change is sustained use—keeping the new and not reverting to old practices;
- benefits are measures of the outcomes;
- disbenefits are perceived negative outcomes.

Thus, Gateway™ informs on and is informed by capabilities used by the Agencies. It acts as a kind of glue that pulls other enablers (capabilities) by assessing and assuring whether a Project's and/or Programme's progress is on track to meet organisational targets—which are also Government targets. The Delivery Confidence given by the review team is indicative of future and forecast progress based upon current performance. The reviews are valid, however the process of them is still scrutinised. It is not always smooth sailing.

Post- and Pre-Mortem Stories of Assurance, Advice, Confidentiality and Double-Edged Swords

In 2010 KPMG/NZ (KPMG, 2011) surveyed Project practitioners in both private and public sectors across all industries and found that 36 percent of organisations reportedly did well on time (leaving 64 percent who did not), less than 50 percent reportedly did well on cost, nearly 50 percent reported failure to consistently deliver stated deliverables, and 29 percent of organisations consistently routinely monitor, control and report performance—making adjustments accordingly (leaving 71 percent who did not).

With a different approach in 2011 (SSC, 2011b, p.4) the SSC's, Project Monitoring Unit (closely aligned to the Gateway™ Unit as Major Projects are high risk[7]) reported trended issues concerning:

- capability/funding/capacity;
- over-optimism and unwarranted selection of leading edge products;
- competing priorities—working effectively with overseas counterparts versus sharing functionality across NZ Agencies;
- infrastructure costs assigned to projects;
- internal project assurance functions.

This report also cited a list of failure lessons submitted by the then Office of Government Commerce (OGC) in the UK. These Project lessons showed lack of the following and were not dissimilar to NZ findings from KPMG and the SSC Lessons Learned report (this was of interest as Gateway™ being a UK product needed to be a best fit also to NZ capability issues and Project context with similar issues requiring similar solutions).

- clear links between the Project and the organisation's key strategic priorities, including measures of success;
- senior management and ministerial ownership and leadership;
- effective engagement with stakeholders;
- skills and proven approach to Project management and risk management;
- attention in breaking down development and implementation activities into manageable steps;
- evaluation of proposals driven by initial price rather than long-term value for money (especially securing delivery of business benefits);
- understanding of, and contact with, the supply industry at senior levels in the organisation;
- effective Project team integration between clients, the supplier team and the supply chain.

From the UK, the National Audit Office (NAO)/OGC, in looking at common causes of Project failure, cited a "lack of clear link between the Project and the organisation's key strategic priorities, including agreed measures of success" (undated, p.1) citing:

- priority and alignment of Projects with other delivery and operational activities;
- critical success factors (CSFs) for the Project ill-defined;
- CSFs not agreed with suppliers and key stakeholders;[8]
- poor planning for delivery and all business change required, and Benefits Realisation.

---

7   SSC has an ongoing Project monitoring function for all Projects with a Whole of Life Cost exceeding 25 million $NZ.

8   CSF can also mean Causes of Spectacular Failure (origins of this statement unknown and unattributed).

From interviews conducted by the author with stakeholders involved with coordinating, commissioning and participating in Gateway™ Reviews, some of the mistakes reported were in applying best practices contributing to successful Project and Programme performance. The use of terminology (Interviewee Comment, 2012) for instance where " . . . we see publications from a range of sources—not just local—on PM, PPM, 3PM, 4PM, P3M, P3M3™, OPM3® etc . . . . you need a dictionary to work it out if it's the same or different," indicates the first element is communication, where Project and Programme jargon is a barrier.

The second element is that of ownership, governance and coordination of the practices *out there.* In interviews some people did not know who authored what, where it was located, when it was last updated and on occasion how to complete the tool or follow the guidance. Another element is seeing the links between the practices, as there is an element of seeing duplication/replication rather than unique purpose. So elements of streamlining, wider training/education and branding are needed. The idea is that the capabilities complement practice rather than compete with it.

A fourth element can be seen as the tools/techniques lack flexibility (this pointed to lack of understanding their purpose/potential etc.) and can be seen as an added burden to work rather than being the work or making the work less of a burden longer term. Also there is no apparent incentive or disincentive for complying with recommended practices and some key decision makers being removed from being able to advise their teams—this points to organisational leadership and follow-up. The other significant element is finding and keeping the talent to focus on the role needed at that time. It is not so much the tools and techniques themselves—it is the vision of how they enable practice as there are some people who consider they disable it.

As already mentioned, in an earlier unpublished PhD study (Ross, 2013), a series of interviews and case study analyses with UK, Australian and NZ Project/Programme results focused on Gateway™ as a capability and sustainability tool. In surveying public and private sectors, both in NZ and abroad, on utility of best practices and Gateway™ as an assurer, the following summaries were received from the reviewers, monitoring unit, users, Agency, Project manager and Programme manager perspectives. These are summarised:

- it's a communication tool, it's objective and it's inclusive;
- it is complementary to all audits and checks an organisation undertakes internally;
- it places accountability where it is needed;
- it is focused on due process and it reminds Agencies to take stock;
- it is about bi-directional free and frank information;
- it highlights external and cross dependencies as well as Programme and Portfolio issues;
- it gives peer review and it offers support and follow-up;
- it gives value and importance to the Project work;
- it is about risk management and uncertainty reduction;
- it offers a tight centralised team and framework in its Monitoring Unit;
- it brings in different reviewer expertise as needed;
- it can inform the Minister and on occasion Cabinet;
- it links and networks people and Projects;
- it offers consistency and it offers confidentiality;
- it offers a brand that is respected;
- it leaves the actions to the organisation's governance structure.

Can't do so robustly—the process at tactical and operational levels:

- it can't enforce compliance with the process;
- it can't enforce the private sector comply in Public Private Partnerships (PPP);
- its place as carrot or stick is ambiguous and thus misunderstood;
- its reports are cloaked in secrecy adding to confusion;
- it doesn't capture just under the threshold radar Projects;
- it doesn't capture Projects and Programmes flying under the threshold radar;
- it has little influence on the SRO post review actions;
- it needs a governance structure above it across the sector.

Table 10.1 shows the different lenses which Gateway™ is seen through.

In removing perception and observation from the equation and looking at data from assured Projects and Programmes from 2008–2013—Gateway™ performs. It may be seen as carrot or stick, depending on the viewer, yet it has made a difference. The numbers speak, as opposed to the members speaking. Table 10.2 shows a comparative between both reports formed the benchmark. Weightings Report 1 shows volume and findings from 2008–2011. Weightings Report 2 shows from 2011–2013 (SSC, 2013). In the first report the six areas of Business Case, Issue and Risk Management, Stakeholder Management, Governances, Resourcing, and Programme and Project Management accounted for 75 percent of the issues identified. In the second report these domains accounted for 64 percent of all issues.

The second report by SSC presented lessons and analysis from 45 Gateway™ reports conducted across 34 Projects and Programmes involving 18 Agencies from March 2011–March 2013 making 540 recommendations. The weightings in column 3, Report 2 indicate movement, if any. Of note is a marked improvement in Business Case and a decline in Governance and Sourcing Strategies with SSC noting that "Positive lessons learned tend to emerge as Projects progress to second and subsequent reviews" (SSC, 2013). Some of these could well have been a continuation to conclusion of Projects/ Programmes cited in the earlier report, with SSC noting that positive lessons emerge as initiatives move from review to review—Building on *recommendations capital*.

Table 10.1 Comparative Dilemmas

Stakeholder Lenses of Gateway™	Summary Viewpoints
Assurance vs. Advice	Advice
Carrot vs. Stick	Neutral, intended to be a helpful carrot-flavoured stick
Confidence vs. Cop Out	Confidence
Critical Success Factor vs KPI	Critical Success Factor
Customised vs. Productised	Customised
Dialogue vs. Monologue	Dialogue
Free and Frank vs. Fear and Favour	Free and Frank
Free vs. User Pays	Should be Free
Inclusive vs. Exclusive	Inclusive
Mandatory vs. Voluntary	Mandatory for all Projects Deemed High Risk
Motivates vs. Demotivates	Motivates
Recommendations vs. Teeth/Bite	Neutral
Responsibility vs. Accountability	Neutral

Table 10.2 Domains of Issue Concerning Delivery Confidence from 2008–2013 as Lessons Learned

Category	Domain Weighting Report 1 2011/100 Percent	Domain Weighting Report 2 2013/100 Percent	High Level Issue Definition/Description—Original from Report 1 2008–2011. 680 Benchmark Recommendations	The Difference or Similarity between the Two Reports. Why the Improvement? Why the Decline? Why the Status Quo? 540 Recommendations
Business Case	21%	15% Measurably improved	The "why" unclear in periods of the lifecycle through to Benefits Realisation. Initial justification and continued business justification—for timing, detail, costing, risk analysis and benefits management.	In 2010 NZ Government mandated Better Business Case Model through Treasury (BBC was introduced by Cab Circ CO(10)2 in 2010) The model ensured structure, progressions, iterations and accountabilities of the Business Case. In particular, Programme Business Cases inform Project ones and vice versa. They are dynamic and support the change implementation and embedding environment. The executive summary should be concise, show vision and alignment and make a compelling case for the investment. Early BC development must support the business decision and should provide go/no go. It should detail, among a range of elements, the business (esp. inter-Agency) impact, change capabilities and stakeholder impact.
Project and Programmes	12%	9% Measurably improved	Governance, reporting, competence, scoping, administration activities (management). Planning, reporting, systems and fully understanding assumptions, constraints and the end visions/ scoping. Hard to report and make decisions—control—if not clear on roles/responsibilities and objectives.	Systems integration common element for failure—consider a Portfolio approach to consider operational impacts thoroughly. In particular, customer facing staff can absorb and adapt to limited change at any time otherwise this affects continuity. Make sure Project work does not overtake Programme decisions. Internal Project delivery must have same rigour as external. Ensure Corporate Centre Monitoring, Gateway, and Independent Quality Assurance (IQA) agreed and managed. Programme documentation should not be dispersed. There should be one complete set with all work streams contributing.

Risks and Issue Management	12%	12% Neutral/status quo	Compliance, guidelines, standards, policies and strategies, tools and techniques. Identification, qualification, quantification, planning; data on daily dashboards/registers incomplete or inconsistent in information and ownership.	Risk methodology in identifying, assessing and controlling still poor with risk registers somewhat ad hoc and not always completed to fullest extent. Should undertake full security assessment, Risks and issues should be separated, shared services/inter-Agency have common and different risks and access to information by vendors/suppliers and their abilities to perform across multiple work streams need to be addressed. Quantitative Risk Assessment is mandatory for all complex Projects but should be considered as a best practice on all Projects. Programme SRO should meet Minister face to face on major change/transformational initiatives.
Stakeholder Management	11%	6% Measurably improved	Identification, analysis, engagement and ongoing management. Communication and multi-Agency stakeholder considerations (diversity, differing Agency missions/outcomes) across shared services needing more attention.	Lack of integrated scope and message in large initiatives. SRO needs to ensure messaging as "one-voice." Integrated stakeholder consultation needed. Establish a Working Group with local organisations as needed for liaison and consultation. Consider multiple ways to attain stakeholder input and engagement. Develop plans for stakeholders and communications.
Resourcing	10%	6% Measurably improved	Under identification/underestimations. Including skill base and preparedness to resource major Projects. Issues of putting rooky pilot in most expensive airplane without back up.	Good human resource planning will keep stability of a skills pool and assignments. Make sure roles and responsibilities known especially for the vendors in managing own people. External resources lack context and frustrate local staff as they back fill positions; they need to be trained as needed.
Governance	9%	12% Measurably worse	Transformational change and roles and responsibilities. Clarity of roles, responsibilities and in particular authority, decision and delegation controls.	Governance needs to be defined at the beginning and roles and responsibilities assigned and accepted and monitored with appropriate level governance structures. The use of independent advisors at Programme level is key, complexity leads to full time rather than part time management roles that should not have to "fit around day jobs" (p.9). Attendances on governance groups should be consistent, regular, focused and well prepared. Develop models for transitioning across sectors/Agencies i.e. Programme Transitional Governance. SRO must be Senior Executive.

(continued)

Table 10.2 (continued)

Category	Domain Weighting Report 1 2011/100 Percent	Domain Weighting Report 2 2013/100 Percent	High Level Issue Definition/Description— Original from Report 1 2008–2011. 680 Benchmark Recommendations	The Difference or Similarity between the Two Reports. Why the Improvement? Why the Decline? Why the Status Quo? 540 Recommendations
Programme/ Project Planning	8%	4% Measurably improved	Proposals not clear affecting Business Case, design, execution, implementation/transformation.	Project Plans not always completed and seen as Gantts. It should cover Change Management transition planning. Phased delivery requires careful documentation of requirements. "Plan the implementation phase using an "unconstrained approach" to scheduling. This will ensure that the timeline to deliver the planned scope of work is understood and will allow informed decision regarding trade-offs before constraints are applied" (p.27). The Project Plan should show Alternatives Analysis for slippages.
Management of Change	6%	5% Marginally improved	Workforce planning, training, user involvement, milestone management.	Insufficient attention to transition requirements—planning and controlling them. Function/utility rather than technical specifications need to be considered. Transition into Service Plans and focus needed. Business Change Managers and Business Change Networks among key stakeholders needed to be formalised.
Sourcing Strategy	4%	12% Significantly worse	Procurement, contracts, market capability, sustainability, negotiation issues.	Agencies must familiarise themselves with Rules for Government Procurement. Contract management should be in place as soon as Business Case approved. Select contract managers before vendor contract negotiations start. Need to document a Decision-Making Framework, develop Risk Allocation Matrix, requirements must be in Tender related documents, develop a Partnership Charter, after Proof of Concept revise any procurement documentation accordingly. Develop resolution and mediation strategies in advance.

Category				
Dependencies Management	3%	2% Marginally improved	Control of outputs by third party contributors not in direct control by Agency/department.	The single most valuable thing that Programmes and Projects can do to help themselves in this area is to develop a detailed critical path diagram that clearly identifies external dependencies and the impact if any of them are delayed. Such a diagram can help governance groups to understand the vulnerabilities so that they can use their wider span of control and influence to keep external activities to schedule (p.31). Dependencies must be clearly articulated.
Financial Management	2%	4% Marginally worse	Capital rationing and funding management.	Cross-Agency complexity impacts this in regard to funding gaps. Need a Funding Agreement between parties in form of a Partnership Agreement. Programmes need to consider how to bridge funding gaps. Options for cash flow and opportunity cost forecasts need to be considered. Detailed Business Cases should include Funding Models.
Methodology	2%	3% (marginally worse)	Coherent structure, rigour, processes unclear, no common approach.	Should be flexible and scalable. Certifications good at relevant levels e.g. PRINCE2 and MSP. Investment Logic Mapping is mandated to understand link from Drivers to Projects to Benefits. Linked to Benefits Realisation Plans. Need method for Quality and Configuration controls.
Transition into Service	Not counted 7%		Too early to assess in 2011. Based upon Report 2 a lack of transition manager, transition planning and management. Go Live does mean Go Smoothly for business as usual.	Projects tend to focus on delivery of capability and not change environment. The Project should expect post implementation issues and prepare for those in advance by making sure business as usual has process/training etc. in place. A lack of detailed Integration Plan for Go Live needed. Risks in readiness for Service need to be considered. Data migration especially is complex. For phased implementation document the process flow models.
Benefits Realisation	Not counted 5%		More Projects progressing to completion. Need clear indicators, milestones, measures and processes to identify benefit and disbenefit levels especially in regard to planning assumptions.	Not done well. Need to develop Benefits Management Framework early and could be part of initial Business Case development. Need Benefits Realisation Plan, Benefits Mapping, Benefits Profiles and details on how suppliers/vendors contribute to these.
Capturing Previous Lessons	Not counted 2%			Establish lessons registers, and act on and incorporate them—not just record them. Use lessons to guide type of announcements made on large complex initiatives. Phased implementation gives opportunity to incorporate lessons as you go.

SSC reported that generally good practice fundamentals (SSC, 2013, p.3) were evidence encompassing many of Gateway's key themes, in that supporting evidence was found (these have been paraphrased below):

- *Strategic alignment* with Government and organisational tactical and operational policy and goals requirements.
- *Top-down buy-in*—from ownership, management and leadership in Government through to the SRO.
- *Governance* arrangements and active sponsorship for ongoing justification as per business objectives and Business Cases demonstrating this.
- Effective *stakeholder engagement* to help identify, analyse, segment and engage and monitor.
- Commitment to follow *method and structures* for good Project and risk management practice.
- Focus on skilling, competency and taking care of talent management of the whole *Project team.*

Conclusion

Capability was broadly defined as the ability to carry out Projects and Programmes to successful conclusion in terms of objectives and benefits. It is evident that this collaboration exists at Government level and decision making organisational levels. Both sectors need each other, they are a supply and distribution chain into each other of competence, resource, guidance, training, legislation and leadership. This study focused on the public sector Projects but could not do so without involving the private sector. At practitioner level, generic Project managers are respected for their focus and expertise. They are fairly or unfairly criticised for lack of Agency context (politics)—what one sees as an advantage another sees as disadvantage.

In summarising, Gateway™, as a form of IQA, has impacted on Project and Programme results by its mandate and by its process using what is effectively peer review. Its findings, reported locally to key organisational stakeholders, such as the Senior Responsible Owner (SRO), are transparent, effective and measurable. Again, by SSC making a lessons report available for the wider Project stakeholder community, lessons, albeit summarised, are available to a broader public and private sector community.

Improvement can generally be seen in NZ public sector results; underpinning this is improved delivery capabilities. Two significant reasons for asking why examine the capabilities are:

1   Striving for value for money in a constrained and increasingly recurring recessionary environment.
2   Gateway™ assures trajectory based upon actual, planned and forecast progress.

Gateway™ has a record of saving time, money and protecting investments in UK and Australia. Measured data for NZ is not available at time of writing. The Gateway™ (peer) Review process as an assurer giving Delivery Confidence (or lack thereof) is able to assess present and future Project/Programme status. It seeks evidence of structure, rigour and accountability at all levels. It also seeks actions on follow-up recommendations made Gate by Gate—whilst reviewers may naturally change depending on progress requirements; it does seek responsibility for actions by placing account-ability on the Project organisation. *It can and does pick up on the presence and absence of capabilities adopted, adapted and embedded.* Those who see Gateway™ as additional work are countered by the argument that, by acting on the recommendations, the Project/Programme is doing the work it should have been doing anyway. Gateway™ also has *soft benefit outcomes* of stakeholder involvement, free and frank discussions with peers that add to organisational lessons and knowledge pool to incorporate on current and future Projects/Programmes. It solicits, represents and encourages buy-in. The process works—Gateway™ works.

Bibliography

ANAO Better Practice Guide (2010) Planning and Approving Projects: Planning and Approving Projects—An executive perspective, June 2010, Canberra, Commonwealth of Australia.

Better Business Case (BBC) introduced by Cab Circ CO(10)2 in 2010.

Cabinet Minute (07) 44/11 (1 January 2008) referring to Gateway™ mandate on all capital Projects started after this date.

Cabinet Office Circular CO (10)2 (1 August 2010), Capital Asset Management in Departments and Crown Entities. 168474v1, (Distributed by Secretary for the Cabinet Rebecca Kitteridge).

Commonwealth of Australia (2012) Administration of the Gateway Review Process, Department of Finance and Deregulation, ANAO Audit Report No.22 2011–12, ISSN 1036–7632.

Department of the Prime Minister and Cabinet (3 April, 2012) Ministerial List: 194972v1.

KPMG NZ (2011) Portfolio, Program and Project Management P3M Capabilities in Government—Increasing Success Rates and Reducing Costs, March. Printed in NZ.

NAO/OGC (undated) Common Causes of Project Failure, pp.1–4 (online) www.ogc.gov.uk.

Ross, S. (2013) Capability Building in the New Zealand Government Sector from a Project Management Perspective Using Best Practice Models—A Capability Breakdown Structure with a Gateway™ (UK Cabinet Office) Focus. Unpublished Doctoral Thesis, SKEMA Business School, France.

State Services Commission (SSC) (2008) The Capability Toolkit—a Tool to promote and inform capability management; developed by State Services Commission, Treasury and Department of the Prime Minister and Cabinet, ISBN: 978–0–478–30350–6.

State Services Commission (SSC) (2011a) Gateway™ Reviews Lessons Learned Report—2008–2011, State Services Commission, NZ, ISBN: 978–0–478–36158–2.

State Services Commission (SSC) (2011b) Guidance for Monitoring Major Projects and Programmes: State Services Commission, NZ, ISBN: 978–0–478–36157–5.

State Services Commission (SSC) (2012) OGC Gateway™ Process—Gateway to Success—Delivery Confidence Guide to Review Teams, Version 1, State Services Commission, NZ.

State Services Commission (SSC) (2013) Gateway™ Lessons Learned Report—2011–2013, State Services Commission, NZ. ISBN: 978–0–478–40968–0 (Online), ISBN: 978–0–478–40971–0 (Print).

The ANO Report (2011/12) and Queensland Department of Infrastructure and Planning (7 February 2011), Administration of the Gateway Review Process. Australian National Audit Office Issue No.22 2011–12, Department of Finance and Regulation, ISBN: 0 642 81227 6 Commonwealth of Australia.

Wooley, P., Barlow, G. and Brame, A. (2011) KPMG New Zealand Project Management Survey 2010: Project Advisory Services, KPMGA3228.

Chapter 11

As All Things Hang Together, Systemic Analysis Is a Requirement for Sustainable Performance When Facing Complexity[1,2]

Murial Walas and Philippe Scotto

Introduction

The contribution of this chapter is to introduce a powerful tool of analysis that is sustainable over the long term. This tool is rooted in cybernetics sciences. The complexity of strategic problems as all things hang together, when driving for instance a risk analysis in project management, and the need to resolve them collectively, force us to use methods that are rigorous and participatory as much as possible so as first, to recognize the problem and second, find acceptable and sustainable solutions. Most of the time, systems, like in risk management, are modelled by using a large number of variables, therefore it is impossible even for a bright human brain to understand the complexity of the relationship (direct and indirect) among all the variables. This tool not only makes it possible to analyse these risks in all their complexity at the present time, but also enables us to recognize trends or future ruptures. In this chapter, we will concretely apply our systemic approach on the risk analysis of the Microgine® project. All details about the Microgine® project and its risks are provided in an annexe. Through the use of a mathematical analysis and software applications, many different graphics were elaborated in order to well describe our study. Of course, even if people cannot be reduced to a rational mind, as they are also driven by intuition and passion, the advantage to collectively conduct a systemic (structural) analysis will help us: to construct a common language, to enlarge our visions, to secure our decisions and finally to build team work.

In this chapter, we deal with the issue of managing complex projects and uncertainty in project development.

The answer contained below is the method of systemic analysis also known as structural analysis. We shall show how this method helps us to analyse the interconnections among project components in order to determine their importance at a given moment in time (t), but also over time by projecting into the future.

We apply this method to the Microgine® project and its risk analysis.

We are thus able to show how to manage the degree of complexity and uncertainty inherent to the project's risks, knowing that risks are not independent and that it is

---

1   Thanks to Armand PORTELLI (Microgine®).
2   Some elements of this chapter are extract from the project plan of the Project Microgine (MSc Web-Marketing and International Project Management 2011–12, project team: Isabel Angulo, Marie Boulanger, Marion Eugene, Apichaya Inprasit, Pierre Josseaux and Sebastien Santucci).

essential to take account of all the interrelationships among these risks to achieve forecasts that are sustainable over time.

Structural Analysis: A Sustainable and Efficient Project Management Method

Origin of the Method

As a reminder, cybernetics is a science of the control of living or non-living systems. It was founded in 1948 by the mathematician Norbert Wiener (1984). The etymology of the term cybernetic has nothing at all to do with the current fashion for "cyber" or video games. Cybernetics comes from the Greek *Kubenêsis* meaning "the action of manoeuvring a ship, to steer". Systems and sub-systems, whether living or not, are an integral part of our world, and they all interact and overlap (Bloomfield, 1986). The following can therefore also be considered as systems: our universe, a galaxy, a solar system, our "blue" planet (Meadows, 1982), a society, an economy, a computer network, an organization, a machine, an individual, a brain, a cell, an ecosystem, and a project along with its risks.

In cybernetics, a system is defined as a set of elements that interact; the interactions among these elements can consist of exchanges of matter, energy or information. To understand more easily, we can also refer to the fundamental principles of the physical sciences (particle physics, statistical mechanics, quantum physics (Heisenberg, 1971), Shannon's theory, the notion of entropy etc.). These exchanges among elements constitute communication that results in the different elements reacting, changing state or modifying their action. Communication, signals, information and retroaction are notions that are central to the dynamics of all systems. When elements are organized into a system, their interactions give rise to properties that the elements taken separately do not possess. We then say, to return to the remarks of Edgar Morin (1977), that "the whole is more than the sum of its parts". For example, a computer has properties that go far beyond the sum of its electronic components; similarly, human beings present faculties that are far superior to the sum of their individual organs.

One of the main advantages of systemic analysis over more traditional methods currently encountered in management is that it takes account of the dynamics of mutual interactions. Indeed, the action of one element on another results in the response of the second element towards the first. We then say that these two elements are linked by a retroactive or feedback loop. We will return to this essential notion later.

In essence, cybernetics is a science of verification and information aimed at knowledge and piloting systems. This chapter gives a practical insight into one of its numerous applications in the domain of strategic management; we examine a structural analysis of the risks identified in the context of the Microgine® project.

Description of the Method

Aim

Structural analysis is a systemic tool that structures the pooling of ideas. This form of analysis describes a system using a matrix that combines the constituent components of the system. These components may be objectives, needs, functionalities, risks etc.

One of the main advantages of systemic analysis over most traditional methods (often encountered in management) is the integration of mutual interactions dynamics. The effect of one element on the other leads to a response from the second element towards the first. It is then said that these two elements are linked by a feedback loop. Indeed, as Michel Godet (2001) suggests: "In a systemic vision of the world, a variable only exists by its relationships." The roots of this approach come from the cybernetics of Wiener (1954, 1984), Forrester (1969), Von Neumann (1966), Von Foerster (1985) and from the School of Palo Alto through the research of Bateson (1973), Bertalanffy (1968) and Waltzlawick (1972).

We use this method to analyse risks because each risk is memorized by the full Microgine® system and by its interactions with its environment (law, competitors, partners, clients, users etc.).

To demonstrate this, we run a three-step structural analysis:

1   the inventory of variables and their definitions;
2   spotting relationships in the Structural Analysis Matrix, that we will henceforth call SAM (or Direct Influence Matrix – DIM);
3   the search for key variables by the Micmac[3] tool (algorithm) based on matrix computation.

Structural Analysis in Three Steps

1. The Inventory of Variables and Their Definitions

The first step consists in listing "all" the variables that characterize the system under study and its environment (internal as well as external variables). This stage should be as thorough as possible and initially should not exclude any line of research (first brainstorming period).

Apart from the prospective workshop, the pool of variables should be enriched by gaining information from non-directive interviews with representatives of actors in the system.

The final result is a list of internal and external variables for the system studied. Experience shows that this list does not generally exceed 70 or 80 variables if the system under study has been thoroughly broken down and outlined.

A detailed explanation of variables is essential to follow up the analysis and recognize relationships among the variables, generating a "database" which is required for any prospective thinking. It is therefore recommended that to give a precise definition for each variable, to note former changes, to identify the variables that started the evolutions, characterize the present situation and recognize trends or future splits (*Past – Present – Future*). In this way, a common language is constructed that can be shared by all participants.

---

3   Micmac: "Matrice d'Impacts Croisés-Multiplication Appliquée à un Classement" (cross-multiplication impact matrix applied to a ranking). This tool was perfected at the CEA (Atomic Energy Commissariat) between 1972 and 1974 by Michel Godet and J.C. Duperrin.

In our case, we identify 34 risks (see Table 11.1) that are more or less directly connected: those that are essential to the management and comprehension of our system's evolution.

2. Spotting Relationships

FILLING OF THE "SAM"

The SAM can be filled in using different methods (brainstorming, questioning, interviews etc.). Generally, before concluding that there is a relationship between two variables and quantifying it, we have to answer three questions:

- Does variable i directly influence variable j, or is it a mutual relationship? (Figure 11.1, case a.)
- Is there an existing influence of i on j, or is there no collinearity through the influence impact of a third variable k on variables i and j? (Figure 11.1, case b.)
- Is the influence of i on j direct or is it relayed through a variable n (indirect relationship)? (Figure 11.1, case c.)

This automatic questioning procedure, to quote Michel Godet, avoids a certain number of errors during the matrix filling stage, the most common mistake being to replace an indirect relationship by a direct one. Even though characterizing and quantifying the relationships are subjective, it is important to take the time to think in order to avoid this mistake. Once the existence of a direct relationship is proven, we can ask ourselves at which level of intensity (high, medium or low) the relationship determines the influence of one variable on another one. This quantification of direct relationships results in more adequate settings than the simple utilization of binary code where the number 1 means the existence of a direct relationship and 0 its non-existence. Even though the binary code is already very efficient, in this study we will use the traditional coding: 0: no direct influence, 1: low influence, 2: medium influence, 3: high influence, p: potential influence, which means that there may be an influence.

Therefore, for each variable i we look to see if it influences variable j and to which degree. Relationships are not always reflexive. For example, a law can influence a company strategy but this law isn't necessarily influenced by the company's strategy. We then analyse then whether variable j is influenced by or depends on variable i.

To fill in the matrix (SAM), we work in rows, spotting the influence of each variable on all the others, and then in columns, noting by which variable each variable is influenced (for example, see Figure 11.2). Even though this procedure is tedious, it

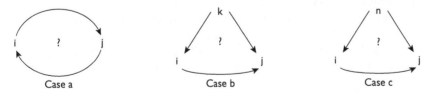

Figure 11.1 The Different Possible Relationships among Variables (Scotto, 2004)

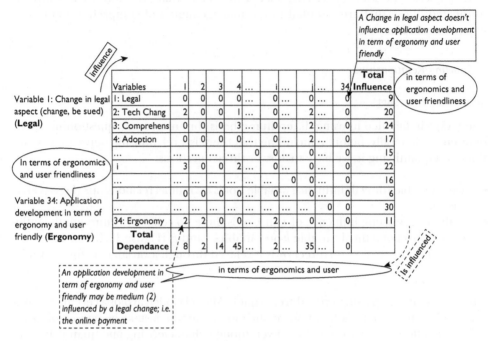

Figure 11.2 Principle of Structural Analysis Matrix (SAM) Conception

needs to answer a huge[4] number of questions, in our case: 22 312 (2 x 34²), it seems essential to us. Usually, the exchange and ideas that such moment induces helps to build a common language and a team spirit. Indeed, the setting of methods issued from systemic analysis proves to be an efficient process in terms of team building.

PRESENTATION OF THE SAM (ALSO CALLED DIM)

Better than a long speech, Figure 11.3 presents the SAM, with a breach only visible in 4/4 according to the difference made between external (and external/internal) variables and internal variables.

Dials number 1 and 4 respectively represent the impact (influence) of external (including three internal/external variables), and internal variables on themselves. Generally, we notice that the influence of external on internal (dial 2) is more important than the contrary (dial 3), which is not the case here in Figure 11.3, mainly due to the fact that we have mixed the three internal/external variables with the external variables. As we can deduce from Figure 11.3, around three-quarters of the matrix is filled in with zeros.

As Michel Godet (2001) reminds us, "the higher the direct fill rate, the less relevant it will be to take account of the indirect relationships given by the Micmac algorithm". In fact, if the matrix were completely filled (i.e. contained no zeros), the indirect relationships would simply be a homothetic multiplication of the direct relationships.

---

4   We can calculate this number with the following mathematical formula: 2 x (number of variables)².

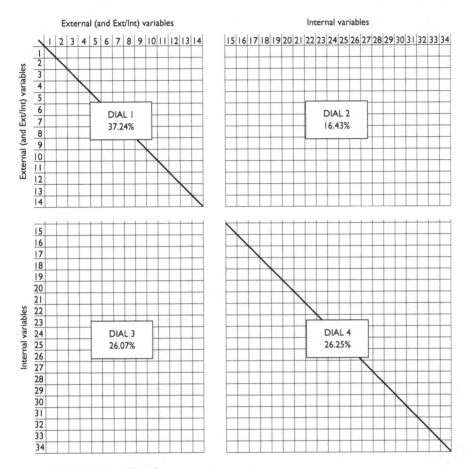

Figure 11.3 SAM the 4 DIALS

3. Looking for the Key Variables

The objective of the Micmac tool (software) is to reduce our system's complexity (currently comprised of 34 variables) by putting forward the key variables to be studied as a priority. Two types of variables appear essential. The first are those that have the most influence on the system. They are said to "drive" the system. The second type are those that are the most dependent on or sensitive to the system. Other variables, specifically those that do not seem to impact the system much (low levels of influence and dependence), will be omitted, thus reducing the initial list. Hence, the Micmac tool elaborates a variables typology in direct and indirect rankings.

Simply reading the SAM allows us to observe which variables have the greatest influence and which are the most dependent.[5] However, as Michel Godet underlines

---

5   The sum of row *i* represents the number of times that variable *i* has a direct influence on other variables in the system. This number constitutes an indicator of variable *i*'s influence. Using the same reasoning,

(2001, p.150), this is not enough "to uncover the hidden variables that sometimes have a great influence on the problem in question". In fact, it is already difficult to imagine all the direct relationships when analysing a matrix of 34; this alone may contain several thousand indirect interactions resulting from chains of influence and other feedback loops. It is then impossible for the human brain to imagine and extract any interpretation from a network of such complex relationships. This explains why we resort to the tools from mathematics (matrix, bubble sort, factor analysis etc.) and physics (notion of intensity, principle of uncertainty) used in cybernetics. As an indication and to give an idea of the inextricable nature of even trying to represent the strong, medium and weak direct relationships, Figure 11.4 gives a graphic representation (Karouach and Dousset, 2003) of these relationships in our system.

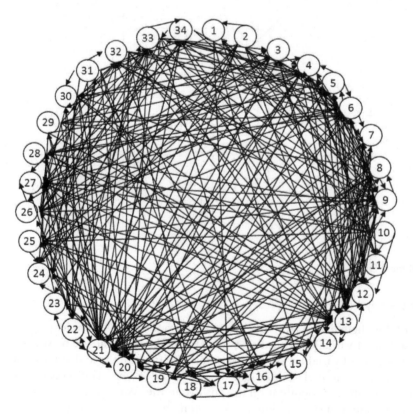

Figure 11.4 Relational Graphic Showing the Direct Relationships among the 34 Variables (Risks)

the sum of the j column represents the number of times that the j variable is dependent on other variables and constitutes an indicator of the dependence of the j variable. Thus for each variable, we obtain their coordinates (the x coordinate being determined by the dependence indicator and the y coordinate by the influence indicator), enabling us to position them on a dependence–influence diagram describing the system.

	1:	2:	3:	4:	5:	6:	7:	8:	9:	10	11	12	13	14	15	16	17	18
1 : Legal	0	0	0	0	0	0	0	0	0	0	0	2	0	2	2	0	1	0
2 : Tech Chang	2	0	0	1	0	0	0	2	1	0	2	0	2	0	0	0	0	0
3 : Comprehens	0	0	0	3	2	3	0	0	0	0	0	2	3	0	0	0	0	0
4 : Adoption	0	0	0	0	0	0	2	1	1	0	1	0	3	0	0	0	0	0
5 : Visibility	0	0	0	3	0	3	2	0	0	0	0	3	3	1	0	0	0	0
6 : Lack of	0	0	0	2	2	0	2	0	3	0	0	2	3	0	0	0	0	0
7 : Payment	0	0	0	0	0	0	0	0	0	0	0	1	2	3	0	0	0	0
8 : Google...	1	0	0	2	2	2	0	0	2	0	1	3	2	0	2	1	1	1
9 : Kompass...	0	0	0	2	2	2	1	1	0	0	0	1	1	0	0	1	0	0
10 : Control	3	0	0	2	2	0	0	0	0	0	1	1	1	0	0	0	0	0
11 : Usbbita	0	0	0	3	0	4	0	4	4	0	0	0	0	0	0	0	0	

Figure 11.5 Zoom on the Direct Influence Matrix (DIM) of the Risks

It is important to understand the difference between direct and indirect relations in terms of time periods. When we are looking at *direct relations*, it means that we are considering the *present time*. Why? Because if we start the clock when a variable is directly affecting the "behaviour" of another variable, we will notice that there is no delay between the effect and the cause. So, it is a picture of the situation at the present time in terms of influence/dependence. We will see later on, the *crucial role* played by *indirect relationships* that will give us a projection of the *future*. The question is: "What is going to happen to the system?" The amazing point is that the level of influence/dependence of the same variables could change drastically compared to their level for the present time.

Analysis of the Direct Relationships

A simple look at the SAM (also called the DIM) enables us to notice which variables have the highest level of influence and which have the lowest level of dependence, see Figure 11.5.

We obtain the influence of each variable by summing the values of its row and its dependence by summing the values of its column (see Table 11.1).

From Table 11.2, we can extract the variables with the greatest influence and the biggest dependence.

Table 11.1 List of Risks with Their Values of Influence (Summing in Rows) and of the Dependence (Summing in Columns) of Each Variable

N°	Variable	Summing in rows influence	Summing in columns dependence
1	Change in legal aspect (change, be sued)	9	6
2	Technical change (new entrants)	20	0

(continued)

Table 11.1 (continued)

N°	Variable	Summing in rows influence	Summing in columns dependence
3	Comprehension (difficult to use for end-users)	24	14
4	Adoption of the product in terms of habits by the end-users	15	45
5	Non-recognition of the Microgine® brand by publishers and end-users (problem of visibility)	16	29
6	Lack of interest from the publishers to provide and update information for the system	21	26
7	Level of involvement of publishers in terms of payment (turnover provided by the publishers)	8	14
8	Global competitors (Google, Yahoo, Bing, Ask.com) may offer the same service as Microgine®	25	12
9	If French local competitors (Kompass, Studyrama, CCI, AEF (*Annuaire des entreprises françaises* – French company directory)) remain independent, they will not join the Microgine® community	15	27
10	Country risk: information controlled by a country (access denied to data)	22	0
11	Country risk: cultural (lack of practice/habits in terms of information search on the web)	16	5
12	Lack of ads from the publishers and partners (to promote the Microgine® network)	6	35
13	Loyalty of partners in terms of duration (at least three years)	13	41
14	Delay (from 30 to 60 days) of payment from customers (publishers and companies)	8	12
15	Size of company (Microgine®)	8	10
16	Disagreement within the team (Microgine®)	8	15
17	Degree of organizational (inside Microgine®)	6	9
18	Members' reliability (inside Microgine® team)	6	9
19	Poor investment in the communication plan to promote Microgine®	13	6
20	Speed of project development	5	33
21	Level of investment in constant innovation to be up-to-date	28	32
22	Complexity of product implementation	11	9
23	Technical issues from databases	15	4
24	Size of project: in terms of workload	7	19
25	Servers go offline/crash	15	10
26	Design of the widget (design of the front office): difficult to use the service	18	11
27	Timeliness of the service	16	19
28	Semantic risks linked to languages: finding the information in different languages (Japanese, Russian, Arabic etc.)	14	7
29	Capacity of translation in different languages to make information accessible (readable, understandable) to the end-users	23	2
30	Security prevention against hackers (destruction of data and database) and theft of engine's search results, platform and information	24	11
31	Use of project management methods and tools to pilot the project well (in particular task allocation/planning)	23	3
32	Problem of data quality (correct, up-to-date, not redundant and complete)	21	14
33	Problem of quality for data use (easy to transfer, speed of access)	18	18
34	Application development in terms of ergonomics and user friendliness	20	10
	Totals	517	517

Table 11.2 Ranking of the Most Influential and Dependent Variables

Rank	Variables	Total influence		Rank	Variables	Total dependence
1	21	28		1	4	45
2	8	25		2	13	41
3	3	24		3	12	35
4	30	24		4	20	33
5	29	23		5	21	32
6	31	23		6	5	29
7	10	22		7	9	27

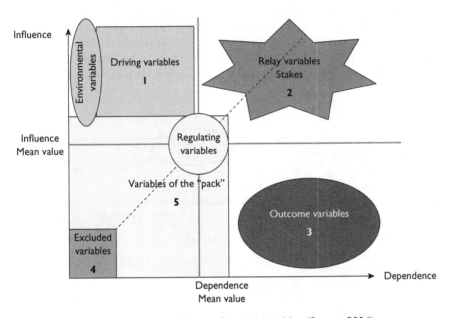

Figure 11.6 Interpretation of the Influence–Dependence Map (Scotto, 2004)

We notice that variable number 21 (up-to-date) has most influence and that variable number 4 (Adoption) has the highest score of dependence.

We also dispose of Influence/Dependence mapping with all the system variables. This mapping could be divided into different sectors (Figure 11.6).

- Section 1 gathers variables that determine the system; these are highly influential driving forces with a very low dependence. Usually, they are known as *environmental variables* (war, conflicts, accidents etc.).
- Section 2 represents variables that are both very influential and very dependent. These are *relay/strategical variables* because of their unstable nature. We generally find the challenges of the system in this section: in this section we usually find those variables that exercise a "leverage effect".
- Section 3 represents variables that have low influence and high dependence. Their evolution depends on section 1 and 2 variables. Variables such as productivity,

added-value, turnover, cash flow and quality are usually found in this section when the system concerns a company.

- Section 4 is made up of variables with very low influence and dependence. Most of the time, these variables are disconnected from the system and don't really determine its future. They have an autonomous evolution and so they can be excluded from the analysis without much risk.
- Section 5 represents variables with a medium influence and/or dependence; they form the "pack" according Michel Godet, and as such we can't deduct any variables from them.

Figure 11.7 shows the results for our projects.

At the present time, we realize that the variables named: "Up-to-date, Google, Security, Comprehension, Translation, PM methods, quality . . ." are the ones with the highest level of influence for our system regarding risk. We also notice that the variables called "Tech change" and "Control" are not dependent on the system, but they still have an important influence. We have two "relay" variables, meaning that our system is not stable. At the same time, it is a surprise to see that the

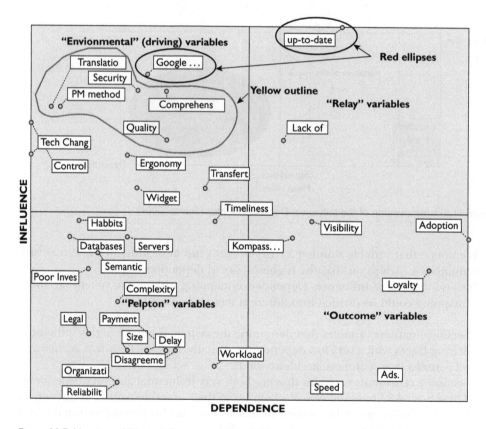

Figure 11.7 Mapping of Direct Influence and Dependence of Risks (Picture of the Present Moment)

risk variables named "Databases", "Poor investment", "Habits" and "Legal aspect" have almost no impact on our system of risks. By experience and/or intuition we can expect that the product visibility and uptake result from other risks. This outcome is indeed confirmed in the mapping above (Cf. the "Outcome" variables quadrant).

Analysis of the Indirect Relationships

In order to avoid going into too much detail about the how the Micmac algorithm works,[6] since it uses certain algebraic properties of squared matrices,[7] we shall use Jean-François Lefebre's (1982) approach. In other words, we shall look at a simple example. Let us consider a system described by three variables A, B and C that act on each other according to the relational system in Figure 11.8.

If we use the binary system, the SAM of this little system) is shown in Figure 11.9.

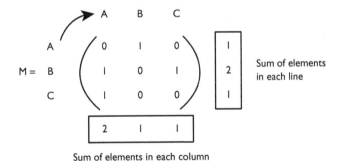

Figure 11.8 Example of a Relational Scheme Relating Three Variables, Directly and Indirectly (Scotto, 2004)

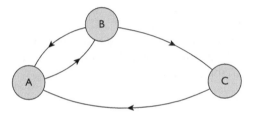

Figure 11.9 Structural Analysis Matrix

---

6 Exponention of the SAM matrix.
7 The most common problems of numerical calculation related to matrices are resolving linear systems, inverting squared matrices and calculating matrice's own values and own vectors. For information, in quantum physics, we often use a matrix representation for modelling a system. We also recall that only a matrix with an identical number of rows and columns, commonly called a "squared matrix", can be exponentiated.

In this first matrix, the diagonal elements are always 0: no account is taken of the influence of a variable on itself,[8] whereas in the indirect effects (updated by increasing the power of the matrix) we take account of the effects of a variable on itself (these effects have to pass via one or several other variables).

Figure 11.10 in row 1, column 1 indicates that there is a path of length 2 going from A to A and in Figure 11.10, for example in row 2, column 1, means that there is a path of length 2 to go from B to A. In fact, we find these paths in Figure 11.8 (see Figure 11.11).

It thus follows that the elements of the cubed SAM matrix (M^3) will show the paths and circuits of length 3 to go from one variable to another. It is interesting to observe that from a certain power of the matrix, the rankings in rows and columns stabilizes. We therefore understand why the indirect effects of feedback loops gradually highlight the importance of the "hidden" variables as the matrix power is increased. As Michel Godet remarks (2001), "This immediate consideration of intensities is understandable in as much as we can think of a relationship of intensity 2 between two variables as equivalent to two direct pseudo-relationships between those variables."

However, as Michel Godet insists, it is essential to "seek out the hidden variables that sometimes have a big influence on the problem studied".

Let us consider the following example (Figure 11.12) where a system of variables can be split into two sub-systems S1 and S2 which would be independent if they were not linked by three intermediate variables (a, b, c).

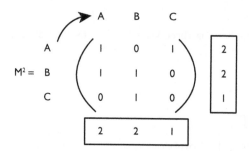

Figure 11.10 Matrice M^2

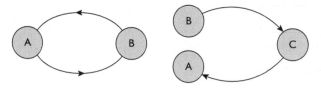

Path of length 2 to go from A to A   Path of length 2 to go from B to A

Figure 11.11 Paths of Length 2 Seen in Figure 11.8 (Scotto, 2004)

8   In fact, a variable has no self-influence from a direct point of view, because a direct relationship cannot exist without at least two variables.

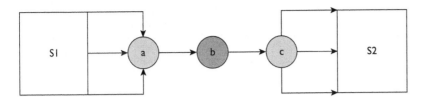

Figure 11.12 Identification of a Key Variable (b)

If we look at direct effects, we remark that variable *a* is very dependent on the "S1 sub-system" and variable *c* dominates the "S2 sub-system".

This is the main reason why indirect effects should not be disregarded. Each time we analyse an indirect relationship, it will modify the influence and/or dependence of the variables. The principle is to undertake all these analyses until reaching stable influence and dependence values. To do this, we literally elevate the SAM (DIM) matrix to the next power until we reach a stable final matrix.

A program running on Mathematica and/or Micmac software (Wolfram, 1995) enabled us to determine the matrix order for which line and column rankings become stable.[9] In our case, we found the stability of the matrix for the order (power) 8 (DIM^8). Finally our Indirect Influence Matrix (IIM, see Figure 11.13) is equal to the DIM at the power 8 (IIM = MID^8).

From this matrix, a new variable classification highlights the most important variables of the system (see Figure 11.14).

	1 : Legal	2 : Tech Chang	3 : Comprehens	4 : Adoption	5 : Visibility	6 : Lack of	7 : Payment	8 : Google...
1 : Legal	22380810	0	223547800	1087860000	824258600	672898000	858600600	328153700
2 : Tech Chang	75060860	0	750115800	3647120000	2762696000	2255771000	2877060000	1100208000
3 : Comprehens	103603200	0	1038432000	5050001000	3825375000	3123128000	3985410000	1521398000
4 : Adoption	62691180	0	627656600	3052965000	2312790000	1888142000	2409539000	920031900
5 : Visibility	55919680	0	560559600	2727136000	2066955000	1686554000	2152815000	821426200
6 : Lack of	80151100	0	802372600	3903191000	2956891000	2413962000	3080715000	1176207000
7 : Payment	25875170	0	269578800	1262741000	956573300	780895400	996851200	380205100
8 : Google...	80009130	0	800293700	3893554000	2949794000	2406110000	3073126000	1173772000
9 : Kompass...	63530420	0	635759000	3092935000	2343113000	1912902000	2441167000	932162400
10 : Control	88140220	0	882162600	4290729000	3250445000	2653693000	3386256000	1293145000
11 : Habbits	74907700	0	750513700	3650591000	2765433000	2257672000	2881375000	1099679000
12 : Ads.	19795160	0	198382600	965342500	731338800	596990300	762216800	290660500
13 : Loyalty	41914820	0	420033700	2043298000	1547891000	1263697000	1612810000	615516300
14 : Delay	33294810	0	333785600	1623599000	1229943000	1004066000	1281641000	488971700
15 : Size	12839670	0	127145200	619170000	469312600	383109700	488598400	187376800
16 : Disannaranna	5400140	0	57509310	255434000	104523000	155040000	201455000	70107220

Figure 11.13 Zoom on the Indirect Influence Matrix (IIM) of Risks

9 The word "stable" indicates that the level of influence and dependence will not change beyond a certain order (power) for the IIM.

Matrix DIM	▼		Matrix IIM	▼
Rank	**Variable**		**Variable**	
1	21 - up-to-date		21 - up-to-date	
2	8 - Google...		3 - Comprehens	
3	3 - Comprehens		29 - Translatio	
4	30 - Security		30 - Security	
5	29 - Translatio		10 - Control	
6	31 - PM method		34 - Ergonomy	
7	10 - Control		26 - Widget	
8	6 - Lack of		6 - Lack of	
9	32 - Quality		8 - Google...	
10	2 - Tech Chang		11 - Habbits	
11	34 - Ergonomy		2 - Tech Chang	
12	26 - Widget		33 - Transfert	
13	33 - Transfert		31 - PM method	
14	5 - Visibility		9 - Kompass...	
15	11 - Habbits		4 - Adoption	
16	27 - Timeliness		32 - Quality	
17	4 - Adoption		27 - Timeliness	
18	9 - Kompass...		25 - Servers	
19	23 - Databases		5 - Visibility	
20	25 - Servers		19 - Poor Inves	
21	28 - Semantic		28 - Semantic	
22	13 - Loyalty		23 - Databases	
23	19 - Poor Inves		13 - Loyalty	
24	22 - Complexity		22 - Complexity	
25	1 - Legal		14 - Delay	
26	7 - Payment		7 - Payment	
27	14 - Delay		1 - Legal	
28	15 - Size		12 - Ads.	
29	16 - Disagreeme		24 - Workload	
30	24 - Workload		20 - Speed	
31	12 - Ads.		15 - Size	
32	17 - Organizati		17 - Organizati	
33	18 - Reliabilit		16 - Disagreeme	
34	20 - Speed		18 - Reliabilit	

Figure 11.14 Ranks Variables by Influences

- On the left (DIM) the ranking of the variables is made downstream from the most influential to the least influential. It is a picture of the current situation in terms of classification (only based on direct relationships among variables).
- On the right (IIM) the ranking is made downstream from the most influential to the least influential. It is a picture of the forecast situation in terms of classification based on all the direct and indirect relationships among variables.

The results in the Figure 11.4 are very interesting and surprising. Indeed, we can see the drastic drop of the "Google" variable in terms of influence when we take into account indirect relationships (Cf. Matrix IIM). We have almost the same situation for the following variables: "PM Method", "Quality" and "Visibility". At the same time, the variable "up-to-date" is still ranked number 1 and the level of influence of the variables named: "Comprehension", "Translation", "Control", "Ergonomy" and "Widget" has strongly increased.

Figure 11.15 presents the classification of variables dependence (downstream from the highest dependence to the least one).

From Figure 11.15, we can immediately notice the very significant increase of the level of dependence for the following variables: "Payment", "Delay", "Google", "Security" and "Poor Investments".

These results seem logical, because in terms of risk, payment, delay, security and poor investments are mostly the consequences of other phenomena. We can visualize their positions (circled in blue dots) on Figure 11.16.

A new mapping of indirect influences will enable us to study the evolution of variables through time. This new mapping is by far the most powerful and interesting result to use and to interpret in this type of strategic risk analysis.

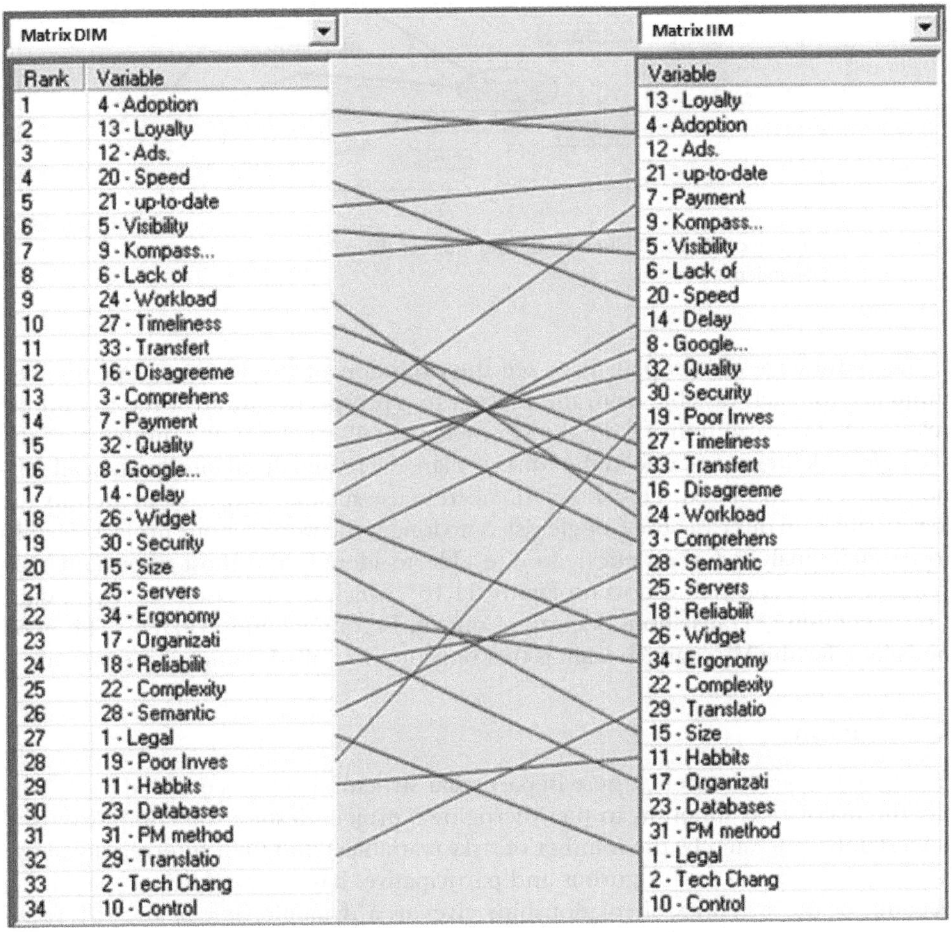

Matrix DIM		Matrix IIM
Rank	**Variable**	**Variable**
1	4 - Adoption	13 - Loyalty
2	13 - Loyalty	4 - Adoption
3	12 - Ads.	12 - Ads.
4	20 - Speed	21 - up-to-date
5	21 - up-to-date	7 - Payment
6	5 - Visibility	9 - Kompass...
7	9 - Kompass...	5 - Visibility
8	6 - Lack of	6 - Lack of
9	24 - Workload	20 - Speed
10	27 - Timeliness	14 - Delay
11	33 - Transfert	8 - Google...
12	16 - Disagreeme	32 - Quality
13	3 - Comprehens	30 - Security
14	7 - Payment	19 - Poor Inves
15	32 - Quality	27 - Timeliness
16	8 - Google...	33 - Transfert
17	14 - Delay	16 - Disagreeme
18	26 - Widget	24 - Workload
19	30 - Security	3 - Comprehens
20	15 - Size	28 - Semantic
21	25 - Servers	25 - Servers
22	34 - Ergonomy	18 - Reliabilit
23	17 - Organizati	26 - Widget
24	18 - Reliabilit	34 - Ergonomy
25	22 - Complexity	22 - Complexity
26	28 - Semantic	29 - Translatio
27	1 - Legal	15 - Size
28	19 - Poor Inves	11 - Habbits
29	11 - Habbits	17 - Organizati
30	23 - Databases	23 - Databases
31	31 - PM method	31 - PM method
32	29 - Translatio	1 - Legal
33	2 - Tech Chang	2 - Tech Chang
34	10 - Control	10 - Control

Figure 11.15 Ranks Variables by Dependencies

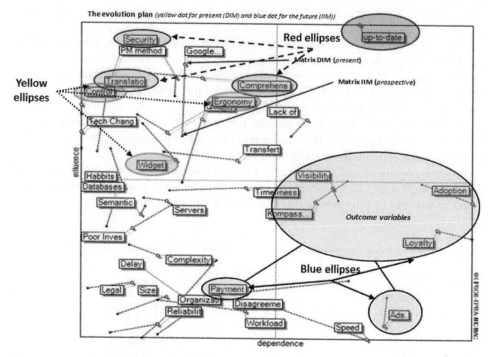

Figure 11.16 Mapping of Direct (Yellow Dots) and Indirect (Blue Dots) Risk Influence and Dependence

The advantage of this plan is to see the evolution of the level of dependence/influence for each variable from the present to a prospective future (due to indirect relations). As we can notice from the "Environmental" quadrant, the influence of the "Google" risk the second one in the "direct" plan, decreased dramatically when all relationships are considered. This shows the need to use such an approach to identify the key variables. In our case, the Google risk is no longer the worst for our project. Thanks to systemic analysis (cybernetics), we are able to identify the most important risks (circled in red and yellow dots on Figure 11.16), which in our case are: "Up-to-date, Comprehension, Translation, Security, Control, Ergonomy and Widget". The good news here for the Microgine® team is that only the risk called "control" is external.

Conclusion

Using tools from cybernetics, here in particular structural analysis enabled us to identify the major risks inherent to the Microgine® project despite the complexity and uncertainty generated by the number of risks (variables) and their interrelationships. This method, that is both rigorous and participative, has several advantages. Taking account of the systemics of relationships gives us a dynamic view of the risk issues involved and enables real monitoring to take place. First, this projection is a graphic representation, so it is easy to read and interpret; second it can be read over two time zones (present and future) depending on whether one considers only the direct relationships between the variables or all the relationships, both direct and indirect, involved. The fact that structural analysis can be easily understood and used makes it a tool of choice for a systematic reflection about a problem and/or for research. In fact, even if 80 per cent of the results obtained often appear obvious and confirm one's initial intuition, this generally strengthens the common sense and logic of the systemic approach, but above all, it adds weight to the remaining 20 per cent of counter-intuitive results. Thus, not only does this method underpin long-term performance on the level of strategic analysis, but also on the level of the work group for it enlarges the group's field of vision, helps construct a common language, aids sounder decision-making and encourages teamwork. To conclude, the Microgine® project will be a success story if the product is up-to-date, secure and multi-lingual as well as being highly ergonomic.

References

Bloomfield, B.P. (1986). *Modeling the World: The Social Construction of Systems Analysts*. Oxford, Blackwell.

Bateson, G. (1973). *Vers une écologie de l'esprit*. Paris, Le seuil.

Forrester, J. (1969). *Urban Dynamics*, Chapter 6. Cambridge, MA, MIT Press.

Godet, M. (2001). *Manuel de la prospective stratégique – Tome 1 & 2, une indiscipline intellectuelle & l'art et la méthode*, Second edition. Paris, Dunod éditeur.

Heisenberg, W.K. (1971). *Physique et philosophie*. Paris, Albin Michel.

Karouach, S. and Dousset, B. (2003). Visualisation de relations par des graphes intéractifs de grande taille. *International Journal of Information Sciences for Decision Making*, No.6, article No. 57, March.

Lefebvre, J-F. (1982). L'analyse structurelle, méthodes et développements, doctoral thesis third cycle, University of Paris IX Dauphine.

Meadows, D. (1982). Whole earth models and systems. *Co-Evolution Quarterly*, summer, pp.98–108.

Morin, E. (1977). *La méthode. Tome 1: la nature de la nature*. Editions du Seuil, Paris.

Portelli, A. (2013). Business Plan Microgine®, Microgine® company documentation.

Scotto, P. (2004). Necessity and Feasibility of a Quality Approach to Information. Application to the case of the International Atomic Energy Agency (IAEA), Marine Environment Laboratory. PhD thesis. Laboratory I3M-Lepont, University of Toulon, France.

SKEMA (2011). MSc Web Marketing and International Project Management, Project Plan Microgine® BOOK 1.

SKEMA (2012). MSc Web Marketing and International Project Management, Project Plan Microgine® BOOK 2.

Von Bertalanffy, L. (1968). *General System Theory*. New York, Braziller.

Von Foerster, H. (1985). Interview with J-P. Dupuy, P. Livet, P. Levy and I. Stengers, genealogies of self-organization, AERC Cahiers No.8, Ecole Polytechnique, Paris.

Von Neumann, J. (1966). *Theory of self-reproducing automata* (edited and completed by A.W. Burks). Urbana, Illinois University Press.

Watzlawick, P. and Beavin, J.H. (1972). *Une logique de la communication*. Coll. Paris, Points/Essais, Seuil.

Wiener, N. (1954). *The Human Use of Human Beings: Cybernetics and Society*. Boston, MA, Da Capo Press.

Wiener, N. (1984). *Cybernetics*. New York, Wiley & Sons.

Wolfram, S. (1995). *Mathematica, le système informatique pour les mathématiques*, Second edition. Paris, Addison-Wesley France.

Appendix[10]

The Microgine® Case, an Efficient, Sustainable New Generation Web Information Research Tool for Professionals with a Systemic Analysis Applied to Project Risks

Currently a small number of online search engines such as Google, Yahoo, Bing and Ask dominate the market. They enable users to select websites without charge. The information available across the web is huge, but search pertinence is questionable and decreases with the exponential growth of data available. This is becoming a real issue for professionals looking for specific, accurate information within a timeframe. Workers spend increasing amounts of time seeking relevant information. At the same time, content publishers struggle to sustain their business model as Google, Yahoo, Bing, Ask and other big players, capture the core of the financial flow through referencing tolls, advertising and paying communications. Alongside the main players, specialized search engines have low visibility and must work hard to survive.

Microgine® is a start-up company with ambitions to change the paradigm of professional search and to organize professional information on the web.

The core concept involves structuring information geographically and by theme (Information Technology, Education, Healthcare, Industry etc.), in order to direct searches towards professional websites and to give access directly to pertinent, pre-screened information. Microgine's® architecture is not just *one* search engine, but a network of search engines. Thus each theme for each geographical entity has its own search engine and these will ultimately work as a network. Each search engine uses the same interface and the same technology resulting in a standardization of the search process. Differentiation is provided through "search links" which are customized by theme.

Microgine® is not a meta professional engine indexing specialized search engines, but a Search Grid, mapping professional web information, using a common interface and filtering data for more pertinence. Microgine® will contribute to solving certain problems of big data management for the professional web and will therefore enable sustainable performance for professional searching by end-users.

Introduction

The first problem that concerns us in this age of "big data" is to find the *relevant* information quickly and not simply to be redirected to other websites or files in the manner of big search engines, not least because these redirections change depending on algorithm modifications. Moreover, the traditional search process used by large search engines is not sustainable, because it fails to create any gradual enhancement through stocking data over time.

The Microgine® project aims at offering an efficient and sustainable solution that transforms big *data* (row data) that is hard to access into thematic *information* (classified, structured data). Through its networked structure that includes multiple

---

10   Thanks: Armand PORTELLI (Microgine®).

partners, the Microgine® project hopes to present itself as an alternative to the current quasi-monopoly. A presentation of Microgine® and explanations about how its risk analysis was conducted will be provided.

Presentation of the Microgine® Project

The Microgine® project aims to create a new generation of information search tools specifically for professionals.

Today, two out of three web users are professionals, 94 per cent of whom want specialized and quick access to information. For example, these professionals can recruit via the web while other users look for IT[11] firms in France. To this end-users have *search engines* or *specialized research tools*. As mentioned above, search engines such as Google and Yahoo propose redirecting links based on their own search algorithms, and not on what professionals need.

There are literally thousands of search tools such as the Yellow Pages and specialized directories. These are not always easy to navigate, moreover, they each have their own interface as shown in Figure 11.A1. Their information is neither shared nor

Figure 11.A1 Specialised Search Engines: A Heterogeneous Technological Environment with Content Dispersed and Varied User Interfaces

11 Internet Technology.

aggregated. Professionals thus waste a lot of time searching without being sure to find the most reliable or thorough information.

The Microgine® Solution

Microgine® enables users to consult the professional web and access information more quickly. The interface is simple and effective (see Figure 11.A2).

The information is grouped and organized. To that end, Microgine has invented a new matrix presentation of architecture on Internet (see Figure 11.A3).

Microgine® possesses four essential assets:

- A network architecture that is easy to extend; thousands of specialized search engines are organized in a matrix on Internet. Each item of the matrix can be hosted on a partner server. The example in Figure 11.A3 shows a search in France (the countries are shown horizontally) containing information relative to IT (the themes are shown vertically). An engine (France-IT) processes the search and supplies links and information (such as white papers, conferences etc.). Results of the search are shown using arborescence as with an "explorer" – (file manager).
- A hybrid indexing technology in a single engine. This technology comprises: (1) mechanisms of engines seeking information in URLs; (2) directories (like the White or Yellow Pages); and (3) a content management system (CMS) that structures the search results as mentioned above, and also offers other functions (see for example Figure 11.A4).
- The data processing power of the large search engines at a lower cost for firms that want to publish specialized information. These firms simply pay a very modest subscription fee.
- Integrated geolocalization.

Microgine® is a sustainable technology that gets richer over time country by country, region by region and domain by domain. Its positioning is unique. Microgine® is both a general search engine, because it indexes web pages, and a specialized one, for it aggregates other engines (such as directories), company information and presents information by specialized themes (see Figure 11.A5).

In order to support and strengthen this project, we first identified the risks involved and then, using a sustainable analysis technique, we identified its major risks.

Presentation of the Project Risks

We identify two major categories of risk throughout the Microgine® project: *external* risks (i.e. legal), and *internal* risks (i.e. disagreements among members of the Microgine® team); and the risks throughout the two major categories regarding the project Microgine®: *external* category (i.e. legal aspect) and *internal* category (i.e. disagreement within the team Microgine®). We also identify five main types of risks: Business, Competitors (sub-category of Business), Financial, Political, and Social, Human and Technical.

The degree of risk is derived from the scale of that risk. The scale depends on the risk criterion. For example, for the criterion project size (weight) the scale is: >300

Figure 11.A2 The Microgine® Search Engine: A Unified Environment

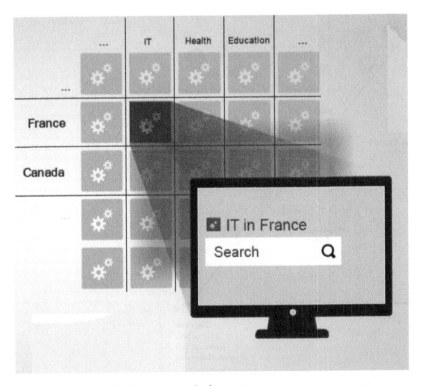

Figure 11.A3 Matrix Architecture on the Internet

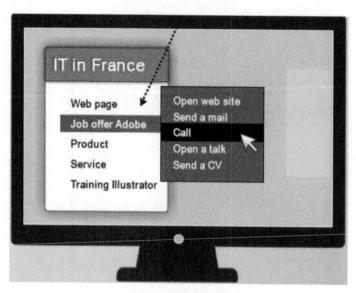

Figure 11.A4 Example of Microgine®'s CMS

Note: A user can make a call and send a CV directly to a company in reply to a recruitment offer.

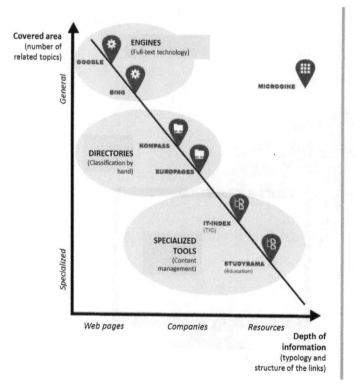

Figure 11.A5 The Law of Dilution: General or Specialised? Microgine® Does Both

Table 11.A1 Example of Criteria, Degree and Scale of Risk

Criteria	Degree (based on scale)	Scale
Duration	1	<= 6 months
	2	<= 18 months
	3	<= 30 months
	4	> 30 months
Weight	1	<= 20 month per man (month*men)
	2	<= 120 month per man (month*men)
	3	<= 300 month per man (month*men)
	4	> 300 month per man (month*men)

men months. The degree is thus 4. Our degrees of risk range from 1 (very small) to 4 (very large). The higher the degree of risk, the greater the impact on the project.

Business Risks

We take into consideration two kinds of risks. First, risks related to the environment involving legal aspects and possible technical changes with new entrants. Second, risks induced by customers and end-users' habits: will they find this interface difficult to use? Will they adopt it? And will publishers be interested enough to provide information and update it? Another challenge is brand recognition, because Microgine® is only a small company.

Risks from Competitors

There is a danger that big global competitors (Google, Yahoo etc.) may offer the same service as Microgine®. On a local level, competitors as Kompass, Studyrama and chambers of commerce etc. could decide to remain independent rather than joining the Microgine® community; this would result in a huge lack of interesting data for Microgine®.

Human Risks

The human risks are internal. Of, course we must take into account the small size of the company, so there are risks concerning potential conflict and the reliability of Microgine® team members. At this stage of the company's development, efficiency and good working conditions are important. The risk of changes within the organization (organizational degree of change) is quite high too because of possible new entrants, a joint venture and everything else related to life as a start-up life in a very high tech and innovative environment.

Financial Risks

We have many high-level financial risks. External risk concerns the level of involvement of the editors. If they fail to promote Microgine® Engines by giving them enough visibility, publishers will not pay to be present on the Microgine® Grid (similarly, a customer would not buy a key word on Google). We have three risks that deal with both internal and external aspects. The first is a lack of ads from publishers: this means that the Microgine® network will not be promoted enough. Promotion is crucial because Microgine® is both young and small, the company must grow fast; its visibility depends partners' level of advertising. The second risk is partner loyalty terms of duration and the third risk involves payment delays because of cash flow difficulties for start-ups. Finally, we have three internal risks. Of course Microgine® depends on its partners to promote it, but it is essential that they invest enough in their communication plan. This IT project needs to be up-to-date, so it is vital to maintain a high level of investment in constant innovation. The speed of project development also presents a financial risk. Delays will result in financial problems: too much investment and not enough turnover.

Technical Risks

Obviously, any IT project carries a lot of technical risks. As the team is composed of high-level engineers, these risks are not about programming issues. Nevertheless, we have to take into consideration the risk of hacking. We also have risks linked to languages (capacity of translation and semantic risks), server crashes and even misuse of project management methods. Another main risk that needs to be taken into account is the workload. Indeed, we need to pay great attention to the time allocated to each task.

Risks concerning data are also important: the quality of data use must satisfy end-users in terms of ease of transfer and access speed.

There are other risks that need to be considered, but they are less important than financial or business risks.

Political and Social Risks

In this category, we highlight risks linked to countries. The first of these is political risk that arises if information is controlled by a country that prevents data access. The second is social risk that involves lack of practice/habits in terms of information search on the web.

Table 11.A2 List of Risks

N°	Group	External/ internal	Definition (criteria)	Degree	Scale
1	BR	E	Change in legal aspect (change, be sued) (**Legal**)	4	Very high
2	BR	E	Technical Change (New entrants) (**Tech Chang**)	2	< 12 months
3	BR	E	Comprehension (Difficult to use for the end-users) (**Comprehens**)	2	Weak
4	BR	E	Adoption of the product in terms of habits by the end-users (**Adoption**)	4	Very high
5	BR	E	Non-recognition of the brand Microgine® by publishers and end-users (problem of visibility) (**Visibility**)	4	Very high

6	BR	E	Lack of interest from publishers to provide and update information for the system (**Lack of**)	2	Medium
7	FR	E	Level of involvement from the editor in terms of revenue generation (turnover provided by the publishers) (**Payment**)	4	High
8	CR	E	Global competitors (Google, Yahoo, Bing, Ask.com) may offer the same service as Microgine® (**Google . . .**)	4	Very high
9	CR	E	If French local competitors (Kompass, Studyrama, CCI, AEF ("annuaire des entreprises françaises" French company directory) remain independent, they will not join the Microgine® community (**Kompass . . .**)	2	Medium
10	PR	E	Country risk: information controlled by the country (denial of access to data) (**Control**)	3	High
11	PR	E	Country risk: cultural (lack of practice/habits in terms of information research on the web) (**Habits**)	3	High
12	FR	I/E	Lack of ads from the publishers and partners (to promote the Microgine® network) (**Ads.**)	3	High
13	FR	I/E	Loyalty of the partners in terms of duration (at least 3 years) (**Loyalty**)	4	High
14	FR	I/E	Delay (from 30 to 60 days) for payment from customers (publishers) (**Delay**)	3	High
15	HR	I	Size of the company (Microgine®) (**Size**)	2	Medium
16	HR	I	Disagreements within the team (Microgine®) (**Disagreeme**)	3	High
17	HR	I	Degree of organizational change (inside Microgine®) (**Organizati**)	3	Medium
18	HR	I	Members' reliability (inside Microgine® team) (**Reliabilit**)	2	Medium
19	FR	I	Poor investment in the communication plan to promote Microgine® (**Poor Inves**)	4	Very high
20	FR	I	Speed of project development (**Speed**)	4	Very high
21	FR	I	Level of investment in constant innovation in order to be up-to-date (**up-to-date**)	3	High
22	TR	I	Complexity of product implementation (**Complexity**)	2	Medium
23	TR	I	Technical issues from databases (**Databases**)	1	>200
24	TR	I	Size of the project: in terms of workload (**Workload**)	4	>300 men months
25	TR	I	Servers go offline/crash (**Servers**)	2	Medium
26	TR	I	Design of the widget (front office design): Difficulty of using the service (**Widget**)	2	Medium
27	TR	I	Timeliness of the service (**Timeliness**)	2	Medium
28	TR	I	Semantic risks linked to languages: finding information in different languages (Japanese, Russian, Arabic . . .) (**Semantic**)	3	High
29	TR	I	Capacity to translate in different languages to make information accessible (readable, understandable) to end-users (**Translatio**)	3	High

(continued)

Table 11.A2 (continued)

N°	Group	External/ internal	Definition (criteria)	Degree	Scale
30	TR	I	Security: prevention of hackers (destruction of data and database) and theft of search engine, platforms and information (**Security**)	3	High
31	TR	I	Use of Project management methods and tools in order to pilot the project well (in particular task allocation / planning) (**PM method**)	2	Medium
32	TR	I	Problem of data quality (correct, up-to-date, not redundant and complete) (**Quality**)	3	High
33	TR	I	Problem of quality for data use (easy to transfer, speed of access) (**Transfer**)	4	Very high
34	TR	I	Application development in terms of ergonomics and user friendliness (**Ergonomy**)	3	High

Notes: There are 3 risks that combine external and internal issues; these concern our partners: cf. risks 12, 13 and 14. BS: business risks; HR: human risks; FR: financial risks; TR: technical risks; CR: competitor risks; PR: political and social risks.

Conclusion

In this particular case, we have seen that Microgine® should contribute to solving some important issues of big data management for the professional web and therefore allow sustainable performance of professional search by end-users. Furthermore, through using sustainable PM Standards, we have been able to identify the key risk variables of our system (Microgine®). By highlighting the most important risks for the Microgine® project, ("Up-to-date, Comprehension, Translation, Security, Control, Ergonomy and Widget"), we now know where the Microgine® team should mainly invest its resources so as to maintain a stable system and to sustain their project. To conclude, to be a successful story and a sustainable project, Mircrogine® has to be an "up-to-date", "secure" and "multi-languages" product that is well designed in terms of ergonomy (good widget).

Bibliography

Portelli, A. (2013). *Business Plan Microgine®*, Microgine® company documentation.

SKEMA (2011). MSc Web Marketing and International Project Management, Project Plan Microgine® BOOK 1.

SKEMA (2012). MSc Web Marketing and International Project Management, Project Plan Microgine® BOOK 2.

Chapter 12

Sustaining Project Management Office (PMO) Performance: A New Focus On Lean and Agile as Standards

Waffa Karkukly

Introduction

Project Management Offices (PMOs) constitute a topic that two distinct groups, academics and practitioners, have been exploring for some time now, thereby enriching the literature and providing industry with answers to many of the questions revolving around PMOs. More recently, the focus of both groups has been on seeking answers pertaining to the performance of PMOs and on what differentiates performing PMOs from the ones that lack in performance. One critical item in PMO performance, on which there is agreement in the literature, is the notion of building value-add through adopting sustainable practices. Lean and Agile are two prominent such sustainable practices that PMOs can leverage in order to ensure their own success and longevity, as well as the sustainability of the organization they support.

Actually, Lean and Agile concepts, methods, and practices are not really new. IT-focused organizations in particular have been implementing a variety of standards for development, and Agile has been one of them; while non-IT organizations have practiced Lean for some time now. Organizations in search of continuous improvement have learned to use these two methods, though they were often heard of separately. More recently there has been a huge buzz around Lean *and* Agile, to the point that, now, one is not mentioned without the other.

The Lean and Agile journey requires structure, champions, processes, as well as an appropriate change management approach in order to ensure successful adoption and attainment of the promised goals.

There is a need to explain in more details the adoption of Lean and Agile and what each entails, so as to allow students and practitioners alike to learn more about their applicability. Further, this would allow IT managers or organizations interested in adopting Lean and Agile to understand clearly what is required to implement these approaches and thus achieve what is called "Leagility." Understanding the applicability of the Agile and Lean standards, as well as understanding what results we can expect from them will contribute to the practicality of the project management field in general, while shedding light on how these standards can sustain the performance of PMOs.

Additionally, this chapter presents the case study of an organization in the Canadian financial industry that achieved Leagility through the adoption of Lean and Agile.

While Agile was adopted by their IT organization, the business side of the organization adopted Lean methods in order to achieve the desired transformation of its delivery model. Thus, what constituted the product function of the organization was aligned with the software development function and the PMO creating a unified model that achieved Leagility through the benefits of both Lean and Agile.

Origins of the PMO

The concept of a PMO originated in the 1950s when it had a role in the military mainly, and in critical projects, and was staffed with specialized project staff to ensure completion. The purpose was to control specific projects and to be closer to the customer (Kerzner, 2004).

The journey since 1960 has changed the PMO in terms of operation and in terms of the expectations of both users and management. Project-based industries (IT, construction and defense), profited immediately from project management—probably because they already had a certain level of project maturity and were the first to establish project offices to monitor their project progress. Non-project-based industries were measured by their functional product line. Hence, project management maturity was slower and adoption of the project office was slower too (Rad and Levin, 2002).

> A project management office (PMO) is an organizational body or entity assigned various responsibilities related to the centralized and coordinated management of those projects under its domain. The responsibilities of a PMO can range from providing project management support functions to actually being responsible for the direct management of a project.
>
> (PMI, 2008, p. 11)

PMOs are called Centers of Excellence (CoE) in some organizations; but these CoE PMOs have to satisfy some specific elements. For an effective CoE, Bolles (2002) identifies four necessary key elements: An effective CoE provides authorization; it assists the organization to align its resources with its strategic objectives. In addition, it also *identifies*, *categorizes* and *prioritizes* projects. Further, the CoE provides a means to manage projects and assists the organization to advance in its project management maturity, doing so through:

- **Standards:** Establishes standard tools, templates and methodologies to be applied to all projects within an organization.
- **Education:** Provides training and education to all concerned with respect to project management within an organization. This is a key component of the cultural change that is often required to implement the authority and standards of a methodology.
- **Readiness:** Establishes a project's readiness to proceed through the required methodologies and may include an evaluative aspect or pre-project assessment as to the likelihood of success for a project. This could involve a pre-project assessment of critical success factors or a preliminary risk analysis.

PMO and Organizational Performance

In a research survey, when participants were asked whether PMOs contribute positively to organizational performance, 98 percent confirmed with "Yes" that PMOs contribute positively to organizational performance. Further, the results indicated that the levels of governance adoption as well as the level of standards adoption have positive impacts on organizational performance (Karkukly, 2010).

Organizations are adopting project management to solve problems. Project-driven organizations should adopt a broader application of the project management discipline as well as the new models, which will make them perform better (Gareis, 2005).

Organizations that have a PMO are believed to have better performance than those that do not have a PMO. Over the last decade, one of the reasons that a number of organizations have created a PMO has been the need for better managing project delivery (Aubry and Hobbs, 2007). Regardless of the role of PMOs or the types of functions they may perform, the expectations of executives of organizations are consistent: Drive better performance through the project organization—which can be summarized in having PMOs (Viswanathan, 2004).

While studies have proved that standards and governance positively impact organizational performance, it is important that every organization determine the specific value-add imperatives that drive their respective organization's performance. If these parameters are left undefined, then what constitutes performance may be different for every function in the organization.

In summary, if PMOs are able to identify the value-add parameters, execute on them, measure them and show better results, then these are well-performing PMOs that contribute to the performance of their organizations.

PMOs and Sustainability Principles

This chapter will now explore what it means for a PMO to sustain operations and be continuously engaged on the improvement journey. Some PMOs are concerned with delivering the right projects and delivering these projects right. For that to happen, they need to have a plan demonstrating to their executive sponsors and their broader organization that the pursuit of improvements is an unending journey.

Sustainability principles call for social-oriented, economical and ecological systems. These systems can be for the medium term or for the long term, and can span from local to global. Most notable is the notion of value-base, which is considered the foundation for sustainable project management (Gareis et al., 2011).

A definition of PMO that emphasizes value-add as defined by the author is that:

> PMO is a critical organizational entity that adopts a variety of roles and structures but should be focused on adding value to an organization and its customers to achieve the desired organizational performance.
>
> (Karkukly, 2010, p. 55)

From the PMO definition above, the PMO should be contributing to add value to its organization and the organizations it services, i.e. the customers' organizations. A more formal definition of value-add is that:

Value added refers to "extra" feature(s) of an item of interest (product, service, person etc.) that go beyond the standard expectations and provide something "more" while adding little or nothing to its cost.

(wikipedia.org/wiki/Value_add)

Bowman and Ambrosini introduce two dimensions to value-add. First, the human resources (HR) as a dimension of an organization and how employee performance can contribute to the organization's profit/success. Second, value capture based on customer perception of the received value (Bowman and Ambrosini, 2000).

To focus on establishing value-add dimensions, the HR value-add and the customer value-add will be explored along with the various elements that ensure sustainability in each dimension. Further consideration will be given to the risk management factors that influence the customer and HR value-add measures.

HR Factor

Employees are motivated through financial rewards, self-fulfillment, challenging assignments, employer's respect and career progression. These motivators are reflected in employees owning their work and being accountable for their deliverables, which ultimately generate performance improvement. As a result, employers will attract talents, minimize issues resulting from bad morale, and improve efficiencies, thus leading to continuous improvements.

Customer Factor

The PMO will need to align with its organization on the type of customer value model its organization needs to satisfy. To be able to quantify the value-add, there are quantitative and qualitative measures for customer value. Quantitative measures can be obtained via customer relationship and measuring customer satisfaction using customer surveys, meetings, one-on-one, and town hall meetings that address wider customer needs. Qualitative measures can be obtained by ensuring that the company has Customer Focus defined as one of their goals and objectives. Further, these customers should feel they are receiving the expected product and service quality factor, on time delivery, and competitive in cost (Karkukly, 2012).

In summary, literature has established that having a PMO improves organizational performance and that organizations having a PMO perform better than those that do not have a PMO. Although the value-add may vary in definition as to whether they were directly or indirectly contributing to organizational performance, the consistent understanding is that PMOs that help their organization identify the value-add elements, execute on them, and are able to measure the value, will contribute to their organization's performance. Further, such PMOs will be adding value through improving standards, better governance, and deepening the human dimension, whether the HR is internal or external to the organization.

Now, while we have established that PMOs do contribute to organizations, the question is how do Lean and Agile further contribute to PMOs own sustainability and the sustainability of such organizations as have these PMOs? In the next section we will explore the concepts of Lean and Agile, and their benefits, before introducing the case study.

Lean and Agile

Organizations are able to deliver value-add through Lean and Agile. PMOs in some organizations can be the champion of Lean and Agile implementation and can be the entity that sustains Lean and Agile practices for value-add. But before we explore the value-add resulting from Lean and Agile and introduce our case study on how one organization was able to achieve value-add, we'll introduce what exactly Lean and Agile are. Figure 12.1 shows the benefits of adopting Lean and Agile (VersionOne, 2011).

What Is Lean and Why Lean?

Lean is an approach that identifies the value inherent in specific products, identifies the value stream for each product, supports the flow of value, lets the customer pull value from the producer, and pursues perfection. "Lean is doing more with less. Use the least amount of effort, energy, equipment, time, facility space, materials, and capital—while giving customers exactly what they want" (Womack and Jones, 2003).

Lean thinking focuses primarily on customer satisfaction through quality and speed. Second, it focuses on improving processes through minimizing defects. Figure 12.2 summarizes the principles of Lean (Forrester, 2011).

Transforming to a leaner organization involves moving the organization through major stages of change. However, becoming Lean is not a final destination, but rather a way of approaching and delivering services that becomes integrated into the

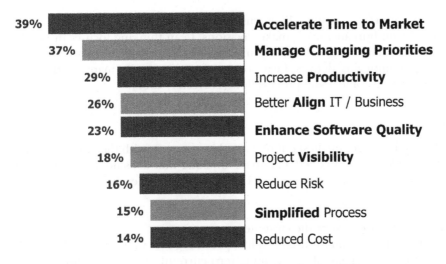

Figure 12.1 Benefits of Adopting Lean/Agile for Technology Product Delivery

Source: Version One: State of Agile Survey (2011, n=6000+), percentages show option respondents marked as "Highest Important"—http://www.versionone.com/pdf/2011_State_of_Agile_Development_Survey_Results.pdf.

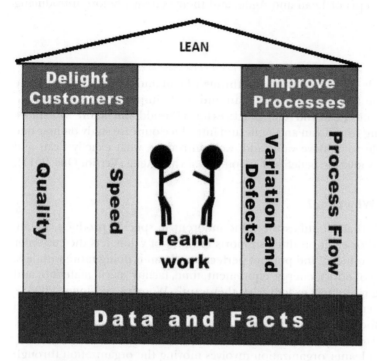

Figure 12.2 Principles of Lean

Source: February 3, 2011, "Transforming Application Delivery" Forrester report.

organization's culture. Fostering a high trust culture through transparency, reduces the need to rely on bureaucracy to make decisions. Lean thinking focuses primarily on customer satisfaction through quality and speed, and second on improving processes through minimizing defects. Lean focuses on value stream mapping through VOC (voice of the customer) and process flow (Forrester, 2011).

Origins of Lean

Lean existed to simply get the best out of limited investments with the understanding that you only build what is needed, eliminate anything that does not add value, and stop if something goes wrong (Harvey, 2004). Womack and Jones distilled these Lean principles even further to five:

- specify the value desired by the customer;
- identify the value stream for each product providing that value, and challenge all of the wasted steps (generally nine out of ten) currently necessary to provide it;
- make the product flow continuously through the remaining value-added steps;
- introduce pull between all steps where continuous flow is possible;
- manage toward perfection so that the number of steps and the amount of time and information needed to serve the customer continually falls.

Lean Today

Toyota, the leading Lean exemplar in the world, stands poised to become the largest automaker in the world in terms of overall sales. Its dominant success in everything from rising sales and market shares in every global market stands as the strongest proof of the power of Lean enterprise. Today, there is such a huge interest in Lean that there are literally hundreds of books, articles, and papers, exploring Lean.

As Lean thinking continues to spread across organizations around the world, leaders are also adapting the tools and principles beyond manufacturing, to logistics and distribution, services, retail, healthcare, construction, maintenance, and even government. Indeed, Lean consciousness and methods are only beginning to take root among senior managers and leaders in all sectors today (Womack and Jones, 2003).

What Is Agile and Why Agile?

Agility is the ability to both create and respond to change in order to profit in a turbulent business environment. Agility is the ability to balance flexibility and stability (Highsmith, 2002).

Agile describes a set of principles and practices for delivering software. Agile business objectives are: Continuous Innovation, Product Adaptability, Improved Time-to-Market, People and Process Adaptability, and Process Adaptability. Every effort should be taken to automate all standardized and repetitive processes and tasks. Agile focuses on innovation, product adaptability, improved time-to-market, and support business growth and profitability. Agile organizations possess the processes and structures to support a convergent business and technology model that requires the management of business requirements and technology capabilities as one, thus resulting in greater collaboration and responsiveness to business needs.

Origins of Agile

Agile started in the 1960s–1970s with the United States Department of Defense (DoD) and NASA—Iterative and Incremental Development. In the 1980s, it evolved to include New Product Development (Takeuchi and Nonaka, 1986). In the year 2000, the foundation of SCRUM was laid and IBM Rational Unified Process (RUP) became more visible, and finally, Dynamic Systems Development Method became the catalyst for the Agile Manifesto in 2001 (Sliger and Broderick, 2008). Figure 12.3 summarizes the Agile journey.

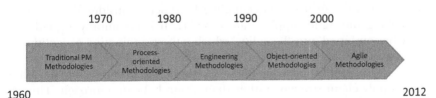

Figure 12.3 Summary of the Agile Journey

Benefits of Agile

- Adaptability: Project weight equally distributed throughout the phases of the project.
- Innovation: Forces teams to focus on business goals.
- Enforces tactical management: Self-organizing and self-management encourages teams to find solutions for their obstacles.
- User commitment: Customer is part of project and feedback is sought throughout.
- Knowledge transfer: Focus on communication and collaboration encourages learning from each other.
- Improved team morale: Teams are empowered to work under minimal supervision, and management trusts they will deliver (Goncalves and Heda, 2010).

HR Management in Agile Source

The Agile approach to HR management is to focus on establishing cross-functional teams with mutual accountability that self-organize. These teams consist of coders, testers, analysts, architects, project leaders, etc. The advantage in this model is having the self-organized team share knowledge that allows for mutual accountability.

The team self-organizes as a result of regular check-ins and analysis of how the team wishes to continue:

- the total ownership by the team of the planning, execution, and review of both the product and the process leads Agile teams to a high level of self-directed performance;
- Agile SCRUM Masters still need to address the issues of planning, acquiring, coordinating, and managing HR on an Agile team;
- having dedicated cross-functional, self-directed teams requires delicate management of project HR;
- Agile SCRUM Masters do not create staffing plans at the initiation of a project that specifies who will be needed when;
- these types of staffing plans never work out as planned because of the inherent changes occurring on projects: late deliveries, new features, existing features take longer than expected.

Instead Agile SCRUM Masters create cross-functional teams that are fully dedicated to the project for its duration (Sliger and Broderick, 2008).

The Thesis of Leagility

Both postponement and information decoupling have been considered as relevant initiatives in making the Agile supply chain a reality. It is commonly argued that Lean and Agile be combined into "Leagility," which is the combination of Agility and Lean capabilities within one supply chain. Based upon a one-year study of Agility in the supply chain, if the Agility approach is to work, though, it is required to fit within a purely Agile supply chain strategy, rather than a purely Lean approach. Thus, it is concluded that the Agility thesis does not fundamentally challenge the Agility concept (Hoek, 2000).

The thesis of Leagility rests on four principles: Management framework for strategy; Paradigm for business-IT alignment; Agile processes and champions; and Enabling technologies and infrastructure (Forrester, 2011).

- Management framework for strategy: This is concerned with the HR factor and on how to foster a culture where people take charge and improve as a result of alignment of work to business goals. Establishing metrics and measures that tie into business success criteria, and, most important, instituting change management.
- Paradigm for business-IT alignment: This is concerned with the process, the alignment of the business portfolio to IT. The outcome is decision around how the business initiative will be understood by IT as well as determining the archetype for delivery.
- Agile processes and champions: This is concerned with the HR factor again, where hiring the right talent that contribute positively to Leagility adoption not only within the development team in IT shops, but more prudently across the entire business to ensure Leagility being thought through from the early stages of ideation, through development, and implementation.
- Enabling technology organization: This is concerned with the focus on tools enablement to ensure process alignment and HR efficiency that drive toward unifying platforms and infrastructure; or, introducing new technologies that support IT and business alignment in order to enable decision making.

Implementing Lean and Agile in Organizations

In implementing Lean and Agile, the focus should be first and foremost on having a structure for the implementation. A structure is important because it will ensure that areas of focus are identified and priorities are addressed in the right order. The structure should identify the following three areas in order: Focus on building people; build and stream line processes; and, implement supporting tools and technologies.

- Building people includes: Training and investing in the HR factor. This is not limited to one level of HR in the organization. Education should be targeted bottom-up and top-down, where the message and the content of training will differ, while the objective will remain the same; and that is, getting the organization buy-in and minimizing resistance due to lack of knowledge in the matter. Training to the senior management of an organization should focus on benefits and outcome; while training for middle management should focus on the techniques to manage through Lean and Agile, as well as on the benefits to them and their teams. Training for cross-functional teams within a department or within a project should focus on the new collaboration techniques, estimation techniques, and learning through retrospectives. Training should vary from Just In Time—JIT—to Group Training, to Hands-on. The diversification of training allows different audiences to better align with specific objectives and improves adoption.
- Building processes includes: Charting the Lean and Agile process. This can be either by looking at existing practices which may have some Lean and Agile aspects to them and better aligning them to the foundations of Lean and Agile; or, one can build a fresh new process that encompasses the new way of doing business through Lean and Agile. The process should focus on building checkpoints

through gates. For successful gates implementation, gates success criteria should be identified for each gate, for example, the governance of members involved in the gate review and the expected outcomes for a go or no-go decision. Last, incorporating retrospectives as a fundamental learning step in the process, in order to allow the teams to reflect on what is working from a process perspective, as well as on the content being delivered as a result of the new process.

- Implementing supporting tools and technologies includes: As mentioned in the process described above, emphasis should be put on Retrospective and on Visualization tools such as Kanban, where the flow of work and transparency are key elements that allow teams to focus on breaking down work and reducing variability. Utilizing Leverage Poker Games for estimation incorporates fun while allowing teams to collaborate and learn how to better estimate.

- Building measures includes: Building the right score cards at the right level. Expectations in the early adoption stage should be less focused on measuring performance and throughput and more on measuring collaboration and adoption. This can be achieved through team self-assessment rather than guided success criteria to measure against. In later stages, the expectations will be to measure performance of delivery, throughput, speed, and efficiency through improving estimation via "poker game," weekly burn down charts, completed work, and remaining work.

Sustaining PMO Performance by Achieving Leagility

For organizations transformed into Lean and Agile, whether their respective PMO was a champion in leading the change or the organizational change was led by other entities, the fact remains that it is the responsibility of PMOs to ensure sustained practices and sustained performance. As seen in the previous section, the Lean and Agile journey requires changes in all aspects of an organization's operations and most importantly the HR factor. While adoption levels may vary by department, the faster PMOs can adopt the change and help their respective organization in managing the change, the more visible the value-add role of PMOs will be perceived. The areas of emphasis should be around people, process, technology, and the ability to measure all these areas of emphasis.

- Building people includes: PMOs should train their project managers in the new ways of managing projects in Lean and Agile. This includes Process training, Tools training, and provides project managers with the opportunity to learn by shadowing those with more Agile experience or by allowing them to manage projects and have Lean and Agile coaches to support them. Having coaches on hand has helped organizations successfully navigate the adoptions period where people, project managers included, know that there is a resident expert to whom they can go and ask questions to improve their understanding and application of the Lean and Agile practices. Since PMO has the cross-functional teams reach, it should leverage that ability into conducting cross-functional training to allow teams to be trained on various collaboration techniques. PMOs can help build and list the new competencies required for project managers to run Lean and Agile projects, as well as partner with HR to support organizations in building competencies around Lean and Agile for all other functional areas within an organization.

- Building processes include: In some organizations, the Lean and Agile way of delivering can be housed in the PMO where the PMO becomes the custodian of all processes pertaining to delivery in the organization, allowing other functional areas to focus on content and deliverables at hand. In that case the PMO can lead the change in ensuring processes are streamlined across all functional areas and that Lean and Agile methods are kept up to date as part of continuous improvement. If the PMO is not in charge of the entire process leading to delivery, at the very least they need to update their current practices to embed Lean and Agile foundations through planning, execution, monitoring, and controlling. The focus should shift from the usual triple constraints of scope, time, and budget to value, quality, and constraints. The PMO can help by being the facilitator and lead the gates reviews to provide neutral assessment, thus allowing executives to make a go/no-go decision.
- Implementing supporting tools and technologies includes: In addition to introducing some of the tools that will require project managers and project teams to work together, the PMO can also assume the role of trainer. The PMO can set policies around the new ways of status reporting and communication structure (team stand-ups), which had already been adopted from SCRUM stand-ups or Sprint stand-ups. Expanding the concept to core project teams, allows the entire team to collaborate and provide status, but in shorter time horizons and focusing more on action and less on the task list reporting. Assign action: This can be further enhanced by the use of Kanban boards which adds to the status the visualization aid which allows teams to follow the flow and to take immediate action and post it on the board as an update. The PMO can facilitate the retrospectives where the project managers and project teams can be neutral partners in addressing the question of how the project performed.
- Building measures includes: The PMO should focus on aligning the right score cards at the right level of the organization. The PMO should update their current dashboard and tracking based on what Lean and Agile requires. Updated PMO templates should correspond with the Lean and Agile structure. For example, long project charters covering all phases of a project might be difficult to write. Therefore, allow project managers to have scaled charters which address the current phase only, and limit planning to either the current phase or to a time box the team has agreed to. The PMO can help set up and establish these policies, as well as monitor their execution.

In summary, the PMO can adopt the Lean and Agile principles and further their adoption by their organizations through:

- First, build people, then products, by means of education and opportunities for people to put into practice what they learn and be supported.
- Second, build processes tailored to the organization that encompass all delivery cycles monitored through gates, and with focus on delivery flow, elimination of waste, and empowering teams.
- Last, foster a high trust culture through transparency, reducing the need to rely on bureaucracy to make decisions, introducing tools and technologies as enablers and coaching people to do the right thing before they are measured on the outcome.

Case Study and Results

About the Case Organization

Interac Association (the "Association" or "Organization") is a recognized leader in debit card services. The Association is responsible for the development and operations of the Inter-Member Network (IMN), a national payment network that allows Canadians to access their money through Automated Banking Machines and Point-of-Sale terminals across Canada. Formed in 1984, the Association is now composed of a diverse group of members, including banks, trust companies, credit unions, caisses populaires, merchants, and technology and payment-related companies. The Association is a not-for-profit organization, governed by a 14-member Board of Directors, appointed annually based on the business sector and the volume of transactions processed. More information about Interac Association may be accessed at http://www.interac.ca. Today, Canadians coast to coast associate the Interac® brand with leading electronic payment services that are trusted, secure, and reliable.

The Organization's Challenge

The organization faces external and internal challenges.

External challenges: First, the external challenge that the payments landscape is evolving at a fast pace as Canadian consumers increasingly adopt newer mechanisms to pay for products and services. Second, is speed-to-market: The need to improve speed-to-market for new products/services. Last, the need to increase offerings and integrate with external partners, which increases project complexity.

Internal challenges: First, the organization is challenged to deliver faster, better, and to produce quality results. Second, the challenge posed by the emphasis put on process alignment and achieving better efficiencies as Interac seeks to achieve continuous improvement and reduced waste. And, finally, the challenge to ensure alignment across the three lifecycle models that Interac employs in the various elements of its business and operations.

The Role of the PMO as a Champion

Reflecting on the role of the PMO within Interac, we found that the PMO sat at the enterprise level, helping the organization's C-level plan and optimize their business portfolio and connect with the organization's strategy and the annual corporate objectives. At the same time, the PMO oversaw the execution of projects through streamlined processes and standard methodology. The PMO was not involved in either product development or IT build, which made the Interac Enterprise Program Management Office (EPMO) the perfect candidate to be a Champion, since the function has vested interest in helping the organization's functions streamline, optimize and speed deliver through the adoption of Lean processes and improved Agile practices. Additionally, the Interac EPMO benefitted from the fact that they were fairly mature in terms of both their practice and their processes. This circumstance would enable them to lead a huge organizational transformation while being flexible in approach in order to achieve the desired results.

The PMO led the initiative as a major change to the organization and structured the project in a manner that ensured governance at various levels and an effective C-level Steering Committee that included the areas that drive content (as in the product group and IT group), where ideas translate into IT builds. The importance of having an effective C-level Steering Committee played a huge role in removing roadblocks since they were at the center of the decision-making mechanism—a fact that facilitated successful results.

Why Lean and Agile in Combination?

For Interac, Agile was already being practiced within the development team, but it was not widely accepted or adopted. To ensure further adoption within IT as a whole, other areas within IT apart from developers needed to be brought in and educated on the value of Agile, more specifically the Business Analysis group, the Quality Assurance group and the Implementation folks. Now, while the reason for adopting Agile could be understood by IT in general once they are fully briefed on its value to them and on how to use it, the outstanding challenge was the business unit. They understood Agile well but considered it an IT process, and were concerned about process overlap and what it may generate in terms of waste, how to align their resources with IT, and how do their two teams interact in general.

At this point, it became imperative to bring in the concept of Lean and to make its primary focus the elimination of waste, the building of quality, and the alignment of teams. So, with the IT and business needs in mind, the Interac PMO charted both Lean and Agile as one initiative of transformation to the delivery model of the organization. The approach required the buy-in of executives and that was obtained through training, where Subject Matter Experts (SMEs) on both concepts presented their respective value.

Once the buy-in and funding support became available, middle management were engaged for bottom-up buy-in and they in turn leveraged champions with background and experience with either Lean or Agile to become messengers of why the transformation into Lean and Agile was needed. As soon as the buy-in on Lean and Agile was in place, the next step was to determine the approach to carry out the change.

The Approach

The approach was a three-step process as shown in Figure 12.5 that took into consideration people, process, and then technology, and it consisted of:

- building people, then building products;
- formal education on the value of Lean and Agile, and their benefit for their organization at all levels, starting from senior management and going down to the team members;
- providing time and support for teams to participate in Lean and Agile tours and conferences;

The Approach—Building Measures

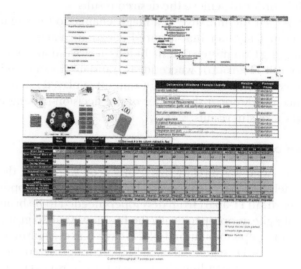

Figure 12.4 The Three-Step Approach

- building a process tailored to the organization that encompassed all cycles, from product ideation to operationalization, all of it monitored through gates;
- providing various tools to implement and measure people performance, and process performance.

Managing the Change

The approach started as early as the initiative started through identifying a vision, validating the vision, then taking action, which meant either pivoting and changing direction, or pressing on and accelerating adoption. The approach covered three core areas:

- cultural and behavioral change;
- leadership alignment and communication;
- process adoption which included ennoblements, capabilities, and tools to help adoption:
  - starting the adoption through champions and pilot initiatives before mass rollout;
  - continuous evaluations and reflection on pilot performance and adoption of teams.

The Learning

The success of Interac's PMO in leading the implementation of Lean and Agile resulted in the following:

- fostering of a high trust culture through transparency, reducing the need to rely on bureaucracy to make decisions;
- focusing on people education resulted in better buy-in and minimized the fear of change;
- inclusion of the various layers of the organization in the design of the process, and leaving tools to the end;
- building enough slack to deliver fast, instead of maximizing utilization;
- moving forward with imperfect information instead of waiting for the perfect plan.

Summary

This chapter summarized the case study of Interac, an organization in the financial industry in Canada that achieved Leagility through their adoption of Lean and Agile. The success of this case study and the Leagility journey of Interac is due to the commitment of its leadership team, the continuous coaching and support from their EPMO to ensure adoption, education and allowing people to go through the learning curve, and, finally transparency through visualization tools that is part of the Lean and Agile practices.

Conclusion

Lean and Agile are two of the many sustainable practices that PMOs can leverage in order to ensure their own sustainability and the sustainability of their organizations.

Lean and Agile are not new concepts; organizations that seek continuous improvement have learned to use these methods for some time. However, these two concepts were often heard of separately. Most recently, there has been a huge buzz about Lean *and* Agile, to the point that, now, one is not mentioned without the other. The Agile and Lean journey requires structure, champions, processes, and well thought-out change management approach in order to ensure the success of the Lean and Agile adoption.

In this chapter we have explained what the Agile and Lean standards are, their applicability, and the results that these standards can contribute to organizations and their PMOs. Further, we have shown how PMOs that adopt Lean and Agile find their performance sustained.

Additionally, this chapter presents a case study of an organization in the financial industry in Canada that achieved Leagility through their adoption of Lean and Agile, and how their PMO was a driving force behind the implementation and adoption of Lean and Agile, and how this very fact provided sustainability to both the PMO and their organization.

References

Appelo, J. (2011) *Management 3.0, Leading Agile Developers, Developing Agile Leaders.* Boston, MA: Addison Wesley.

Bolles, D. (2002) *Building Project Management Centers of Excellence.* New York: AMACOM.

Bowman, C. and Ambrosini, V. (2000) "Value creation versus value capture: Towards a coherent definition of value in strategy," *British Journal of Management,* Vol. 11, 1–15.

Derby, E. and Larsen, D. (2006) *Agile Retrospectives: Making Good Teams Great.* Pragmatic Bookshelf.

Forrester (2011) "Transforming Application Delivery." Forrester Report, February.

Gareis, R. (2005) The management strategy of the project oriented company. In *Handbook of Management by Projects,* ed. Roland Gareis. Vienna: MANZsche Verlags, pp. 35–47.

Gareis, R., Huemann, M., Martinuzzi, R., Sedlacko, M. and Weninger, C. (2011). Relating sustainability principles to managing projects: First reflections on a case study project. Proceedings for IRNOP 2011, Montreal, Canada.

Goncalves, M. and Heda, R. (2010) *Fundamentals of Agile Project Management Overview.* New York: ASME Press.

Harvey, D. (2004) Lean, Agile. Paper for Workshop, "The Software Value Stream".

Highsmith, J. (2002) *Agile Software Development Ecosystem.* Boston, MA: Addison Wesley.

Hobbs, B. and Aubry, M. (2007) "A multiphase research program investigating project management offices (PMOs): The results of phase 1," *Project Management Journal,* Vol. 38, No. 1, 74–86.

Hoek, V. (2000) "The thesis of leagility revisited," *International Journal of Agile Management Systems,* Vol. 2, No. 3, pp. 196–202. http://www.lean.org/whatslean/history.cfm referenced in March 2013.

Karkukly, W. (2010) *Outsourcing PMO Functions for Improved Organizational Performance.* Bloomington, IN: Trafford Publishing.

Karkukly, W. (2012) *Managing PMO Lifecycle—The Set-up, the Build-out, the Sustainability.* Bloomington, IN: Trafford Publishing.

Kerzner, H. (2004) *Advanced Project Management: Best Practices on Implementation,* 2nd Edition. Hoboken, NJ: Wiley & Sons. Inc.

Rad, P. and Levin, Gi. (2002) *The Advanced Project Management Office: A Comprehensive Look at Function and Implementation.* Boca Raton, FL: CRC Press.

Sliger, M. and Broderick, S. (2008) *The Software Project Manager's Bridge To Agility.* New York: Pearson Education Inc.

Takeuchi, H. and Nonaka, I. (1986) "The new product development game," *Harvard Business Review.*

Version One (2011) http://www.versionone.com/pdf/2011_State_of_Agile_Development_Survey_Results.pdf, accessed February 2011.

Viswanathan., V. K. (2004) "PMO—The value Proposition."

Womack, J. and Jones, D. (2003) *Lean Thinking: Banish Waste and Create Wealth in Your Corporation.* New York: Free Press.

Index